WHAT IF WE GOT AI RIGHT?

WHAT IF WE GOT AI RIGHT?

How to stop catastrophising and
build an ethical future

ELEANOR DRAGE

Profile Books

First published in Great Britain in 2026 by
Profile Books Ltd
29 Cloth Fair
London
EC1A 7JQ

www.profilebooks.com

Copyright © Eleanor Drage, 2026

1 3 5 7 9 10 8 6 4 2

Extract from T. S. Eliot's 'The Hollow Men' from *Collected Poems 1909–62*
(London: Faber, 2002) reproduced with the permission of Faber and Faber.

Typeset in Sabon by MacGuru Ltd
Printed and bound in Great Britain by
CPI Group (UK) Ltd, Croydon CR0 4YY

A CIP catalogue record for this book is available from the British Library.

Our product safety representative in the EU is BGC Sustainability & Compliance,
7 avenue du Général Leclerc, Paris 75014, France https://baldwinglobalconsulting.com

ISBN 978 1 80522 544 7
eISBN 978 1 80522 546 1

Contents

Introduction: Panicking about AI   1

Part I: What's Wrong with AI?
1. The Pernicious Myths on Which AI Is Built   25
2. Misdirections, or Apocalypse vs Utopia   51
3. The Triangle of Doom   72
4. Building from Better Visions   93
5. Beware False Promises   114
6. The Fight for Control   146
7. Feminism by the Back Door   165

Part II: How Can We Get AI Right?
8. The Case for Controversy   193
9. Nerds, Arise: Data Scientists Behaving Badly   207
10. Trust Your Instincts   224

Conclusion   231

Acknowledgements   237
List of Illustrations   239
Notes   241
Index   271

Introduction: Panicking about AI

Everyone is talking about AI. We're plagued by mixed messages about how much of a threat AI is: on the one hand, we hear that it poses imminent, existential risks, but on the other that it's ushering in a new dawn for the human race. Paradoxically, the very people and enterprises that are most vocal about their alleged concerns are also those most zealously engaged in the race to build artificial general intelligence (AGI). Big Tech companies are firing their ethics teams and rolling out AI products they claim to be bigger, better and smarter. They say we have no choice but to swallow unacceptable risks in our bid for global AI supremacy. With opposing views about which kinds of collateral damage are worth tolerating and whether the most pressing issue is the day-to-day harms caused by AI or hypothetical future catastrophes, it's hard to know what to think, and where we should direct not only our fear but our optimism.

Meanwhile, workers in almost all industries are having to make their own decisions about whether to use AI and which products to buy. They know these are high-stakes choices, and that in-house guidance is often severely lacking. While AI speeds ahead, our understanding of the technology itself – both the technical aspects and the ideologies and motivations that go into its creation – lags behind. This is often as true for the people developing AI as it is for new users. If computer scientists can't fully explain how their AI systems produce outputs, and aren't considering what the short- and longer-term effects of their products might be, is there any hope for those of us still struggling to unmute ourselves on Zoom?

In 1951, my great-great-grandfather's company, Ferranti Ltd, collaborated with the University of Manchester to create the Ferranti Mark 1, the first computer to play an AI-powered game, and generate music and poetry. The launch of its grandchild, ChatGPT, in November 2022 coincided with my umpteenth year of using dating apps. I suddenly received an influx of AI-generated poems from hopeful suitors who had spotted 'AI ethicist' on my profile. What was intended to be a discouraging filter was interpreted as an invitation to send me GPT 'poetry'. The poems were mostly dreadful. On the rare occasions that I would respond I sent them the following:

DUCK DUCK
YOU ARE MY WISTFUL ENCHANTMENT. MY PASSION CURIOUSLY LONGS FOR YOUR SYMPA-THETIC LONGING. MY SYMPATHY PASSIONATELY IS WEDDED TO YOUR EAGER AMBITION. MY PRECIOUS CHARM AVIDLY HUNGERS FOR YOUR COVETOUS ARDOUR. YOU ARE MY EAGER DEVOTION.

YOURS KEENLY
M. U. C.

The Manchester University Computer. This was programmed on the Ferranti Mark 1 in 1951 by computer scientist Christopher Strachey, rumoured to be Alan Turing's one-time lover. He would pin poems like this on to the university notice board for confused computer lab workers to furrow their brows over. The MUC could type out letters at the rate of about one a minute for hours without ever repeating itself. This is now considered the first piece of digital literature and of digital art, predating the next earliest examples by a decade. The BBC later commissioned Strachey to program a computer-generated medley; he chose 'God Save the King', 'Baa Baa Black Sheep' and the twentieth-century big band classic 'In the Mood'. Strachey also managed to impress Alan Turing, then a senior colleague at the university's computer lab, with his plan to create a draughts-playing program on the Mark 1. Turing subsequently commissioned him to write the first program that would allow the computer to monitor itself, a nod to Big Tech's current ambition to create a self-aware AI. It's hard to know what to make of Strachey, who despite struggling to concentrate at school and university was widely commended for his terrific teaching when he became the first Professor of Computation at the University of Oxford. What is obvious is the joy he took in making computers write nonsense poetry, games and music mash-ups, mostly in the dead of the night when his colleagues at the lab were fast asleep.

As the highly educated nephew of another famous queer, Bloomsbury Group writer and friend of Virginia Woolf, Lytton Strachey, Christopher would have been familiar with poetry. But instead of simulating the intense, sincere lovers of Anne Bradstreet's 'To My Dear and Loving Husband', Elizabeth Barrett Browning's 'How Do I Love Thee?' or Byron's 'She Walks in Beauty', his generated love poem produces a most unserious opening line: 'Duck duck'. Whereas Samuel Taylor Coleridge's 'sacred flame' burned for his Genevieve in what has become one of the most celebrated love poems of all time,[1] Strachey gives us the slightly terrifying 'covetous ardour' – surely worth a restraining order – and the ick-inducing 'yours keenly'. He makes the computational narrator a clingy, cutesy, besotted little psycho with an ambivalent sexuality, apparently not bothered about the species, let alone the gender, of its lover. Given that Strachey largely kept his sexuality private, his public expressions of love in his computer lab era appear to have been enjoyed only through the queer musings of his poem generator. It's an important moment in LGBTQ+ history, which is all about reading between the lines and looking for titbits of personal expression. We know much more about queer gestures towards freedom through writing, dance and music than via computers. Some people don't know quite what to make of the idea that a gay computer scientist's tongue-in-cheek lovesick narrators were making fun of standard heterosexual romance. But many, particularly queer students, are delighted that he used his rebellious intellect to prank the serious computer scientists in Turing's lab. I only wish the wooers-in-waiting on my dating apps would have sent me something quite as subversive.

There is so much potential to use computers to prod at the common tropes and queasy metaphors of lovers' exchanges. In 2024, I joined the Ethical Dating Online group run by Natasha McKeever and Luke Brunning of the University of Leeds. We wrote an open letter to UK, EU and US government departments asking them to pay attention to the use of generative AI in dating apps.[2] Part of what we were concerned about was generative AI tools making all user profiles and talking points the same. Thanks to standardised prompts and AI-enhanced photos, it's a sea of mediocre brunch-loving, Netflix-watching cloned profiles out there, and no one looks like themselves in their pictures. Strachey showed that this isn't the destiny of computation. Computers can process information in novel and surprising ways that could give us the freedom to appear as weird and wonderful as we truly are.

AI, everywhere

When Turing wrote the world's first programming manual for the Mark 1, it hardly made the papers. This was partly because the computer it described was so enormous, expensive and slow that it held little apparent interest for the general public. By contrast, when ChatGPT was released in 2023 it broke records for the fastest-growing consumer application since the origin of apps, way back in 1997 with the Nokia 6110 Snake game. Now we're using AI when we book holidays online, open our unnecessarily powerful smartphones, and – according to dubious but persuasive advertising – interact with smart fridges and freezers. Companies like OpenAI, Google and Microsoft have made AI capabilities available to the public and other companies have dived in, building and purchasing AI products to turbo-power their enterprises. Speed and scale are critical business factors, and AI can satisfy these ambitions in spades, transforming the consumer experience far beyond what we might currently be aware of. If, like me, most of your tech products are Apple, you're necessarily opting into a life with AI: Apple MD Tim Cook has stated that AI is fundamental to 'virtually every product that we build'. It's increasingly difficult for even the most tech-averse among us to avoid AI. It's there when we cross borders, open bank accounts, and call for an engineer to fix our gas boiler.

With each development in AI breathlessly reported by tabloids and academic journals alike, every journalist worth their salt is trying to find the newest and most apocalyptic story. Panic sells, but so does fantasy, and stories about AI ending the world jostle for space alongside claims that AI could find a cure for cancer, lift the global population out of poverty or offer a silver-bullet solution to global inequality. Steering a course between the hype on the one hand and the terror on the other is the only way we can make good choices about how we create and interact with AI. This book examines the many ways, big and small, in which AI affects our lives today, debunks the myths about what AI can and can't do, and lays out some ground rules for how we can all participate in making the technology better – and safer – for everyone.

One of the biggest falsehoods about the era of AI is that it's the first time the relationship between humanity and technology has been thrown into turmoil. Technology has never been, as we will discover, separate from humanity; Western mythology dictates that since the advent of fire, tools have been as much a part of our species as the bacteria in our gut. Like all technology, AI doesn't exist in a vacuum – and so to understand how to voice our enthusiasm for and anxieties about it, we need to investigate the ideas, infrastructures and histories that drive its progress. In Part I we go back to basics, exploring the myths, ideologies and ideas behind AI and its relationship to humankind. From Greek mythology to da Vinci and Darwin, we unpack the origins of current mania around AI's perils and possibilities. In Part II we delve deeper into how AI toes the line between destruction and salvation, arguing that it has been fetishised, made into an obsessive, guilty pleasure, by Hollywood blockbusters, unrestrained tech monopolies and by philosophical and social movements like utilitarianism and effective altruism. From facial recognition and machine objectivity to control and intelligence, I debunk some misleading language that tells us AI can do things that it can't. From there, I outline how we can revamp AI innovation and ethics, make it a little more controversial, and give the technology a chance of being both safe and fair for many generations to come.

AI ABC

You don't have to have any prior knowledge of how AI systems work to read this book, nor do you need to be up to date with the AI news cycle. As an AI ethicist, corporate speaker and podcast co-host working in AI ethics, governance and education, I've found that people generally know more about AI's uses and limitations than they give themselves credit for. Take Sneha Revanur, who as a high-school student stopped the state of California from implementing a racist algorithm that claimed to predict recidivism rates.[3] Without much technical insight into how the algorithm worked, Sneha gained international youth support for the campaign and overturned the proposal. Her 'way in' came from her understanding of how the disproportionate incarceration of African-American men drives cycles of poverty and injustice. Equally, HR professionals often tell me that they have a hunch that AI recruitment products can't actually 'de-bias' hiring. They know that making their companies more diverse means more than 'colourblind' recruitment, as many AI companies promise to be able to achieve on behalf of their clients. Diversity at work hinges on eliminating pay and childcare inequalities, tackling racist and sexist aggressions, preventing people from scheduling early-morning or evening meetings that might interfere with domestic obligations – an all-round cultural transformation![4] With a little more knowledge and confidence, millions of people worldwide can be empowered to select safe, positive and effective AI products, know their rights in relation to AI they encounter at work or in public spaces, get to grips with the risks of AI products that they bring into their homes, read news about AI more critically, engage in AI-related activism or tech union activity, and have more informed conversations with their friends, parents and children.

We are mostly unable to choose how we interact with AI: whether we like it or not, an increasing number of companies are implementing AI tools for things like customer service, push notifications or simply to recommend our next watch or listen. To have more control over our interactions we need to be literate in AI – which doesn't just mean knowing what AI is and how to interpret its behaviour, but also being able to debunk some of the false claims made by AI companies about what their systems can do. AI literacy involves understanding how state bodies like the police are using AI, and getting clued up on the ideological rifts at the heart of corporate and institutional politicking around companies like OpenAI. When I met the brilliant Audrey Tang, who transformed Taiwan's democratic governance during her tenure as Minister of Digital Affairs from 2022 to 2024, she was adamant that it isn't enough to be 'literate' in AI. We need to be actively involved, she said, in how it's created and regulated, just as we're required to take part in the judicial system as jury members and democratic governance as voters. Only through this kind of civic participation can we become proficient at interacting with AI, which Tang calls 'AI competence'.[5] Governments and regulatory bodies around the world don't seem to be able to follow in Taiwan's footsteps and allow citizens to have a say in how AI is created and deployed. This is an underestimated crisis that makes us more susceptible to threats like cybercrime and misinformation. As part of its broader AI and the Futures of Learning initiative, UNESCO is now developing 'AI competency' frameworks that support teachers and students' understanding of and involvement in AI creation. It's a start, but the scheme needs to be implemented nationwide, and globally.

Attempts at AI competence-building also need to work towards clear and informative labelling of AI products. Just as it's a requirement for a can of tomato soup to feature a food label that allows you to check on the tomato and genetically modified corn syrup content, it should also be obligatory for AI companies to tell you where the data that's used to train AI came from, who annotated it, and perhaps even who their other clients are. The military? Law enforcement? Governments? Only with this kind of information can we exercise our democratic rights to choose which tools we buy and from whom. More attention should be paid to AI systems built for local use, like autonomous servers and private, self-hosted AI applications that can run without much compute power. These tend to be more sustainable and can also increase community trust in AI, because tools and services are separate from large corporations and can establish their own data privacy and sovereignty principles. Plenty of such tools have emerged, especially in Latin America: their primary purpose is defending the public from Big Tech's chokehold by changing the way AI is currently produced. Without having to make money for shareholders and C-suite executives, organisations can concentrate on producing useful and good things like free software designed to promote knowledge about AI. If you used one of these tools, created by your local community, or even by your own family, would you trust it more? Would it be more likely to solve the issues that matter to you? More useful in your daily life? Less likely to be globally harmful? It's a challenge to change people's mindsets about the locations and people we think should create AI: we think it happens in companies or commercially sponsored university labs, not in rainforests or slums in Latin America. But first, let's reconsider what AI actually 'is'.

What is AI?

AI is many things. Systems are often labelled 'artificial intelligence' if they involve machine learning systems (the umbrella term for techniques like deep learning and natural language processing). Machine learning, which needs data, energy and compute power to function, is a statistics-based way of training algorithms to make predictions and classifications. Some, but not all, robots use machine learning. AI is mostly found in unglamorous, banal contexts like IT and telecoms, which have used AI for many years to assist with maintenance, provisioning and administrative tasks. What AI can do right now is limited by the corporate imagination – how companies believe AI is likely to generate profit. Here are seven ways in which AI is commonly, and often misleadingly, clustered today:

Task automation, which is a euphemism for technologies like social media posting and client invoicing that displace human labour. But when people say, 'AI is taking our jobs', it's not so much that AI is now sitting at your desk doing everything you did before, as actioning specific tasks that have traditionally been a core part of job descriptions – and, in the process, changing what it means to be a marketing manager, a lawyer, an engineer or a truck driver.

AI data analytics helps human data analysts by automating the data crunching process and, crucially, using AI to make sure the data is good enough to analyse in the first place. From combining data from lots of sources, checking for missing data, detecting anomalies and discovering if the source of data has changed, AI is now used at most stages of data preparation and analytics to do some of the grunt work on behalf of data analysts from all sectors, including operations, strategy, marketing, finance and PR teams.

Chatbots, which can also use generative AI and which you might interact with when a company doesn't want to link you to a human agent. Chatbots work by categorising what you're writing and then retrieving information that matches your query (not always successfully). Often they take your conversations and turn them into data about what their customers are saying and why. Chatbots can be powerful AI tools, or really basic ones.

Prediction tools claim to show you future trends based on what is happening now by analysing historical data, from how consumer behaviour will change to how a protein's 3D structure might look based on what we know about its amino acid sequence – or whether a bus contains soldiers or children (as seen via a military drone).

Content generation tools are a huge category, because lots of AI tools make things. We mostly use them to create text, video and images. You can ask a generative AI tool to come up with a music video for a jazz tune featuring Mr Bean riding an elephant, write a sonnet in the style of a nineteenth-century adolescent boy, a job description for a penguin specialist, a deepfake of the Pope inside a bouncy castle, or a vocal clone of Donald Trump. These work well because there are lots of jazz standards, audio of US presidents, poetry, teenage boys and job descriptions online that generative AI tools can learn from. This online content is grist to the mill, becoming the data that AI models are trained on. The more audio there is of a politician that a tool learns from, the fewer weird mistakes it will make when replicating the sound of their voice and the content of their speech.

Recognition technologies are really technologies that claim to know something about your body and categorise you accordingly, like voice, speech and gait biometric technologies.

Human augmentation is a huge market oriented towards medicine, life extension and everything in between, like the brain chips Elon Musk is making through his Neuralink venture.

These technologies span all industries, from science and medicine to arts and culture, and are widespread in the business world. It's important to recognise that the categories I've selected here are not terribly meaningful beyond their commercial applications. Many of the terms we currently use to describe AI miscommunicate what it can actually do. Trying to figure out how different kinds of AI systems work is even more challenging when there isn't a universally accepted baseline definition of AI, even as a general concept. Every regulatory body, organisation and policy observatory under the sun takes its own approach, with definitions of AI often divided along national lines. This means a government doesn't just come up with a perspective on what AI is by asking itself the question, 'What is AI?', but, as was the case for the UK, 'How can we stand out from how the EU defines AI?' Because the EU sought to define AI in order to better regulate it, companies with a vested interest in remaining outside of the scope of regulation applied pressure on the EU to define AI such that their own products were exempt from the most stringent obligations. What the EU takes to be a 'high-risk' AI system was the product of extensive lobbying from tech giants, who often seek to underplay the potential impact of their products while simultaneously overstating their tools' AI capabilities to the public. Relatively unadvanced systems, therefore, are being labelled as AI even though they contain only very basic or optional AI features. I've seen this with some recruitment tools that are branded 'AI' but have limited machine learning elements, which can also be 'switched off'. Many fairly rudimentary chatbots are also being touted as AI, even though technically speaking they are really glorified decision trees. Essentially, AI has become a buzzword that helps startups get funding, companies sell products, and Hollywood pitch dystopian futures, just as much as it's a tool that usefully automates aspects of domains like drug discovery and contract law.

AI is a massive, intimidating concept. The first step to knowing how to use it safely is to break it down into digestible chunks. Then we can ask again: what do we want AI to do, and how should we create it? The key is to get a variety of answers that speak to different people's life experiences and bring technology's relationship with society sharply into focus. This is why we need definitions of AI which make it clear that hardware and software don't exist in a vacuum but are related to people, the material world and culture. If we look at AI this way, it begins much earlier than we think it does, in water-intensive lithium fields and geopolitical tensions over access to Taiwan's silicon shield. It also ends quite a bit after we might believe the technology is completed. The course of AI development depends on wide-eyed marketeers, vendors at startups with ambitious sales targets, and the success Big Tech lobbyists have in wining and dining regulators. Where systems are programmed to learn from customer behaviour, the interactions that we have with AI on a day-to-day basis, whether it's deployed in our homes or at work, are also part of the AI training process. This is our – often unwitting – contribution to AI development, and it's crucial we also treat this as a component feature of what AI is today.

Breaking AI down into a series of stories allows us to focus in on mined quartz superheated into silicon and hardware assembled by Apple's suicidal iPad factory workers, photos taken for Google Maps' Street View by contractors on $15/hour salaries, and the traces of our online and offline lives that are captured as data fed into large language models (LLMs). LLMs are models good at interpreting and generating language; ChatGPT, for example, is a form of LLM. These phenomena are just a fraction of what AI is – and, collectively, they're a far cry from the totalising, hype-saturated messages that we're exposed to from the powers above, be it from Big Tech marketeers or the mass media. Of course, AI isn't just the sum of its parts, but something that inspires and forecloses new futures. We're told that superintelligence is both the desirable and inevitable future, and there's no room for any other version of events. AI will apparently eradicate doubt and uncertainty about both the future and ourselves by revealing who we are, what our purpose on Earth (and beyond) is, and what will become of us in the 'next stage' of human evolution. This is good branding, because AI isn't an oracle, and nor are its makers. Even at a technical level, there's more doubt and uncertainty inside an AI system than you might think. AI is probabilistic, which means it uses statistics to make decisions – unlike calculators, which are deterministic because they follow strict mathematical rules at all times. There's no randomness or uncertainty in a calculator, because all the arithmetic is written in advance. A generative AI tool tasked with creating a flamingo picture, on the other hand, learns on the trot, which means that it uses probabilities to come up with the image it thinks you want. Writing the same prompt twice won't get you the same picture twice – the input doesn't always produce the same output. This makes the outputs of these models uncertain (on purpose, so it's more creative for the person using it). And unlike calculators, the impact of an AI system isn't always immediate – the impact of an output might only become visible much later, for example when a person is denied a loan by a bank's vetting system.

Deep learning models like Stable Diffusion or DALL·E that we might use to create our flamingo pictures are also rife with uncertainty. This is because we don't know for sure what's going on inside their hidden layers, where information is processed. Each layer of the model, which is a type of 'neural network' system, learns from the information given to it by the previous one. How its hidden layers behave when you ask it to create the flamingo image depends on how it has learned to recognise the shape of the bird, and how much it associates it with visual elements like pink feathers and long, spindly legs. How the model works is contingent on all these variables. The more variables, the more uncertainty. The more hidden layers there are in this deep learning model, the more doubt there is about how it's actually working. If you can't observe how the system functions as easily as you could the mechanisms of a watch with a transparent case, it's tricky to know if it's operating as it should. This is true of all neural networks, not just those that are known as 'black box' models. There's no question that this inherent uncertainty feeds into AI's reputation as an enigma, a technology that can't quite be pinned down because it is both reality and mythology. When I asked over sixty workers at a tech multinational what AI is, they suggested a range of answers. 'The definition of AI is unclear to a lot of people,' one engineer said about their own workforce, which wasn't reassuring.

The fantasy of AI being able to do anything you want it to is upheld by nebulous definitions that focus more on abstract concepts like autonomy than on material infrastructure and human labour. This allows the industry to maintain hype and mystique. Governments use AI's definitional ambiguity to serve nationalist and imperialist interests, to the extent that historians like Thomas Haigh suggest AI is little more than a brand.[6] To Haigh, this brand was collectively established by both the universities that pioneered and continue to dominate AI research, like MIT, Stanford and Carnegie Mellon, and the Big Tech players who turn academic brainpower into products. The commercial sector requires AI to signal quality, just as a Gucci suit might conjure images of class and craftsmanship. This is why marketing is AI's bread and butter. Images of human data labellers and quartz mines don't inspire the same sense of wonder as do those of transparent humans covered in data points or self-driving cars racing along motorways in the sky. Like the rest of us, AI innovators are seduced by the possibilities for AI expressed in film, literature and digital media, which is why analogies between AI systems and *The Terminator* (1984) are still rife in AI companies, even though their products are nothing like killer robots.

Even if we boil down what AI is to the less expansive term 'algorithm', we find that it remains just as elusive. Derived from 'algebra', which dates from ninth-century Arabic, it indicates that algorithms relate to calculus, but says little about what they actually 'do'. In Tamil, on the other hand, algorithms are often called *Nerimurai*, where *neri* means 'norm' and *murai* means 'the way to do something'.[7] This is a brilliantly constructed word, because it highlights how algorithms favour 'norms' (socially dominant or accepted rules and ideas), and therefore do not merely perpetuate the status quo but exacerbate it by making inequalities proliferate more quickly and at scale.

I also like 'Tequiologies' as a substitute for 'technologies', a portmanteau created by Yasnaya Elena Aguilar Gil, a linguist from Ayutla Mixe in Oaxaca, Mexico.[8] She took the word *tequitl* – meaning work, contribution, duty – from the central Mexican language Nahuatl to describe AI that might be specifically designed to support collaborative work. *Tequio*, she says, is community-level, small-scale efforts that contribute to a larger issue. There are many such words in Hispanic languages that signify collaborative community work within Indigenous societies. This often happens in places where the construction of communal buildings, irrigation systems and farming relies on informal economies of semi-voluntary quid pro quo, or where there is an expectation of social involvement in helping the elderly, orphans and the disabled. Some variations refer to collective education, a community or generational knowledge, or other forms of political social organising, like rallying together to claim their rights against an oppressive regime. In areas of central and southern Chile community work is called *minga*, and in Peru, Bolivia and Ecuador *minka*, but across Central and South America many other terms are used, like *ayni*, *yanapa*, *mita*, *andecha* and *sextaferia*.

During my PhD, I spent six months in the Spanish city of Granada. In a bid to make friends and eat some delicious produce, I joined a co-operative farm. This meant at least two Saturdays per month working the land in baking heat – followed by beers and chocolate churros in the local bar for those who managed not to get sunstroke. There was also an unhurried, gossipy weekly meeting that more often than not stopped just short of a shouting match when discussing social and agricultural issues. Even with my limited understanding of what was going on, these meetings possessed all the tensions of collective organising. There are few niceties in democratic practices. As biologist and historian of science Donna Haraway brilliantly put it, living in a way that's 'terrestrial' (down to earth and connected with the Earth) is not the same thing as living innocently.[9] Sixty people piled into a small, unventilated room debating whether short-term workers were more unhelpful than helpful, and disagreeing about what vegetables to plant, did not feel like an innocent utopian Marxist idyll. But it achieved, somehow, considered and purpose-driven innovation.

Tequio communicates scale and usage: where its development occurs and how. It tells you exactly how the system should be used – not as a replacement, but as a contribution to existing processes. It gets us better acquainted with informal economies, survival mechanisms, and ways of performing our social obligations. And it invites our consideration of which kinds of AI are contributing to essential work or ways of living. We may think that AI is a neutral term, by which I mean it represents exactly the technology that it refers to, but of course it has now taken on its own meaning in contemporary usage, becoming synonymous with Big Tech, commercial use and big data. We need to keep the term flexible, up for debate and self-reflexive – aware of its own shortcomings.

Necroethics or pharmakon?

While most people lack a clear understanding of what AI is, they do share a fear that it might prompt the end of life as we know it. In the spring of 2022 I was grilled by four resident panellists of the BBC Radio 4 programme *The Moral Maze* about whether AI was going to kill us all. It's a question that's pretty easy to get behind, and one that I am asked with increasing urgency by all kinds of frightened faces from across the political aisle, and from different generations and industries. The question is posed so often, I suspect, because it's the one concern about AI that we know how to formulate: is it going to be the end of us? This is also the only answer that people often want to hear in response to the question 'What is the most important issue in ethics right now?' If I don't say 'imminent death', I can see their eyes glaze over and I find myself on the back foot, trying to defend a subject that is at most adjacent to their actual interest, like biometric surveillance, Big Tech monopolies or the homogeneity of the AI workforce.

Later that year I was invited to speak at the Southbank Centre in London with a number of other panellists including computer scientist Stuart Russell. These events are always a mixed bag for me because, understandably, the audience loves to be afraid of AI, believes that AI is both scary and necessary, and only sees AI experts as people like Russell: male computer scientists whose speciality is building technology (rather than doing ethics work). We were tasked with answering the question on everyone's lips: 'Should we be afraid of AI?' Yes, Russell said, we should be very afraid of an AI extinction event. Fine, I replied, but what about the issues underlying those risks, like geopolitical tensions, pervasive systemic inequality, Big Tech's 'move-fast-and-break-things' mantra and other unethical work practices? And have you considered that tackling catastrophic risks means ending the monopoly over compute power and AI development, the ongoing lack of diversity in the workforce, and the power shareholders have to make companies churn out AI products that are, as one engineer told CNBC, 'a big pile of nonsense'.[10] It's this 'Any AI is better than no AI' outlook that's resulting in dangerous and socially detrimental tech products being released into the wild, and yet this is rarely mentioned as an important cause of potential AI extinction scenarios. Equally, disempowering predictions that AI will turn on humanity make it seem like an inevitability, when there's plenty we can do to prevent catastrophes from happening and to influence AI's direction of travel.

You might have noticed that the people most worried about the apocalypse are also those who are building the machines which they claim will cause it. This is an odd paradox, unless you're former Google engineer and 'futurist' Ray Kurzweil, who believes that it's a risk worth taking because humanity must fuse with AI if we are to reach our true potential. Of course, not all of us will fuse with AI, just the select few who can afford to embody progress on behalf of the human race. As I will discuss, philosophers and tech opinion leaders have determined via back-of-the envelope calculations that the probability of being saved by AI is slightly better than the chances of it exterminating us. The lack of social consultation no doubt makes them feel very big. I'd take tech that's mildly useful or beneficial over devices that offer salvation or extermination any day.

The Greeks had a word for things with both positive and negative consequences: *pharmakon*, which can mean a poison, a remedy or a scapegoat. AI embodies this variability of meanings well, because it's considered to be both the root of all our problems and the best hope we have for a prosperous future, while also being a good scapegoat – there are countless examples of it facilitating social and political blame-mongering. I'll explain this by returning to tales of humanity's technological origins. Technology transformed the human body just as writing changed our physiology, resulting in specialised musculature and specific regions of the central nervous system that control it. Shifting the conversation from 'death by AI' to 'a good life with it' means recognising that humanity is never merely organic and the organic is always partly technological. There is no nature versus technology. Those two things have been bound together since the beginning.

We need to regain our focus: the important thing now is

to learn how to sustain and heal each other in a technological world. It's the difference between living well and killing well. This view also gives ethics a wider reach, so that rather than homing in on AI and obscuring broader contextual issues, we can explore the social and geopolitical conditions that affect our experience of AI. You don't have to be an AI ethicist to do this – your knowledge of the labour force, the environment, society and culture, and your experience of being subjected to AI in any context are important contributions to working towards making AI better and safer for everyone.

The question about whether AI will kill us all shows that AI has become mired in 'necroethics' – ethics centred around death. This includes training drones to kill people 'well', or, in the case of self-driving cars, coming up with the correct utilitarian response to the 'Trolley Problem' – the dilemma of whether and how the driver should intervene in an emergency. If it had to, should the car swerve towards the cyclist with or without a helmet? A mother and child or a solitary grandmother? Who is more worthy of life? This utilitarian bind is a professional version of a game of 'would you rather?' Everything is set in competition with everything else for the most deserving life. The quantification and valuation of different life forms often appeals to scientists, to whom the numerical assessment of risk and reward comes most naturally. But when we think like this about death and dying, we contort ourselves in odd ways. For example, if you spend five minutes reading into the ethics of drone technology in warfare, you will notice that 'ethics' in a time of war is dubious. Yes, there are internationally recognised rules of war, but the fact is that war is where ethics goes to die. As Greek tragedian Aeschylus said, the first casualty of war is truth. AI can estrange truth even further by adding statistical uncertainty into the mix. A killer drone, for example, might indicate that there is a 67 per cent probability that an observed van is carrying terrorists rather than, say, schoolchildren. More information doesn't dissolve the fundamental ambivalence of these impossible choices. As anthropologist Deborah Bird Rose says, 'An ethical response to the call of others does not hinge on killing or not killing. It hinges on taking responsibility for one's actions.'[11] Simplifying ethics down to who should die, and who should not, distracts from the question of how companies can take responsibility for the products they create, deploy them responsibly, and be responsive to consumer complaints. None of this, unfortunately, is currently the norm.

AI ethics, in my view, needs to be extracted from moments of crisis and conflict and focus on what it means to live a good life alongside one another, a life mediated by technology. This doesn't mean turning away from hard problems. On the contrary, as Donna Haraway says, 'There is a fine line between acknowledging the extent and seriousness of the troubles [that we face] and succumbing to abstract futurism and its effects of sublime despair and its politics of sublime indifference.'[12] Often, turning on the news, we feel either total paralysis or something akin to a psychological shrug of the shoulders. This is the effect produced by cycles of televised violence broadcast to numbed audiences who have seen it all before and feel like they can't do anything about it. In this book I explore how we can avoid succumbing to an abstract sense of fear, hopelessness and insensitivity. Running alongside concerns about being run over by Teslas or rogue robots turning us into paperclips is the claim that humanity cannot progress as a species if we don't pursue AI, or that, optimistically, AI can resolve humanity's greatest problems. The truth about what AI's overarching effect will be, I argue, is somewhere between annihilation and salvation. I explain this by returning to tales of humanity's technological origins. We begin with the Prometheus myth, where technology isn't some terrifying externality but part of the human identity. Shifting the conversation from death by AI to a good life with it means recognising AI's humanity, not just our own.

Part I

What's Wrong with AI?

1

The Pernicious Myths on Which AI Is Built

Stealing fire from the gods

In the beginning we were 'just' human, and then AI came along and disturbed our peace. This is what we are told. But there are other stories.

It has been said that there were once two fraternal gods, Prometheus and Epimetheus. Epimetheus was responsible for handing out physical attributes to all earthlings. To the giraffes he gave long necks; to the birds wings so they could fly. But by the time he came to the humans he had run out of special qualities. Seized with a new idea, Prometheus stole fire from the other gods and gave it to the humans in lieu of, for example, blubber to keep them warm or humps to store water in. And so, the tale goes, while animals are well *adapted* to their environment, humans used – or *adopted* – fire to make tools and sculpt their way into the future. Humanity is nothing without technology. If you look around, you'll see signs everywhere of just how poorly our bodies are prepared for life on Earth, and how reliant we are on technology to survive and flourish. I was born with two rows of teeth like a shark, eyesight so myopic that, by the time I was thirty, if I wasn't wearing contact lenses I couldn't tell who I had woken up next to in the morning, and a wheat allergy that could have cost me my life. I dread to think what would have become of me without orthodontics, optometry and medicine (and acupuncture, and therapy, and homoeopathy).

At eighteen years old, I had maxillofacial surgery to resolve some dental-related breathing issues. My jaw is now partly made of metal, and I've always felt a little bit cyborgian. The medicine I've taken has also played a part in making me who I am: from immunotherapy to SSRIs, my humanity is a pharmacological condition – it's nothing without drugs, bio-engineered food and supplements. And that goes for my gender too. With my intrauterine birth control device which controls my hormones, and a whole host of other products which bio-engineer my femaleness, I'm living proof of what philosopher Paul Preciado calls 'the fiction of bio-femininity',[1] the fantasy of the natural woman. I am as much a woman as I am 'a modern industrial artefact',[2] as he puts it. Femininity is nothing without industrially produced chemical agents which are terrible for our health, as personal care product studies repeatedly show us.[3] We are integrated with the technologies that we use to make ourselves human. This means we are not necessarily more artificial than AI. Whether or not you are prepared to take an ontological leap and reconsider what it means to be human, it's important that we acknowledge the artificiality of humans and the human-ness of AI. What we perceive to be human intelligence is also engineered through a variety of socio-technical mechanisms from health and food to safety and education.

Technology is so closely entwined with humanity that it has influenced how we evolve, too. The discovery of the 1.75 million-year-old Olduvai Hominid 7 hand in 1960 showed how early human tool use made our hands evolve to be powerful and precise. When humans started cooking with fire, Prometheus' gift to humankind, it drastically changed our gut microbiome. Philosophers of technology like Bernard Stiegler and Gilbert Simondon argue that technology is actually part of the human race: it defines us, because we wouldn't be who we are without it.[4] Simondon urges us not to push technology away like a 'strange or foreign being', but instead discover it as human.[5] I suggest that we give this a second thought. You will find humans everywhere in AI, from administrators and technicians in Texan data centres to Amazon's data labellers who train AI models in Kenyan warehouses.[6] Systems are piloted by and operated on people, like Microsoft's prison surveillance systems across Africa,[7] because of choices made by Big Tech executives and by a stream of thoughtless, power-grabbing bureaucrats. Further behind the scenes, there are mine operators in Spruce Pine quartz quarries in North Carolina and managers of design teams at Taiwanese semiconductor manufacturing plants. There is no technology without people, which is why we need to recognise AI's humanity, and not just our own. The more automated life becomes, the more humans have to get involved. There is no longer an 'AI industry', as AI is integrated into almost every industry. It's merely an illusion that the labour force is disappearing: work is simply shifting, from artists to data labellers and from marketeers to engineers.

Some rather prophetic lines written by Simondon in 1958 predict the attitude of today's titans of Silicon Valley:

> Men who have knowledge of technical objects and appreciate their significance try to justify their judgment by giving to the technical object the only status that today has any stability apart from that granted to aesthetic objects, the status of something sacred. This, of course, gives rise to an intemperate technicism that is nothing other than idolatry of the machine and, through such idolatry, by way of identification, it leads to a technocratic yearning for unconditional power.[8]

In this marvellous bit of foresight, we can almost see Elon Musk parking a Tesla on the White House's front lawn ahead of the 2024 US elections. Yes, technology has been elevated to something sacred by technologists, who want to be more than just engineers or entrepreneurs; they hanker for the status of pioneers, adventurers and prophets of a new era. As historian of science Theodore Porter said, 'scientists, under conditions of modernity, assume many of the functions of priests',[9] whose seminary formation includes bypassing regulatory frameworks and disengaging from civil liberties obligations. For Porter, the fact that cutting-edge research is now geared towards a profit motive is partly why science is no longer a public good, echoing twentieth-century economist Friedrich Hayek's view that establishing a technocracy goes counter to what the scientific revolution was trying to achieve and will put us back on 'the road to serfdom'.[10] Indeed, as we've seen with Musk, building tools has become an exercise in accruing power rather than simply providing a service or fulfilling a function.[11] Aspirational characters like the Tesla and SpaceX founder now go to Washington on secondment from Silicon Valley. Aptly, the acronym for his Department of Government Efficiency under Trump's regime is DOGE, also the name of the rulers that led the Republic of Venice for over a hundred years until the eighteenth century. The doges may have had sizeable ambitions for Venice's spectacular wealth, but Musk has his sights on the colonisation of the universe.

If, as the Prometheus myth goes, technology is how we as humans make ourselves, then technocratic governance is a symptom of the power we have attributed to AI and its creators to decide what it means to be human. We are constantly sold the message that we must better ourselves using technology in order to fulfil our destiny, accompanied by famous icons of Renaissance humanism. Chief among them is Leonardo da Vinci's Vitruvian Man, which has become a kind of mascot for the belief that humans must craft the ending to our own evolutionary journey. Enter VMan, human perfectionism's spiritual leader.

VMan

In the eighteenth century, the European Enlightenment aimed to use science to displace the power of the Church and its Christian God and put human life at the centre of the world. Of course, the Enlightenment failed to make a dent in the human need for worship. Leonardo da Vinci's Vitruvian Man became the icon of this new human-centred ideology: he is Adam without Eve, and free from God. While few have seen the original – VMan is fragile and rarely on loan from his home in Venice's Gallerie dell'Accademia – we are familiar with his lean, muscular limbs of perfect mathematical proportions that flip between two forms, as though they were moving through a jumping jack or turning on a medieval breaking wheel. In one, his limbs are taut and elongated – a male gymnast in the Iron Cross position on rings – in the second, they are stretched into a starfish. It's significant that this is a drawing composed of pencil-like stains of pen, brown ink and watercolour, rather than a painting. The stripped-back form imitates da Vinci's ambition: to reveal the human laid bare. Yet the meticulous line drawing is a fantasy. It lies to us in its claims: first, that man(-kind) in its purest form is a self-sustaining island, dependent on no one and nothing; second, that science and technology can make us perfect; and third, that this is what the ideal human looks like. Compared to him, we are subhuman and subpar.

What strikes me most when I compare myself to the image is my own lack of symmetry: one of my legs is slightly shorter than the other, one foot larger, and one breast smaller (although, of course, there is no Vitruvian Woman). Yet in the sciences, VMan has become the poster boy for humanity's insatiable quest for knowledge and territory. Google DeepMind hangs his image above the reception desk at its London King's Cross office, NASA stuck him on its Expedition 37 crew patches and the Human Genome Project made him an emblem of its attempts to unravel the secrets of the body. Like Rodin's stunning, long-toed and thickly biceped *Le Penseur* (*The Thinker*), VMan's phy-sique reflects his intellectual capability. He represents the best of human endeavour, not only because of how well his neurons are firing but because of how good he looks when they are. When tech companies use this image, they take up da Vinci's quest for a perfection so absolute as to be transcendental, whether through ever-smarter AI or by projecting humans into outer space. The implication is that we are using technology to fulfil our human destiny; somewhat paradoxically, this logic dictates that we can become 'more' human by becoming 'more than' human.

VMan is not only the future that tech companies and space missions alike desire, but a Western origin story. This is because whatever is presented to us as our future must tap into long-standing myths about the past, as Trump's 'Make America Great Again' slogan does in aligning with fantasies about a bygone utopia (a pipe dream). In being the founding father of civilised and able humankind, VMan establishes its strategic direction. He shows that the archetypal human is definitively male, by which I'm not merely referring to his penis and other physical characteristics but to how he expresses the real marker of traditional maleness: his independence. He doesn't look like he'd be confined to domestic spaces, and surely would never be required to spoon-feed children or elderly relatives. Da Vinci cuts out of the frame the relations that allow VMan to live his life, eat his meals and file his tax returns. He also dispels any part of VMan that might not be 'human', like walking sticks and spectacles. His microbiome has not yet been discovered – he is not made of bacteria, just human flesh. He is pure lines and musculature. He has not heard that democracy is about other people. He is autonomous, agentic, free: an island, not doubting his ability to act or be listened to. He is God's nepo-baby, untouched by the demands of social and economic life. If eighteenth-century notions of progress were geared towards the ultimate emancipation of man, VMan is its greatest apostle.

NASA's Extravehicular Activity (EVA) insignia. This embroidered emblem is worn on the right shoulder of US spacesuits used in Extravehicular Activity (EVA) or spacewalks

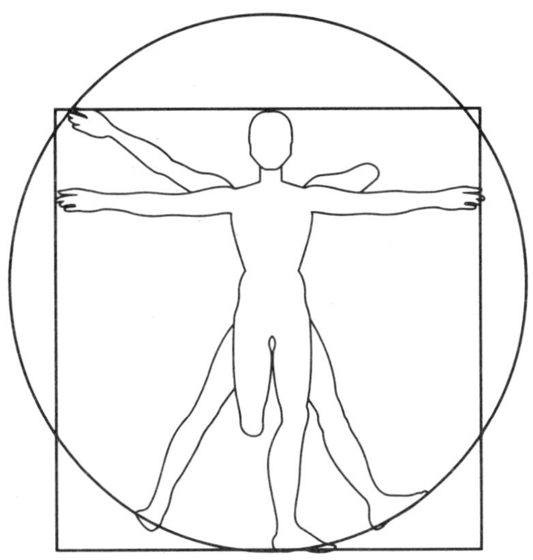

Disabled Vitruvian Man by Déborah 'Debs' Rodrigues

Auguste Rodin's *Le Penseur*, completed in 1904,
now in the garden of Musée Rodin, Paris

It's important to note that this is the archetype of a human being that we not only idealise, but that we design technologies for. Infrastructure has been built around him, car seats moulded to his height. The generic is bespoke to him because it has been crafted to his specifications. Beds are sized to his height, his average calorie intake dictates the government's recommended amount. Even the kerb bend on the street is moulded to his gait. He epitomises able-bodiedness, and this disguises his reliance on a built environment tailor-made for him. This is why a disabled VMan would be a contradiction in terms, because the disability would highlight his reliance on a chair, a cane or a carer. I love Brazilian motion designer

Déborah Rodrigues' disabled VMan,[12] whose amputated leg is impressed upon the frame of perfection. As a long-term *Rocky Horror Picture Show* fan, it was the ultimate gift to see a life-size neon VMan on stage in Richard O'Brien's 2024 revival,[13] framing the birth of Frank n' Furter's human sex toy, Rocky. Rocky, like VMan, is born a fully grown muscle man, and therefore does not endure the debasement of total dependence as a baby, nor the humiliation of evolution from apes. Instead he bounces out of his multicolour liquid birth tank, peels off his bandages, and carries his groom straight into the wedding chapel to screw.

Part of what makes this scene appealingly perverted is the reminder of how appalling it is to be born helpless with our mouths seeking out our mothers' nipples. We lie to ourselves that these days of total dependence are long gone by pretending that technology does not sustain us all the time in invisible ways. We have pavements and lamp posts and gravel, steps and ramps and elevators and escalators and tamed horses and cars, and tubes we've engineered to carry hundreds of people into the sky. As the Prometheus myth tells us, we are poorly adapted to the environment. In the UK the average life expectancy of a homeless person is around half that of everyone else.[14] The human body extends beyond our organs to our support systems, medical care and financial assistance. This is what is particularly noxious about 'the American dream', where the exceptional success stories are touted as examples of how meritocracy is alive and well, and individuals need only take responsibility for themselves in order to be lifted out of poverty and achieve genuine equality. What do we have to put out of mind for fantasies to seem true? Responsible for what exactly, we might add? If fine particulate matter is a third higher in poorer regions of Europe, are the inhabitants of these regions also responsible for their lower health outcomes due to environmental inequalities?

This is why the popularity of VMan as a stock image for AI and an emblem for NASA missions is so telling about the kinds of futures tech companies are trying to usher in. We will, they tell us, finally be free of material constraints on our bodies, as we were at the beginning of time. But our task is not to pretend that our social obligations and the material constraints on our bodies will cease to exist in the hunt for total control, but to accept interdependency and mortality as that which binds us together. Our reliance on each other and on our fragile, shared social and ecological infrastructures is not a negative thing. Vulnerability, in philosopher Judith Butler's conception of it, is not about you or me feeling vulnerable. It's about recognising that our shared lives rely on peace, nourishment, good air and water.[15] The neoliberal view that equality is about the individual often fails to take this into account, and so cannot think of redistribution as the final issue. Ethics should be concerned with repairing social bonds to make life liveable, together. This is why it's wrong to focus on the AI apocalypse as something binary, an instant ending: it hides from sight the 'slow death' and everyday dispossessions that are actually happening now – and which we can address. Focusing on threats to reciprocal global bonds and obligations is tricky when society teaches us that (technology-mediated) self-sufficiency is something we should strive for. Any illusions of autonomy that we might have are repeatedly undermined in the course of life; you might get ill and require support, you might have a disability, you use utensils to cook and clean and biotechnologies to help or prevent you from conceiving. AI, which is itself heavily reliant on human workers and purpose-built infrastructure, changes none of this: self-sufficiency is a mirage that AI cannot achieve on our behalf.

From ape to AI

I'm looking at the image accompanying Yuval Harari's essay on 'Our Nonconscious Future' from the online *Encyclopedia Britannica*.[16] On one side of the image there is a gorilla, and on the other an erect hominid walking into a posthuman future, its body shattered into datafied dust. This is evolution along the straightest of lines. In a Radio 4 Harari feature, the evolutionary line-up is once again a male-bodied affair, with an Egyptian in a bob cut on the far left and the modern man glued to his phone on the right, and a cast of history's protagonists in between, from Romans to Shakespeare's Hamlet.[17] This is not just a string of Western icons but a metaphor of evolution that engineers our understanding of the connection between apes (one moment in time) and Romans (and another).

Along with the Vitruvian Man, one of the key aspirations shared by the tech broligarchy (to borrow Brooke Harrington's coinage)[18] is that we will be able to meld with machines and achieve a 'transhuman' future – the final step in our evolution. This fantasy depends on the belief that evolution is a straight line – a fixed, determined march towards progress. When exploring the possibilities of what it will mean to live well with AI, we need to understand that this doesn't mean turning our back on our origins – instead, it requires us to gain a better awareness of how our species has always grown up alongside non-human life.

Commenting on one of Darwin's diagrams from the 1850s, Tim Ingold writes that 'the life of every individual is condensed into a single point; it's we who draw the connecting lines between them'.[19] Points and lines represent time and inheritance in one continuous flow, where one person originates neatly from another person. But for Ingold this is entirely misleading, because human life intersects with non-human life all the time, making every living being 'a bundle of entangled lines' rather than a straight line of connecting points. Of course, the messy reality of our interdependence with other species doesn't signal capital P 'Progress' in quite the same way, nor does it lend itself to species hierarchies. Darwin's 'artificially reconstructed skeleton of points and connectors',[20] as Ingold puts it, sucks the life out of the vibrant ecology we participate in as humans. Darwin's diagrams condense the tree of life into a fan of dotted lines, so that the tree is 'shattered into thousands of generational segments, each compacted into a dot'.[21] While maximalist representations of family trees from the thirteenth century onwards often brought lines of descent to life in mini-portraits of descendants floating on branches embellished with leaves, Darwin's tree is datafied into impersonal, featureless points on a page. In trying to establish life at specific spots, Darwin's diagram makes human 'beings' of us, disguising the 'becomings' that occur even at those fixed points. What I mean by this is that the word 'being' implies that we are a fixed thing – consider how differently we might see ourselves had we called our species 'human becomings'. We need to bend our minds a little and accept that the human body is not a fixed entity but a thoroughfare of hormones and chemicals that keep us in a constant state of transformation.

As I've shown, when used by AI companies, VMan is not just a mascot but a blueprint for a predefined future. It's crucial that the public buys into this idealised vision of human destiny to 'sign off' on various sacrifices and trade-offs that we must make of ourselves and our planet to support their vision. We are asked to turn a blind eye to the exploitation of data labellers in countries like Venezuela,[22] and hope that the influx of data centres planned for the next decade assumes control of some other city's real estate and local energy supply instead of our own. The content moderators working for OpenAI's ChatGPT in Kenya suffer psychological trauma, receive extremely low wages and are at risk of abrupt dismissal at any time.[23] These

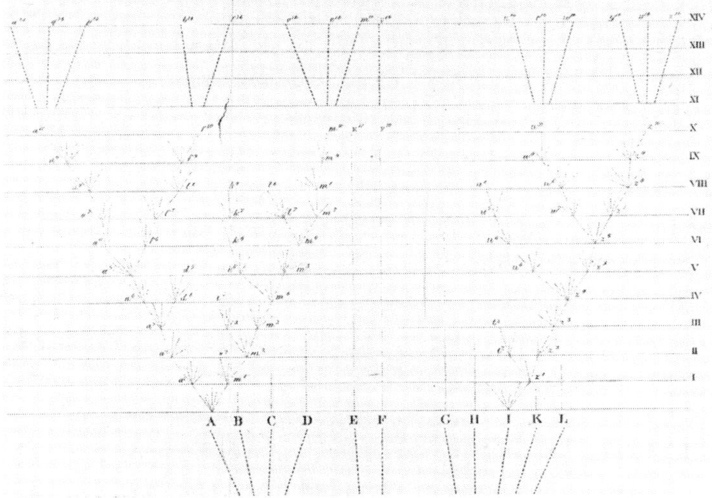

Known as 'The Tree of Life', this celebrated schema for evolution is the only illustration in Darwin's *On the Origin of Species* (1859).

are treated like uncomfortable and unavoidable speed bumps on the road to a utopian future.

OpenAI's mission statement claims that 'Our primary fiduciary duty is to humanity. We anticipate needing to marshal substantial resources to fulfil our mission, but will always diligently act to minimise conflicts of interest among our employees and stakeholders that could compromise broad benefit.'[24] Like so many Big Tech statements, this is both utilitarian, cryptic and euphemistic. Whom are they prepared to throw under the bus, and for what 'broad benefit'? Who is most disadvantaged by their claim on substantial resources? How substantial, exactly? These companies are selling us a future which they also claim is the only one worth desiring, but it's not anyone's job to say what is the ultimate goal towards which we should be striving. Big Tech mission statements have an authoritarian bent in their demands that we share the same view – or else face being left behind. That perspective is communicated as propaganda to a primed and coerced public awaiting Apple's reassurance that life will be easier with the latest iPhone.

There's an arrogance, however, to anyone telling you that there's just one way to optimise your life. This is why the march of progress proposed by transhumanism is particularly nauseous. Those that march under its banner call for technology to be oriented towards the perfection of the human mind and body, such that disease and death are oddities of the past. Transhumanists advocate for the use of advanced technologies such as gene-cloning, nanotechnology and AI on humans to achieve their goals. They hope that, one day, the human body can be encoded into the mind and replaced when necessary with new, artificial organs prepared using advanced technology. Part of why this is so appealing to transhumanists is that they believe that 'in the wake of such interventions, humanity will emerge from childhood and enter the posthuman age', as physician Osman Elbek puts it.[25] Like neoliberalism, transhumanism stems from the triumph of the free market and privatised science, as well as the belief that a fully autonomous, rational being is both humanity's destiny and its origin story – the final stop on the Roman road from ape to AI. As Mike Federowicz (who, tellingly, dubbed himself Mike Darwin), president of cryonics organisation Alcor Life Extension Foundation (1983–8), once stated: 'expanding our own futures, extending our own lives, that is the final frontier and the only truly endless one'.[26] The goal is to cross the frontier into secular heaven, where death no longer looms. Think of NASA's VMan armbands: off we go, away from global food shortages and environmental turmoil with our vacuum-packed potato purée.

This ideology is incompatible with the ideas we discussed in the Introduction which state that we have always been 'more-than' human, in the sense that we are also bacteria and prosthetics. Transhumanism aims to use AI to make the earthliness of humankind nothing more than a bad memory, like an embarrassing aunt or an acned adolescent. It's the difference between wanting to be cryogenically frozen at death or doing all you can to avoid dying, Bryan Johnson-style (the tech entrepreneur billionaire who received blood transfusions from his son), and making peace with inevitably turning into compost. This mission is qualitatively distinct from the diasporic LA health kick movement marketed to global consumers, which has given rise to what *The New York Times* has recently called the Wellness Elite. What Johnson is trying to do goes beyond bespoke diets and wellness retreats. He believes he is prototyping new life-extension techniques and perfecting long-running ones to suspend time itself. Such ambitions rest on a very specific philosophy of success, progress and perfection that defines the meaning of life and humanity's place within it. This heady network of ideas is preventing us from tuning into the mutual dependence of plant, animal and machine life by providing us with a smokescreen of relief: the possibility of using transhumanism to opt out of mortality altogether.

In LA, breaking natural cycles of growth and decay isn't too much of a stretch, but for many people across the world it's an absurdity. Speaking about the Aboriginal Australian peoples she lived with for many decades, Deborah Bird Rose notes that 'in a world of hunting and gathering, death and continuity are core aspects of the integrity of life, and are always unavoidably present in people's lives and minds'.[27] By extracting ourselves from that cycle we also risk disengaging from, as Thom van Dooren says, 'a system in which we live and die *with* others, live and die *for* others'.[28] In other words, our lives end so we can make space on Earth for subsequent generations. Dying is not just inevitable, it's an obligation to the planet and to each other. I am reminded by this of the Indonesian Toraja people, for whom deceased relations are an important part of the living family.[29] Relatives take loved ones out of their coffins each year to clean their clothes, give them a cigarette to smoke, and involve the mummified body in family activities.[30] Why, exactly, are they expressing their gratitude to the dead? For living with them, and then dying for them! For allowing subsequent generations to live in their stead! What's also interesting is how death is seen by the Toraja not as an empty nothingness but as a change in state. These views are often built into language. In Swahili, death is also described as a transition into another stage of existence, as scholars like John Misana Biseko have pointed out.[31] Religions like Jainism also stress that human life is a mere moment in time and space, which is exactly right, because if time on Earth was encapsulated in twenty-four hours, then modern humans have only been around for just over a minute.[32] Extending individual lifespans to take up more space in the history of the planet seems a bit desperate.

Transhumanism's attempts to scale up human significance can be nicely contrasted with the oldest living human on record's total lack of interest in longevity. Jeanne Calment (1875–1997) enjoyed the occasional cigarette, daily desserts and morning coffee. Each night Calment would pray about the afterlife that was still, somehow, being kept at arm's length. Johnson, by contrast, is desperate to avoid death, a mission to which he sacrifices living his life. He uses technology to compose that prayer. What he's asking for is more than just to not die. He wants a metaphysical revolution of sorts – a change to human reality on behalf of all humankind. Without scale the result is merely impressive, it's not a rupture in humanity's relationship to space and time. While he aims to achieve immortality 'on behalf of' all of humankind, this is particularly unlikely. Yes, the average global life expectancy has doubled since 1900, but inequality in life expectancy continues to grow. In the UK, the social gradient of how long we live has steepened appallingly in the past decade. If transhumanist immortality becomes feasible and some people can live forever, you can guarantee that the already substantial gap will part more quickly than the Red Sea. This is why I contest the view that a transhuman era will usher in a good life for everyone, and why we cannot allow these myths to dictate the future of AI.

Metamorphosis – becoming another creature – captured the human imagination long before seventeenth-century Dutch biologist Jan Swammerdam noticed caterpillars morphing into glorious, winged lepidoptera.[33] The desire to reach the 'next stage' of human life is the beating heart of transhumanism, which asks that we fulfil the call to human perfectionism and become other, thus surpassing the 'limit' of what we define as Homo sapiens. For transhumanists, not even VMan is a perfect human – perfection doesn't exist, and won't unless we allow them to continue to make themselves perfect transhumans. So, while transhumanism presents itself as the next step of human evolution, it also claims to do this by investing in initiatives that interrupt and change what it means to be human. The idea is that we can then finally shrug off our earthly attachments and opt out of the cycle of living and dying. As Donna Haraway says, their view that 'we've moved from the primal soup and are going to bliss off earth into total AI is truly silly'.[34]

There is an arrogance to this conviction that humanity can and should rip itself out of the mortal world, particularly at a time where we are learning, however unsuccessfully, to nourish our earthly obligations to the planet and to each other. The one-way metamorphosis that transhumanists are hankering after is like butterflies forgoing their caterpillar progeny and choosing to manufacture the next generation of winged off-spring. Transhumanism has lodged itself into an orthogenetic view of evolution, which sees the history of life on Earth as an upward trajectory – with our quadruped ancestors at the bottom, and modern man (and his cyborg descendants) at the very top. Now is our time to break through the ozone layer with rockets and pollutants, the orthogenetic view tells us, and reach the next stage of our evolution with the assistance of AI-powered tools; there is no alternative. To resist the kind of future that transhumanists would like to usher in, we must reject dominant myths about where we came from, who we are today, and what we might become in the future. We see anachronistic, out-of-touch ideas about what it means to be human impressed upon AI development all the time, making AI behave in ways that limit and constrain all the diverse and subversive ways in which people express themselves today. Transhumanists tell us that our purpose on Earth is to use science to become perfect, superhuman entities, which makes it seem as if such a future is inevitable and closes the door to other, more interesting possibilities for humanity going forward.

If we see the story of humanity as a strange parade of orthogenetic evolution – from ape to serf to iPhone user to AI-powered Übermensch – we block off the possibility of finding new ways in which to relate to technology and each other. Simplified narratives of a preordained human story might be convenient for tech opinion leaders and transhumanists who peddle their own bizarre fiction of staying alive at all costs. But the reality of evolutionary history offers us far greater possibilities than the anaemic, hollowed-out lives we are directed towards, where living forever means having more time on Earth to purchase goods. It tells us that the human imperative hasn't been just to survive, but to co-survive. While 'the survival of the fittest' was the best-known and most popular metaphor to come out of Darwinian evolutionary science, symbiosis is a far more truthful one, as this is what keeps us alive and kicking. There is a microorganism in the human gut which helps humans metabolise the sugars in seaweed.[35] *Bacteroides plebeius* is commonly found in the microbiome of Japanese people who eat seaweed, making them better adapted to their diet. So symbionts (two or more species dependent on each other for day-to-day survival) determine how we evolve.[36] But they can even result in the formation of new species by influencing how a species mates and which genes are passed on. Take the bacteria that play a role in the mating preferences of fruit flies. They actually direct how fruit flies respond to chemical signals issued by potential mates. These bacteria, which help the flies' microbiota function well, encourage flies to mate with other flies that have the same diet. Studies have shown that if you give some fruit flies a diet of molasses, and others a diet of starch foods, then over several generations the flies will only mate with flies who eat the same thing.[37] This is their microbiome telling them that their offspring would be better off with parents who are good at digesting the foods they will be reared on. But giving the flies antibiotics kills the bacteria and reverses this mating preference, which means that it's the genetic material of both the host and its microbiota that affects how a species evolves.

You can see from these examples that species evolve based on the services they provide for each other. If the symbiont–host relationship works well enough, the species is more likely to survive. Evolution, therefore, is more a selection of *partnerships* than an arms race between individual species. The orthogenetic image of evolution, with the gradual march from ape to hominid through the passage from older (ancestral) to newer (descendent) species and the accumulation of random mutations, 'has not been demonstrated in the field, nor in the laboratory, nor in the fossil record'.[38] Biologists Lynn Margulis, Ricardo Guerrero and Mercedes Berlanga were considered radicals by their peers for attempts to demonstrate why gaps in the fossil record can be explained (rather than explained away) by the fact that evolution did not happen continuously but in spurts. During these bursts of activity, interactions between the human genome and its bacterial symbionts formed holobionts, an ecological unit made up of coexisting species.

These two (or more) now mutually dependent species no

longer appear like separate entities. In fact, the holobiont can usefully be seen as a species of its own. Humans – like fruit flies – rely on a sea of bacterial symbionts. In our guts, mouths and on our skin, bacteria both prevent and cause cavities, regulate our immune system and assist digestion. Biologists now frame the human as a holobiont in itself rather than a 'single species' per se, because if it wasn't for our symbioses with bacteria we would be far less able to stave off disease.[39] Health-nutritional strategies to improve gut function rely on patients treating their bodies not as individual units cordoned off from the rest of the world but as the host to other species on which our bodies depend for their well-being. We are, therefore, starting to wake up to the careful balances of a healthy 'more-than-human' body. I am introducing some cutting-edge biology here with the hope of warding off, or at the very least redirecting, the completely uninteresting question, 'Who are we in the age of AI?' That query is nothing more than a revitalised, dressed-up version of the perennial existential conundrum 'Who am I?' I have always thought 'Who am I?' was hopelessly individualistic and self-centred. It expresses fears around human distinctiveness and the kind of narcissistic self-doubt society fosters when we are encouraged to ask ourselves, 'What makes me *me*?' or, 'How am I unique?'

Let's probe in a different direction. We can ask, 'Who have we always been?' 'Who is excluded in this "we"?' 'How do we relate to one another?' What I want these questions to express is an interest in living and dying *well*, and *together*.[40] Of course, this is not so straightforward. Symbiotic relationships are often far from the friendly kumbaya of sitting around a campfire holding hands. As Donna Haraway puts it so well, these are 'non-innocent practices' full of unpleasantness, complicity and difficult choices.[41] Viruses engage in symbiotic relationships with their hosts, either to their benefit, as a neutral tag-along (like the mysterious anelloviruses that hang out in blood and urine but don't directly cause disease), or as a harmful addition, as the COVID-19 pandemic made all too clear. Then there are endoparasitic wasps that lay their eggs in insects, supporting the virus that suppresses the host insect's immune defences which would otherwise kill the eggs. You may know that when you bite into a fig, you're also enjoying digested wasps. Fig trees cannot survive without the females from the *Agaonidae* wasp species that crawl into the fruit, laying their eggs within the seeds while simultaneously pollinating them. The wasp then dies and is digested by the fig. When its offspring emerge they mate with each other, the males then die, and the female wasps continue the cycle by leaving the fig tree, taking with them pollen to fertilise another fig tree where they will also be composted.

This is possessive, cannibalistic. In holobionts, caring practices are not sentimentalised as 'being nice'. It's the relationship between a host and the parasite it depends on for day-to-day life. Would that it were only clownfish teasing the tentacles of sea anemones, feeding off invertebrates that might harm them while the anemone benefits from the clownfish's faecal matter. Or anemones hitchhiking on the backs of hermit crabs, or oxpecker birds eating ticks from the backs of elephants and buffaloes. There are an estimated one million different parasitic wasp species worldwide, and yet Darwin could not quite stomach their evolutionary success. Speaking of the *Glyptapanteles* wasp that stuffs its larvae into living caterpillars until they look like a loaded condom, he says: 'I cannot persuade myself that a beneficent and omnipotent God would have designedly created the *Ichneumonidae* [a family of parasitoid wasps] with the express intention of their feeding within the living bodies of caterpillars.'[42] Symbiosis is the right metaphor for human/non-human relationships not because it's nice, but because it's our reality.

As appalling as some types of symbioses are to human

tastes, they create a worse kind of anxiety for us as a species: the realisation that the individual human is a collection of queasy, mutualistic relationships. As developmental biologist Scott Gilbert argues, we are as much bacterial as we are human; the cult of the individual, he says, is a farce.[43] We are nothing without our gut microbiota: on the anatomic level, nine out of ten of our cells are microbial, on the physiological level we have joined metabolic pathways, and on the developmental level our gut microbe prevents cell death. Quite radically, even genetically speaking we are not individuals either, as 'our' (our in the collective, multispecies sense!) genome evolves with other symbionts, like bacteria. With all this in mind, and armed with the knowledge that we cannot think about our advancement into the age of AI as the final step on an evolutionary ladder, let's ask a far more interesting question instead: who have we *always been* in relation to the non-human?

Co-operation, not competition

How we view our future with technology has much to do with the story plugged to us about humanity being the 'Masters of History' by people like Yuval Harari. This idea originates in religious creation narratives: Christianity and Judaism have plugged it for centuries with the Garden of Eden myth, while in Islam's human origin story Allah creates life from water, and Adam and Hawwa follow. Even though just under 25 per cent of the global adult population identify as atheist or agnostic, the myth that humanity is the pinnacle of life reigns supreme.[44] Other origin stories offer different possibilities: as Déborah Danowski and Eduardo Viveiros de Castro have shown, in certain Indigenous mythologies from across the Americas, humans were the first to exist and then morphed into all sorts of critters, including 'geographical features, meteorological phenomena, and celestial bodies that comprise the present cosmos'.[45] Humanity is not the pinnacle of evolution here, it's merely compost for the diversification of life into plants, animals and spirits. This is the transhumanist nightmare: the human body as a compost heap that provides nutrition for – and is therefore ingested into – other forms of life. Like Catholic dogma, which states that humans must be buried, not cremated and scattered, transhumanists would rather that we were immortal and our bodies were not recycled back into the planet. Catholicism and transhumanism share a distaste for bodies getting mixed up with other 'lesser' life forms on their journey to immortality. Take cryonics, a transhumanist medical procedure that seeks to preserve the body at low temperatures in the hope that resurrection technologies will exist in the future. This is not dissimilar from Catholic burials. Both require the body to remain intact with a view to resurrection. For cryonicists, eternal life takes place on Earth. For Catholics, it's Heaven. Still, whether the body is stored in a cryochamber or a graveyard, what is crucial in both is that it continues as an individual and doesn't disappear into the ecosystem.

The cryonics movement was inspired by Russian-American writer Ayn Rand, proponent of extreme individualism, who believed that human progress and goodness stemmed from self-awareness and self-worth. Rand accrued a cult following for her suggestion that a collective of people was nothing more than the rights of its component individuals.[46] If you believe in the sanctity of human life, or that we exist in a hierarchical relationship to other, lesser creatures, you are likely to want a coffin funeral so that you can be put in a special box not to be forgotten among the trees, as is the case with most desert religions except Buddhism, or frozen with your fingers crossed, like the cryonics crew.

For both transhumanists and the religious, defeating death is not so much about living forever as becoming perfect. In Christian doctrine, faith allows believers to defeat death through eternal life in Heaven, where 'we shall be like him; for we shall see him as he is' (1 John 3:2).[47] The cryonic body is also one that, awaiting (in faith) the right technology, people can live again in a more perfect state. Optimisation, of varying kinds, is at the heart of both modes of deathlessness. We'll now explore how transhumanism was also influenced by Social Darwinism, made famous in the optimisation metaphor of 'survival of the fittest'. Nineteenth-century engineer turned psychologist Charles Spencer's aphorism (often wrongly attributed to Darwin) makes humanity's adeptness at the struggle for existence *against* the competition its major distinguishing achievement.[48] Indeed, the twentieth-century Neo-Darwinists called mutations 'sports', imposing competitive human games on the evolutionary story. But, as we will see, this metaphor turns competition into a battle among individuals rather than symbionts. Lynn Margulis argued throughout her long career that evolution is the product of co-operation between organisms (symbiosis), rather than competition. While humanity tends to configure society into a game of winners and losers, life is actually about 'the living together of unlike organisms'.[49] That is, living alongside creatures and people that don't appear at first glance to have anything in common with us, and making it work.

Darwin himself did not subscribe to the idea that everything exists in violent competition, trying to survive at all costs, and that different beings want each other to die in order to create more space in the ecosystem for themselves. He knew that there are ecological, empirical, mathematical and economic reasons why we coexist rather than always try to 'beat' one another in the game of evolution. Innovations in the biological sciences have demonstrated to what extent evolution is improvisation and collaboration. The immune system was once considered to be a protective barrier, but is now better understood as an adaptive mechanism for securing successful host–microbial relationships. The analogy that likens the immune system to an army that protects the body from bacterial invasions has since been replaced by that of a nightclub bouncer, guarding the doors, letting some customers in while attempting (not always successfully) to differentiate between a fake ID and a real one, and strong-arming rowdy patrons to the door if need be.

The point here is that we are not, and can never be, static individuals because we are always 'becoming' by living together. We know now that evolution is symbiotic: in other words it's not about group selection but the development of co-operative ecological communities. So 'natural selection' is not individual species competing. Instead, over time and with the right environmental conditions, symbiont–host complexes (holobionts) evolve through successful partnerships. We'll talk more about how this reality can substitute control-of-other-species metaphors in Chapter 4. In the meantime, these narratives of natural competition have been essential to the justification of capitalism. Capitalism is to transhumanism what light is to rainbows, yet it's rarely explicitly mentioned in the transhumanist literature it so pervasively infuses. This is, again, why it's unlikely that transhumanism and ultimate human optimisation will result in social equality, because capitalism depends on relations of inequality. In capitalism, profit is the only function that needs to be optimised for. In fact, political scientist Herbert Simon claimed in an explosive talk at the Operations Research Society of America (ORSA) in 1957 that 'physicists and electrical engineers had little to do with the invention of the digital computer – the real inventor was the economist Adam Smith.'[50] And yet there is little mention of capitalism in books about computation, as if AI had something inherently terrifying in it that couldn't be blamed on the profit motive, labour exploitation, bids for global supremacy, and masculinist and militarised visions of technology. We must pay closer attention to the evolutionary optimisation metaphor because it produces the world rather than merely describes it (more on this later). Similarly, from inventing the computer to moving markets, capitalist apparatuses have the material, financial and narrative power to make what they imagine. And, as the ultimate transhumanist singularity narrative tells us, they have the capacity to break time.

From VMan to Harari's march of progress, survival of the fittest to a cryonically sealed denial of death, we have digested plenty of misleading myths about AI and humanity. They're not supported by the latest research in biology and evolutionary history, and they reflect a vision of the world as transhumanists would like it to be, not as it actually is. It's these dull, homogenous world views, played out in comics, games and films, that have most obviously persuaded us that AI will supersede humanity and that apocalypse is inevitable (which it's not). And that it's an issue more important than and different to climate crisis, geopolitical tensions and global inequality (which it's also not). So let's get stuck in.

2

Misdirections, or Apocalypse vs Utopia

The singularity

I'm crouching against the wall of the largest room in Helsinki's biggest conference centre, Messukeskus, on Day 4 of the 2017 Helsinki WorldCon. The room's capacity is 3,300 and it doesn't feel too far from full. This is, by a long stretch, the best-attended event of the week. A panel of science fiction writers, Charles Stross, Lettie Prell, Mikko Rauhala and David G. Shaw, are gathered before a salivating audience to discuss 'The Singularity: Transhuman Intelligence in Fiction and Futurism'. The singularity has many definitions, but a common one is an event followed by the invention of a superintelligent AI system which makes technology improve exponentially so that humanity is eclipsed by machines. Chaos is inherent to the singularity, making 'out-of-control' computers which pose a major threat to civilisation a core theme. As with other discussions about speculative advancements in technology and potential mass destruction, the room is erotically charged. Men wearing 'science investigates the unknown' T-shirts in bubble writing lean against the side walls to get a better view. I have experienced this atmosphere many times since, and traded notes with others who have similar stories. A colleague once told me how, at another event, a fellow panellist on her 'AI Revolution' session explained that the revolution was 'now' and we had to 'ride it'. 'I was the civil society/academic type who asked, "But what is AI *for*?"' she recounted. 'It was so silent you could hear bubbles popping.' Asking useful questions about the role of AI has the same effect as weakening an erection. The disgust, the loss of momentum, the embarrassment. No wonder, then, that Ursula Le Guin called these narratives which foresee and desire an invention that changes what it means to be human 'prick tales'.[1] Le Guin's lifelong friend Donna Haraway also insists that the idea that history is continuous and that it's suddenly going to end because of an AI explosion is self-obsessed delusion: 'What arrogance "the end of history" – that history is Western!' I remembered these words as I sat in that Finnish conference hall, watching an almost entirely white, male room decide that the singularity would be the end of the world, while ignoring all the other ways in which genocide, war and extinction make worlds end across the globe all the time.

The problem is not whether AI will prompt the end of the world. The issue is that by sitting in that room, having that discussion and writing stories about it, we are stimulating our fascination with it. SF is at the core of science, directing innovation. Tech entrepreneur Josh Wolfe has said that he invests in technologies which remind him of inventions from the Isaac Asimov novels that captured his imagination as a boy. No surprises there – science fiction is, after all, an enormously prolific genre that can trace its origins back thousands of years. Some critics identify the ancient Mesopotamian *Epic of Gilgamesh* as proto-science fiction because it features flying machines that penetrate outer space, but certainly SF written by women writers begins at least in, if not before, 1666 with Margaret Cavendish's *The Blazing World*. My PhD in SF gave me only the briefest of insights into what is a vertiginously vast genre. It's a great shame that male tech investors turn only to a small section of its history, mostly written between 1938 and 1946, and a very few – mostly male – authors from which to source inspiration. In the late 2000s, there were more SF books published about the apocalypse and life afterwards than during the

Cold War. Publishers have decided that the apocalypse sells, and so it dominates our imagination. By the way – what gets published doesn't even scratch the surface of the genre, which mostly appears informally on websites or zines. In particular, women, people of colour and anyone else not accepted by the mainstream use these channels to get their work out.

One of the reasons why the singularity is presented as '*the issue*' of AI today is that it's a convenient way of channelling our anxieties about war, fascism, extremism, economic crisis, a changing cultural landscape – whatever they may be – without having to engage with the difficult, unglamorous truths about what causes these crises. Go to any conference, speak with any venture capitalist in the field, and you'll realise how a fetish for the apocalypse sucks the air out of the practical and productive debates we could be having about AI. As I said in the Introduction, if I don't respond to questions about the major problem in AI today with the answer 'AI will result in total destruction', my answer is often not taken seriously. This is unsurprising: when we're thinking orthogenetically, a qualitative change in what it means to be human would indeed be major news – an epistemic atomic bomb. Whether, though, discussions about the singularity really should eclipse everything else is another question. I would invite you now to think of the singularity as a kind of messianism – the belief that a saving force will liberate us. Extracted from its religious roots, the idea of the singularity has been, as Donna Haraway puts it, 'modified to fit the conventions of secular realism'.[2] As the second coming of Christ is to Christians and followers of Islam, so the singularity is to transhumanists, who see it as an inevitability. The singularity is therefore 'proleptic', a word used to describe a 'flash-forward' in films and TV shows when the viewer is told, 'This is what's going to happen.' Prolepsis comes from the Greek term for anticipating, and squarely describes the way Big Tech confidently presumes that 'this technology is the future' and 'this is what comes next for humanity'. Their inventions, they claim, will interrupt time and 'change everything'. When the iPhone launched in 2007, Apple's accompanying slogan was exactly that: 'This changes everything.' In 2015, iPhone 4's marketeers used the phrase 'This changes everything. Again.' Apple has always led on self-congratulatory marketing, but this particular rendering got the special attention of journalists (a favourite headline of mine by Digiday's Mark Duffy read: 'The unending arrogance of the iPhone tagline marches ever onward').[3] There's an irony in the decisive game-changer doing another victory lap.

In *Star Trek: First Contact* (1996), the captain of the USS *Enterprise*, Jean-Luc Picard (from the twenty-fourth century AD), says to a human from the twenty-first century, 'I envy you, you get to take steps into a new frontier.' As a society, we long for newness: freedom from the things we find tiresome and the problems we can't solve. We have plenty of such issues today; as I write, fifty-five armed conflicts rage around the world, and I long for lasting peace in Gaza and Ukraine. At the same time, the banal problems persist: my kettle has broken for the umpteenth time and no amount of drain unblocker appears to be alleviating the small pool of backflow in my bathtub. We continue to hope that technology will allow us to reach new horizons away from both the mundane and the terrifying aspects of our existence, and fresh foundations to underwrite an era of prosperity. Transhumanists argue that an AI singularity would remedy all of life's problems, because it would stimulate the economy so much that abundance would be assured for all. To be unanchored from reality enough to believe this, you also have to buy into a number of contradictions: the belief that total rupture from existing economic and social systems is possible, that capitalism can be bereft of greed, and that there is a threshold at which inequality ceases to exist.

In contrast to John Maynard Keynes's imagined 'age of

leisure' brought on by task automation, technology is making us more time-poor, says sociologist Judy Wajcman and economist Juliet B. Schor.[4] Wajcman argues that the problem is not just that technology does not save time by helping us get through our tasks faster, but that a 'culture of busyness'[5] has become a measure of self-worth and status in the West. Even the fantasy of leisure is misaligned with what is currently socially valued. For the majority of people across the globe, online and digital work have become extra labour-intensive. The platform workers who support technologies making life more convenient for wealthier users are working longer hours, and the global wealth gap is only increasing, as Shamira Ahmed, Tapiwa Chinembiri, Mpho Moyo and Alison Gillwald have demonstrated.[6]

One explanation for why the fantasy of AI-induced permaleisure for all persists is that improvements in health and social care in some minority-world contexts are misread as indications that technology will usher in a better quality of life for everyone, everywhere. The European Commission's Competence Centre on Foresight points out that 'although the overall trend globally for people is that of improved health and longer lives, growing inequalities in education and income are translating into growing health inequalities'.[7] Technology can improve the quality of life en masse in specific regions, but its benefits are never experienced equally. Across the world, women enjoy on average 20 per cent less leisure time than men, rising to 25–35 per cent for women of colour. Abundance will not miraculously cure inequality, because inequality is not merely socio-economic, but cultural and political.

While in *First Contact* technological advancements have transformed the economy so that Captain Jean-Luc Picard can proudly state that 'the acquisition of wealth is no longer the driving force in our lives',[8] in the real world this would mean that technology's production and distribution ceases to be dependent on cheap labour and the exploitation of finite natural resources. So, when AI is produced without water, lithium, quartz, silica, polluting data centres, human content moderators, data labellers, and without humans used as training data, or subjected to its unseen use on the street or at border control, then we can start talking about AI's potential to liberate us all. The promise of prosperity is merely a way to justify the creation of increasingly costly and exploitative AI systems. The reality is that progress is hard, incremental work – there is no silver-bullet solution. Words like 'foundation' and 'frontier' can make us forget that tomorrow is determined by today. The three richest Americans currently hold more wealth than the bottom half of the US population. Working against socio-economic inequality and political polarisation should be front and centre of how AI is created, discussed in the media and regulated, so that AI companies don't mislead or overpromise by suggesting that it can magically induce utopia.

The apocalypse fetish

I'd managed to dodge *The Terminator* screenings for many years before a friend cornered me into watching two back to back. By the end I almost started to enjoy Terminators dropping down naked from the sky on to rainy bridges in North America. There is a reliable thrill to the arrival of fully grown newborns dressed only in slippery musculature, like James Bond emerging for dinner in a good suit.

The US has long had a monopoly over apocalypse: it happens in LA, New York, San Francisco and Washington DC, but rarely in Loughborough, Birmingham or Hopton-on-Sea, and rarer still Phnom Penh, Vientiane or Khovd. SF writers across the world have made their quiet complaint by reimagining the where and when of apocalypse. If you're looking to diversify your apocalypse intake beyond the anglosphere, in the glorious

Il Cuore Finto di DR (*The Fake Heart of* DR, 1992) by Nicoletta Vallorani, life in the post-apocalypse is narrated from the perspective of a sarcastic former sexbot who reluctantly rebuilds a community in the ravaged Brera district of Milan. Equally terrific are Nnedi Okorafor's *Who Fears Death* (2010), set in post-apocalyptic Africa, Lauren Beukes's cyberpunk apocalypse *Moxyland* (2008), which takes place in South Africa, and Manil Suri's Mumbai-based disaster story *The City of Devi* (2013). It feels perverse to call for more variety in the settings of imaginary apocalypses, but when all goes to shit the place where the last man is standing – and, bar *The Terminator*'s Sarah Connor, it's almost always a man – is the only one which matters.

In *Deluge* (1933), a phenomenal pre-CGI movie, the destruction of New York is beautifully rendered using miniatures of the city. The enormity of its skyline was a perfect way to display scale – if a tsunami was twice the size of the Empire State, it had to be huge. Suddenly, a nation that aspired to be the greatest by harnessing scale was defeated by nature in outsize proportions. The legendary flood scene, which features cruise ships smacking into the Empire State while the Statue of Liberty topples into the ocean, inspired a series of NYC-based apocalypse movies, from *When Worlds Collide* (1951) and *Moonfall* (2022) to Roland Emmerich's 2004 *The Day After Tomorrow*. In the latter, *Deluge*'s opening scene is copied verbatim – albeit with all the special effects money could buy in the mid-noughties. The redemptive purge and salvation of the flood narrative has captured global imaginations since *The Epic of Gilgamesh* and Noah's Ark, because the destruction/renewal dialectic has a perennial allure for the human psyche. The Greeks harnessed the perverse pleasure of catharsis when they created an entire genre dedicated to watching heroes fall from greatness. In the tumbling of skyscrapers and the demolition of global hubs, centuries of carefully curated civilisation are turned to rubble.

Despite the geographical variety of the flood narrative, Hollywood disaster movies rarely pan to anywhere other than the US. It's no doubt more ethical to destroy your own toys rather than someone else's, and it's more satisfying to watch wealth crumble than poverty. Audiences are also invited to see the fall of the US as shorthand for the end of civilisation, with the iconic New York skyline standing in for the whole world. Only the end of North America, these films imply, can conjure legitimate existential fear. And so, during two hours of the familiar made unfamiliar, all eyes are turned to the mighty USA as it's contorted into a vertiginous, uncanny universe sickened by apocalypse. When we watch these films, we feel the same perverse pleasure as we do when we have a day that's gone so badly wrong that the final catastrophe that tops it all off can be almost liberating. The domino effect of buildings sinking into the ground, the satisfaction of total detonation, the relief of entropy. Perhaps we have always known that extinction is what we deserve, now that more than 99 per cent of all creatures which ever lived on the planet are extinct. It's not a 'world without us', that is, a world after the end of the human species, but 'us without a world', a humanity bereft of its environment – which we're headed towards if we do not curb our population and climate crises, despite the attention given to the effect of shrinking populations on the economy.

Extinction may be the crisis of the Anthropocene, the era in which we live, but it's also an eternal fear: all species are destined to die before the end of time. We will eventually become the ancient Mesopotamians whom Noah left behind when the flood came, and future Earth dwellers, whoever or whatever they may be, will have to reckon with the sun swelling and vaporising the planet in around seven billion years' time. That will be the collapse of time, but the hour isn't up yet. Instead we can focus on the imminent apocalypse of today, which is undoubtedly the climate crisis. One way of making this happen faster is to build lots of environmentally unsustainable AI-related infrastructure. As AI and climate researcher Kate Crawford emphasised to a forum of AGI enthusiasts just before the start of the 2025 Paris AI Summit, there is no scientific evidence that AI's environmental costs can be justified by its potential to restore the planet to health.

In 2020, I interviewed workers at a tech multinational to find out what they saw as the key AI ethics issues of today.[9] No one said the environment. Lots of people mentioned SF films. A hundred per cent of these films featured a humanoid wielding a gun. Some employees had even nicknamed the projects they were working on 'Project Terminator'. They were using the franchise as a moniker for their AI projects, even though it centres on an evil superintelligence called Skynet. Not exactly a role model for corporate tech development! Why, we might ask, would a company want to name their AI system after a murderous, psychopathic robot? What can we expect, with so many movies depicting an AI apocalypse, prompting a great deal of fear in workplaces everywhere? Often these movies feature aspirational heroes for tech workers. The trope of the scientist-entrepreneur (think Iron Man) has become 'a new form of cultural hero', as Theodore Porter puts it;[10] so has the computer scientist who destroys the world by working at the vanguard (as in the 2014 flop *Transcendence*), defying what's possible; the modern-day Icarus who takes down the world with him.

Referencing Hollywood blockbusters does get people on the same page; even if you haven't seen *The Terminator*, you can imagine Arnold Schwarzenegger as a cybernetic assassin and the potential of a murderous AI to induce chaos. But the page everyone converges on isn't necessarily helpful or informative. These movies make viewers both afraid of and enthralled by AI: yes, *The Terminator* is about scary robots, but they're played by the former Governor of California as slick and sexy.

A mainstream branch of cinematic BDSM, the Terminator's message is that it's going to kill us all, and we're going to enjoy it. Sex and death have always been intertwined, not least through the orgasm, '*la petite mort*', of which Shakespeare was a fan ('I will live in thy heart, die in thy lap,' puns *Much Ado About Nothing*'s Benedick). If, as Oscar Wilde is thought to have said, everything is about sex, except sex itself, which is about power, then *The Terminator* reveals our longing to yield to a higher authority. Loss of control over AI is widely seen in the minority world as *the* greatest AI risk, and therefore it's also reflected back to us by Hollywood as our ultimate fantasy. What we fear most, we desire most.

The issue with fetishised total destruction is that it's distracting. In French, *distraire* also means to entertain, which is exactly the point. Hypothetical apocalypse is turning our heads, which is not so much an issue at the cinema, but is a problem when it's dominating the conversation and detracting from the less sexy structural problems that underpin AI innovation. Once again, the AI issues that are of actual concern to most of the world are at best a side dish to what bothers the US and its allies most about AI. Speculating about an AI takeover is not a top-priority conversation in the majority world; researchers, scientists and opinion leaders beyond the West are concerned with more present, pressing and tangible suffering. This is why it's highly concerning that the fears which appeal most to the minority-world agenda are currently standing in for the rest of the globe, and are the only ones we see in the media. The narrow scope of AI apocalypse not only often excludes famine and genocide, but sees them as inconsequential. Next, we'll take a look at the philosophers who are encouraging out-of-touch perspectives on AI's existential risks.

A world that shrieks

When I give talks about apocalypse narratives, I often begin with a chilling verse from T. S. Eliot's interwar poem 'The Hollow Men'. It goes like this:

This is the way the world ends
This is the way the world ends
This is the way the world ends
Not with a bang but a whimper.

From this poem, Nick Bostrom, a philosopher of existential risk, plucks key words to describe a four-type taxonomy of apocalypses: bangs, shrieks, whispers and crunches. Bangs are sudden apocalyptic events – AI killing all humans instantly, biowarfare, nuclear exchange, comet strikes. Shrieks refer to an AI consciousness with a death wish. Whispers are collapses incurred by alien life (Bostrom explores the plausibility of alien existence) or humanity overexerting itself in the pursuit of interstellar exploration. Finally, crunches are events that 'drastically curtail human potential', though they are still defined as existential threats because Bostrom views anything that inhibits 'human progress' (high-tech and scientific exploration) as being a kind of apocalypse.[11] Technological stagnation or collapse are two such crunches, which means that parts of the planet and human society that live without advanced technology are not 'doing' humanity correctly. He also claims that reproduction that promotes socially 'undesirable' features is another 'crunch'. This belief in and concern about the reproduction of 'undesirable' features is called dysgenics, and was described as 'eugenics on steroids' by the *Guardian* writer Andrew Anthony following the release of some emails in 1993 in which Bostrom argued that white people are more intelligent than Black people.[12] Having read and taught some of the negative aspects of Bostrom's work, I would urge you to view what happened not as an old, misguided email blown out of proportion but as an expression of the incorrect and violent hierarchies that are foundational to his views about humanity and its future with AI. History has taught us that it doesn't take much for one man's thought experiment about group hierarchies to turn into genocide. Whether or not you believe that the relevance of race to intelligence in this case is just a hop and a skip away from past and present eugenics programmes, work of this kind on the optimisation of intelligence has a strained relationship with a genuine belief in the equality of all peoples.

Bostrom has attracted a substantial following with his dramatic thought experiments. In one, an AI system programmed to produce as many paperclips as possible ends up turning the whole world into a paperclip manufacturing facility. In a paper from 2004, Bostrom stated that 'there is a negative correlation in some places between intellectual achievement and fertility. If such selection were to operate over a long period of time, we might evolve into a less brainy but more fertile species.'[13] This dysgenic fantasy is the subject of Mike Judge's 2006 comedy *Idiocracy*, whose movie poster features none other than – yep – the Vitruvian Man, but this time his beer belly is popping out of his vest. The film tells the story of a world 'degraded by insipid popular culture, crass consumerism, and rampant anti-intellectualism',[14] which has given rise to endemic homophobia, populism and a widespread derision of education (what we have now, but more of it). Consumerism has gone so insane that adverts are no longer the stuff of billboards, allocated TV slots or even paid Instagram posts but real-life product placements – words sprinkled by politicians into their everyday conversations. In the opening sequence, a series of images pulse on screen: Einstein, Mozart, Darwin (all accompanied by the Vitruvian Man in the left-hand corner!), then Botticelli's *Venus*, American adult performer and wrestler Chyna, and two WWE fighters in the heat of a throwdown.

It's the female form (starting from the Botticelli) that marks the perversion of 'good' human values and interests as they shift from the intellectual to the carnal.

But the sensible and smart elites aren't the heroes of this movie. They turn out to be silly, insular and unable to recognise that the core of the problem is capitalism and health and social inequality – not to mention the politicians manipulating the disenfranchised. The movie invites the question of whether the concept of intelligence that it seeks to satirise is altogether broken. Similarly, in his commitment to capitalist-mediated 'Progress', Bostrom misses the complicity of the systems he is advocating for in the future that he so fears. The term dysgenics has been traced to eugenicist and ichthyologist (a marine biologist specialising in fish) David Starr Jordan who, in 1915, commented that disabled men were not going to war and therefore procreating in larger numbers than 'able-bodied' fighters, giving rise to a generation of sub-par humans. You could apply Social Darwinist logic and say that, given humanity's insistence on war, survival of the fittest means the eradication of those who are willing and able to fight it.

War is central to 'The Hollow Men'. Written in 1925, the poem has all the trappings of postmodernist literature: life has been hollowed out, stripped of purpose. Its titular lost souls embody a breakdown of meaning, morality, reason, sense, hope and religion. A century later, its depiction of alienation and despair still points to that which is pointless, insufferable, beyond repair, out of action and irremediable. The hollow men signify death without fully being able to die, a kind of deathlessness that permeates the realm of the living. In this technological age, you can read the hollow men as transhumanists, seeking to dodge death through life-extension technologies, but subsequently unable to enjoy a full life. Donna Haraway calls this, in her perfect phrasing, 'commitments to deathlessness',[15] which means being so anxious about dying that you forget how to live well. Deathlessness – a life without death – is not the same as living. Eliot's apocalypse mourns vitality, the collapse of time and truth. For essayist and philosopher Lauren Berlant this is a 'slow death':[16] 'the physical wearing out of a population and the deterioration of people in that population that is very nearly a defining condition of their experience and historical existence'. A slow death is like an unannounced wearing-out, and is caused by the sustained attrition of social life: 'a reduction of our physical force under global and national regimes of capitalist structural subordination and governmentality'. These are the structures and systems that can make our lives unliveable. Berlant's focus is not on the singularity but on the state of distractedness, incoherence and degeneration that life under capitalism and its technologies creates. Even deathbots, the AI avatars of deceased persons, attempt to relieve us from the final resolution of death by uploading the digital footprint of our loved ones to the cloud. That's not death, it's digital purgatory.

The kind of digitised lives and deaths we're being invited to experience by new technologies are ones that are never truly fulfilled: the finality of death is being deferred/surrendered to the cloud by apps that claim to preserve a loved one's data, but even before then, our engagement with life is increasingly undermined by time spent scrolling online. As part of a slow death, we are doomed not to live life to the fullest because we are glued to our phones or monitored and manipulated by surveillance technology.[17] We are pitched 'connectivity' by the tech companies we purchase products from, when these devices also obliterate social bonds. Unlike the definitive, satisfying annihilation of disaster movies, slow death doesn't offer the total destruction from which renewal can arise. It's a catastrophe without relief. It defies the trope of redemptive rebirth represented by the seed that grows from The Plant at the end of *Wall-E* (2008), or Morgan Freeman's velvety narration over images of sprouting fauna in the epilogue of *War of the Worlds* (2005). Instead, like Eliot's hollow men who are bound to purgatory on Earth, with no sign of a metaphysical life to come (because religious hope has been crushed in the aftermath of war), those who endure war, disease, protracted illness, food insecurity and genocide know what it is to experience apocalypse without salvation. As Deborah Bird Rose has emphasised, it's a reality all too familiar to Aboriginal peoples in Australia. In the following lines she talks about one of her Indigenous teachers, Old Tim Yilngayarri, and his community as survivors:

> But something more than death had stalked these Aboriginal people for decades under the name of colonisation and in the form of massacres, starvation, influenza, syphilis, leprosy, and much more. Old Tim and his people had faced the possibility of their own extinction. They'd seen clans die out, and they'd grouped countries together so that there would be someone living who would be able to take care when the last remaining clanspeople were gone.[18]

It's very important that we understand the message of impending AI apocalypse as a misdirection, away from ongoing climate and society-related catastrophes. What Donna Haraway calls the 'all-too-ordinary urgencies of onrushing multispecies extinctions, genocides, immiserations, and exterminations'[19] are the final issue. Whether it's peacekeeping, co-operation, citizen participation, public welfare or freedom from incessant exposure to surveillance technologies, the methods by which we avert these calamities are also the escape routes from existential threats to AI. But by directing our attention towards a hypothetical out-of-control AI, rather than its true causes, rules and people are broken in the rush to re-exert control. The message is 'anything goes, just save us at all costs!'. Ethics is stripped of all meaning and becomes a euphemism for self-preservation.

We cannot make good ethical decisions while mired in the former kind of apocalyptic thinking. The message of Eliot's poem is that wartime has no ethics. Next, I'll explain why we cannot think ethically about AI if we overlook real ongoing catastrophes and claim that hypothetical AI scenarios require a 'state of emergency'. As with periods of austerity, in a state of emergency efforts to solve structural issues end up at the bottom of the pile, even though they are at the beating heart of what's wrong.

The (nation) state of emergency

In March 2023, something akin to a state of emergency was called by AI opinion leaders. They saw themselves as pioneers of AI panic over large language models. Stuart Russell, writer and historian Yuval Noah Harari, Canadian computer scientist Yoshua Bengio and Apple co-founder Steve Wozniak joined around 20,000 academic AI researchers and industry CEOs in signing an open letter published by the Future of Life Institute, calling for a six-month pause in building what they called 'digital minds' (there is no evidence to suggest that these systems are digital minds, but we'll come to that). Only 13.5 per cent of those who signed were women. The signatories, many of whom have computer science backgrounds, admitted that they had created the problem by building unmanageable systems, but at the same time they were insisting that they should be the ones to design the solution. What they came up with was a suspension of time – a pause – a state of emergency. For some ethicists, many of the signatories' concerns appeared to be disingenuous. Two years earlier, Google demonstrated how it was restricting the work of its ethics team by firing some of its top employees who had raised the alarm about the risks of large language models:[20] Timnit Gebru in December 2020 and Margaret Mitchell in February 2021. Google subsequently used a wave of cuts in March 2023 as an excuse to get rid of key safety teams, while telling the *Financial Times* that same month that Responsible AI remained a 'top priority at the company, and we are continuing to invest in those teams'.[21] In January 2024 Google reportedly dismissed its key Responsible Innovation team. Google wasn't alone in its mixed messaging. In spring 2023, Microsoft laid off its entire AI ethics and society team, while Amazon's downsizing of its own ethics teams heavily weakened its ability to moderate content, notably on its online gaming platform, Twitch. Renowned for sexually suggestive content, a relatively young user base (thirteen-plus years old), and strong language characteristic of gaming, Twitch really needed all the content moderators who were sent on gardening leave. In a bid to cut costs, Meta dissolved its responsible innovation team in September 2022, and then disbanded a fact-checking tool in spring 2023 – previously touted as a key technology for 2024, a year of twenty-three presidential elections and twenty-four general elections, all of which were subject to attempts to manipulate voters through mis- and disinformation. By 2025, Meta had taken its lead from the Trump administration and quit fact-checking altogether.

So what was particularly irksome about the open letter was that these prominent (and largely male) computer scientists were saying that AI ethics isn't impactful enough, rather than using their platforms to speak out against Big Tech. Male AI opinion leaders were repeating the warning message of the female ethicists who had been unceremoniously fired for issuing the same message, carrying it off as their own and gaining far more attention. Suddenly, the voices of doom were also the voices of reason – even people who didn't trust Elon Musk were quoting him on the radio and dismissing calls to confront AI-related social inequalities (for example, slower loan approvals and lower credit ratings for low-income and Black families), saying that they were a distraction from impending apocalypse.

By October 2023, British PM Rishi Sunak had declared: 'the risk of extinction from AI should be a global priority', while somewhat contradicting himself with the caveat that 'this is not a risk that people need to be losing sleep over right now'.[22] Not terribly reassuring. How likely it is that Harari and the other signatories' fears will come true is difficult to predict, but we do know how to prevent this from happening. We need to combat antitrust violations and Big Tech monopolies, put a diverse range of people at their helm and those of other AI companies, encourage investment in ethically minded AI firms such as Hugging Face and the Distributed AI Research Institute (DAIR), and ensure that companies comply with robust AI legislation, like the EU AI Act, which protects the public from engineers' off-the-cuff thought experiments.

When the Future of Life's open letter was released, Gebru, Mitchell and other AI ethicists were quick to point out that there is no evidence to suggest that we are anywhere close to what it described as 'digital minds'.[23] But it was too late – the public was soon drowning in scare stories and misinformation, setting back the accurate communication of AI capabilities several steps. Once we have decided that the major threat is the Terminator rising up of its own accord and crushing humanity between its plastic fingertips, nothing except a panic button is deemed an appropriate and proportionate response. The phrase 'hard problems need hard solutions', with all its phallic implications, gets bandied around in tech firms, government buildings and policy bureaus. It's powered by another accompanying idea: that 'AI is moving so quickly we can't keep up.' But, as I've shown above, the problem is not that AI is moving too quickly, but that fundamental changes to the way we build AI (the form it takes, the purposes it serves, the kinds of people who make it, and the pseudoscience peddled by AI companies) are consistently being undermined. Another reason why this idea is disingenuous is because it pretends not to know how much frenzied work civil society, academics and activists are doing behind the scenes. The European Commission laboured over its AI Act for six years before it came into effect, and it could have been much more impactful and authoritative if some of the same individuals who signed the letter weren't also lobbying for weaker regulatory obligations. Tech giants hired public affairs professionals in their droves – and I've spoken to quite a few – to water down the Act through intense politicking and lobbying efforts. These third-party contractors had one goal: make sure the products sold by their client companies are exempt from the most stringent layer of the EU's regulations, the 'high-risk' category – AI used in education, infrastructure, biometrics, employment, immigration and in the judicial system. Meta spent $8 million lobbying Brussels, Apple $7 million. Ranked just below are Bayer (the pharma heavyweight), Google, Shell and Microsoft.[24] Perhaps most significantly, US-based companies spent almost double on lobbying efforts compared with their European counterparts (20 per cent versus 10 per cent), meaning that smaller and non-US based AI companies have the least say in how their products are regulated. For Brussels, that's a lot of free lunches.

Calling for a pause in AI development does not address any of this. As I have said, states of emergency are never called for the reason they claim to be. In December 2024, South Korea's President Yoon Suk Yeol declared martial law with the aim of maintaining power by suspending civil rights and the freedom of the press. A state of emergency is outside of normal time, and therefore the rule of law doesn't apply. Exceptions are made and unsafe policies implemented without scrutiny in the name of security. The effects of an emergency declaration can also endure long after it officially ends. In 2023, a briefing published by the White House argued that the national emergency that began on 14 September 2001 should endure 'because the terrorist threat continues … and the powers and authorities adopted to deal with that emergency must continue in effect beyond September 14, 2023.'[25] So while states of emergency are by definition temporary, they are effectively protracted periods of governance that become the norm. As Judith Butler pointed out following the November 2015 Paris attacks, they can 'set a tone for an enhanced security state, legitimating the suspension or watering down of basic rights, particularly for immigrants and people of colour, forever'.[26] As we will see later in the context of AI used by the police in the UK, the threat of terrorism results in a permanent lack of transparency for citizens. In 2022, with Federica Frabetti, a media theorist who spent her early career programming Nokia phones while campaigning for sexual freedom and gender equality in Italy, I collaborated with an investigative journalist called Max Colbert to get the UK's Metropolitan Police to admit to using an AI-powered system deployed by US police to track and shut down Black Lives Matter protests. Max's freedom of information requests were repeatedly met with the response that it would be a threat to national security for the public to know whether the tool was being used.

There is no evidence to suggest that 'terrorists' would benefit from knowing whether such a system is in use or not. What is certain, however, is that these tools are a threat to *citizens*, particularly people of colour; as Federica and I proved in a 2023 paper, AI policing tools are more likely to flag crowds of predominantly Black and Brown people as a potentially dangerous protest, because they were trained on images of BLM protests.[27] Terrorism can become a phantasm, an ephemeral target for 'national security' to hide behind. If you have ever experienced martial law first-hand, you'll know that the word 'state' in 'state of emergency' does not just stand for a condition or moment, but the inappropriate and dangerous strengthening of state powers. Coupled with unregulated tech companies selling snake oil, a manufactured scare about domestic security is a perfect storm for bad uses of AI.

Like martial law, the open letter's hyperventilating approach calls for a system override. 'Drop everything and press a panic button,' it seems to say. Its single-minded attempt to consolidate authority and skip over democratic processes mirrors the dogged tunnel vision of the post-11 September crackdown on the civil liberties of US citizens on the basis of race and religion. This is why diversity and inclusion and Sustainable Development Goals are swiftly binned following, for example, breaches (alleged or proven) to national security. We have nothing to gain from a one-solution approach to remedying AI harms. It creates an illusory line between AI issues deemed 'most urgent' (existential risk and what is known as 'AI safety' – technical approaches to solving AI problems) and those viewed as smaller or less pressing (social justice and structural approaches to combatting AI dangers). But the latter problems, such as AI's relationship to the gradual degradation of life, are not tangential to urgent issues: they are at their core. Assessing and addressing structural fault lines is the only way to truly tackle the source of what might initially appear to be the new, sudden terror of impending apocalypse – from capital, greed and entente to the privatisation of regulation. Panic buttons and safety mechanisms are important, but they are band-aids on a trauma wound.

3

The Triangle of Doom

One day, as I headed to the bus stop after giving a talk at Cambridge's Applied Mathematics Faculty, a young attendee came up to me, asking how he could pursue his three passions: utilitarianism, effective altruism (also known as EA) and existential risk (Ex Risk). Utilitarianism is a group of ethical traditions that prioritise doing the most good for the most people, which is great until it involves awkward calculations about who is the most deserving of help. EA is a movement aimed at maximising the impact of charitable donations, in other words, making your money go the furthest when you give. Ex Risk, as we've seen above, is the study, prediction and mitigation of low-probability high-impact events. These three movements have become increasingly popular among tech entrepreneurs, and indeed EA groups target bright young things in Silicon Valley as the next potential big donors to recruit. Taken together, I call them the Triangle of Doom. I would like to be clear that I am not referring to these areas individually; the triangle emerges only when they coalesce. Fans of that intersection include Sam Bankman-Fried, in jail for fraud following the 2023 collapse of his crypto exchange business FTX; Nick Bostrom, the aforementioned de-throned ex-director of an AI ethics centre at Oxford; and Geoffrey Miller, a psychologist who said fat people can't complete PhDs and who supports China's position on eugenics.[1] A cryptocurrency entrepreneur and convicted fraudster, Bankman-Fried was a prominent spokesperson and donor for the EA movement since meeting one of its originators, Will MacAskill, as an MIT student in 2013. He also has strong credentials as a utilitarian; when his ex-partner Caroline Ellison was prosecuted for her role in the FTX scandal, she told the courts that 'the only moral rule that mattered [to Bankman-Fried] was doing whatever would maximise utility'.[2] Finally, he was also vocal in his long-termist concerns about an AI apocalypse. Bostrom, meanwhile, who used the Effective Altruism Forum to post articles on similar themes, sent the community reeling after the release of his racist emails.[3] A utilitarian impulse is central to his approach to existential risk, which argues that the benefits AI might have for future generations outweigh the risk of a potentially catastrophic impact on those of us currently on the planet. Miller, meanwhile, taught a course on 'The Psychology of Effective Altruism' at the University of New Mexico, which included long-termism and the 'powerful moral philosophy',[4] as he sees it, of utilitarian ethics. And so the list of people who buy into the Triangle of Doom goes on.

The Triangle of Doom often appeals to these kinds of unfortunate characters, not least because the combination of EA, utilitarianism and Ex Risk is used to justify the possibility of an AI singularity. Apocalypse, they say, is worth the risk because more people in the future would stand to gain from an AI explosion than those on Earth right now have to lose from being extinguished. This laughable logic is typical of how the Triangle of Doom justifies unsafe AI. It provides the foundations for calculations of risk and reward that happen behind a closed door by people who mistake statistics for ethics. Whether we live or die comes down to whether Silicon Valley ringleaders think our deaths (from, for example, AI-exacerbated climate crisis) are worth it if it increases the likelihood of creating AGI.

The individual vertices of the Triangle of Doom are not an issue on their own, because, for example, EA at its best is a movement of people working out how their money can go furthest when they give to charity. But some effective altruists are so attached to their definition of utilitarianism that they've ended up making naive choices about how to help others. In most cases, after all, they are people who have no particular connection to or expertise in poverty, destitution or disease, and yet who are convinced of their abilities to solve these problems. Who needs to be a charity worker when you can be a statistician! It's now well known that anti-mosquito bed nets provided by charities, including EA initiatives such as Give-Well, to knock malaria on the head are instead used for fishing. These strong, light, insecticide-treated nets are resulting in the overfishing of sea and swamp creatures – with potentially disastrous consequences for the ecosystem, as Benjamin Jones at Stockholm University and Richard Unsworth at Swansea University discovered.[5] The framework of utility isn't terribly well suited to charity, where the concerns of the donors are often different from those of recipients. For those who received GiveWell's mosquito nets, having enough to eat was more of a priority than being protected against malaria.

Where there is money, there is murder, and some EA campaigns have been criticised for refusing to disclose the deaths that result from their charity donations in situations where people will do anything to intercept the money.[6] Any charity-sector expert will tell you that because the recipients of charity exist not in vacuums but in complex situations, and are presided over by regimes ranging from governments to gangs, helping people is no easy feat. Deciding who is 'objectively' more or less deserving is also an ugly pastime. Mother Teresa said, 'Never worry about numbers. Help one person at a time and always start with the person nearest you.' She turned out to have plenty of flaws, but she knew what poverty was. She believed that it was impossible to eradicate it while socio-economic inequality persists, and so our purpose on Earth will always be to look after the needy. What is also crucial, she advised, is that we learn not to be disgusted by each other, but compassionate and inspired by those society casts out. This can be very difficult to do, and is often harder the more money you have and the more removed you are from the plight of others. This is why EA's utilitarian bent does not lend itself to helping people. The other reason is that EA is not interested in coming to the aid of individuals – it wants big numbers, big calculations and big victories, even at the risk of big failures. The fantasy of saving the world is strong for those who would rather be Iron Man than a care worker.

Without utilitarianism, Ex Risk is also, for the most part, a discipline that is helping to predict and mitigate low-probability high-impact events. At its best, it includes more than just AI killing us all: volcanoes and biowarfare, climate change and ecosystem collapse, pandemics, geopolitical tensions and global conflict. The media – following the lead of selected computer scientists and entrepreneurs – is mostly focused on *Terminator*-esque AI scenarios. Bostrom views genocide as 'a mere ripple on the surface of the great sea of life' because after a genocide there would be at least some humans left standing – the kind of sentiment that only makes sense if you've never personally experienced one.[7] To Bostrom, what is paramount is that 'intelligent life' persists, because life without intelligence has less value. His obsession with the survival of intelligent life makes different kinds of violence irrelevant by comparison. When I first encountered these statements, their detached, unassuming cruelty stung. I hear people paraphrasing him all the time, often to set up a comparison between his definition of apocalypse (the whole of humanity dying) and climate, hate or war-fuelled extinction events (where lots of people die but intelligent life survives). The phrase has since dulled; it has become merely depressing. Again, a quotation often attributed to Mother Teresa has a different view of ripples: 'I alone cannot change the world,' she said, 'but I can cast a stone across the waters to create many ripples.'

The logic that an AI apocalypse is a much more important threat than – and one distinct from – genocide and war shows how utilitarians are limited in their approach to what's worth their time and money and what's not. Issues that are more immediate, and harder to solve without direct engagement, somehow end up at the bottom of the hierarchy. Suddenly, we are in the realm of making calculations about narrowly defined apocalypses, the poor scientific practice of throwing large numbers into the air so that philosophers and tech billionaires can catch them in their open mouths. One example from Bostrom's work over the past two decades that has stuck with me in this regard is a 2003 article in which he worries that every second we don't spend colonising star systems is an astronomical loss to humankind. His sense of value is oriented by the impact of technology on the economy, which he believes has much to gain from using star energy to support advanced computers. 'Few other philanthropic causes', he says, could match its benefits.[8] Geopolitics is suspiciously absent from this projection. The World Population Review reports that forty-two countries were engaged in war in 2024, and Statista estimated military spending in 2023 at $2.44 trillion.[9] Given global commitments to peacelessness, it's difficult to imagine states refraining from slaughtering each other (using better AI, of course) for their stake in star energy. And then there's the environmental cost of such a mission, though no doubt ecosystem collapse would long precede it.

Another extreme is also presented to us by Bostrom: the possibility of total destruction if the star colonisation mission were to go wrong and the sun-powered supercomputers ended up wiping out humanity.[10] Then come the attempts to justify total destruction with the logic that dying of old age is qualitatively the same as keeling over in an AI catastrophe.

It ultimately won't matter, Bostrom says, what your cause of death is. Is this secularism taken to its logical extreme, where dying is so meaningless that a violent death is the same as a peaceful one? When I present this work in my classes it gets split reactions. Some students recoil, finding it painful, distasteful and pointless. Others enjoy the approach. My concern for the latter group is that treating intelligent life as supreme and violent death as acceptable in any circumstance is not only unhelpful but encourages heartlessness. It's difficult to see these thought experiments as anything other than obscenely out of touch, when the day-to-day experiences of starving and war-torn people globally would no doubt resemble hell on Earth to Bostrom and his followers.

The detachment of these conversations from the real world is gloriously reflected in the venues where they take place. In May 2024 the *Guardian* reported that the Effective Ventures Foundation had put their £14.9m castle, Wytham Abbey, up for sale.[11] The manor had previously been used to host discussions with billionaire tech entrepreneurs about how AI could be considered a charity investment, under the logic that powerful AI could cure world hunger. Visitors included Bankman-Fried, Jaan Tallinn of Skype and Facebook co-founder Dustin Moskovitz. The scheme failed after two years. An Effective Ventures spokesperson reportedly said they had found 'higher-impact' uses of their capital (a very on-brand message). To an outside observer, it doesn't seem surprising that Effective Ventures could get more bang for their buck by spending capital on something other than hanging out with rich and famous people in an expensive building. I myself have watched uneasily while wealthy people give their two cents on 'big themes' in philanthropy while gathered on a yacht or private beach. The experience for everyone present was, quite frankly, a bit awkward. And yet this is how fundraising with the mega-rich takes place – at balls and gala events, on private islands. It's the queasy side of giving, as anyone who has worked in the charity sector will know. My concern is not with needing to ship the wealthy to luxury events for them to care – it's a non-issue – but that discussing charity in the context of EA and AI encourages conversations about life extension and becoming more intelligent: the preoccupations of those who have everything else already. This results in increased investment into, in Bostrom's words, how to 'expand our mental capacities and indefinitely prolong our subjective lifespan'.[12] This is the pet pursuit of so many of the most prominent advocates of a utopian, AI-powered future, and the oxygen they give to it shifts focus away from inequality and violence around the globe. Frankly, this is very wrong.

There is an understandable pleasure in casting daily tragedies to one side to speculate about larger brains and the risk of an AI-induced black swan event. Tech entrepreneurs who give to this cause are no doubt relieved to be involved in a charitable venture that is sexy rather than sad. There is also an odd masturbatory energy in fantasising about saving people from a situation they are responsible for creating, as we saw in the Future of Life open letter. These dramatic impulses can easily distract the public from the everyday uses of AI that are resulting in apocalyptic scenarios – in Gaza, for example, where facial recognition is used to target civilians, or in the many nations where AI is misused by law enforcement, at borders and in the education system.[13] We need Ex Risk that explores apocalypse *through* these everyday nightmares. There is lots of this going on, it just doesn't get the same hype and attention as Bostrom's version of it does. Many Ex Risk centres, like the Cascade Institute, which counts the Centre for the Study of Existential Risk (CSER) at Cambridge as a partner, do not share his concern about a potential plateauing of human intelligence.[14] This is very much beside the point when there is quite visibly little correlation between how humans perform on 'IQ' tests and how well they manage their biosphere. Bigger brains – at any cost – are the wet dreams of philosopher-tech bros like Bostrom. The collateral damage of the energy consumption required to achieve this goal, including water supplies poisoned with toxic metals in the Atacama Region in Chile, which is home to a vast swathe of global lithium reserves, doesn't appear to be dampening transhumanists' spirits. And yet our future depends on the symbiotic relationships we participate in – whether we like it or not – with the rest of life on Earth, from the bacteria in our guts to the billions of humans with whom we share our planet. This is more in line with the thinking behind most good Ex Risk centres that focus on geopolitical violence, failure to keep emissions below the 1.5-degree centigrade target and other Earth system tipping points, pandemics and their long-term effects on health and society, the widespread popularity of authoritarianism within supposedly democratic regimes, ecosystem collapse, and widening rich/poor gaps. When Ex Risk researchers focus on these things, as they do at CSER, they can be a powerful ally in producing climate strategies, supporting Indigenous peoples' collective right to participate in global governance, and improving responses to and recovery from disasters like volcano eruptions and pandemics.[15]

It's crucial that we do not see existential risks stemming from AI as divorced from these other threats but *emerging from them*. No crisis is a single issue. We need a healthy, holistic understanding of the relationship between injustice and catastrophe. Any plan of action that addresses this must draw on the expertise and experience of those most at risk. By taking into account the interconnectedness of things that go wrong in the world, we see how layered issues turn situations from bad to perilous. There are plenty of poor choices we would need to make first before we reach the stage of a supercomputer bent on ending human life; rogue AI would be the last in a long line of dominoes to fall. The rise of authoritarianism, for example, is the result of polycrisis – compounded social, environmental, political and technological problems, from increasing social divisions to the cost-of-living crisis. These constituent crises interact to create existential risks. As CSER attests, 'global risks are not exogenous to human civilisation, they are the products of choices and decisions taken (or not taken) at all levels of human society. The backdrop to these decisions is one characterised by global injustice: profound inequality, corruption, and structural discrimination (such as anti-Black racism and white supremacy).'[16]

I'm therefore invested in how ideas about justice can underpin Ex Risk research, and equally, how Ex Risk experts can direct activist and other pro-justice work. Ultimately, we need to draw the people affected most by particular crises together and ask *them*: what does it mean to you to live a good life? Which ways of living and dying are acceptable to you? What do you value most? What kind of world do you want to inhabit? Is mere 'survival' the goal if it means being starving and homeless in a subterranean bunker devoid of plant life? These are the questions I wanted the student at the bus stop to answer.

Unsurprisingly, as my colleagues point out quite often, there are few researchers in the majority world asking, 'Will AI kill us all?' And it's not because the minority world has a more limited perspective about future risks. The reason is partly that the fantasy of total extinction is caught up in Western control-or-be-controlled narratives that center on interspecies battles over North American civilisational strongholds. We saw that Hollywood's on-screen apocalypses either take place or are instigated in the West. The centre of the ripple is LA. That's the Western lens through which Bostrom approaches his speculations about the apocalypse. Guillermo del Toro's 2013 disaster movie *Pacific Rim* even begins with the Golden Gate Bridge.

We urgently need a change of perspective and focus. By

breaking out of the narratives peddled by the Triangle of Doomers, we can see that calamities don't occur in a vacuum; they're the result of incremental poor choices, institutional thoughtlessness and misguided AI opinion leaders who tell us they're the only voice worth listening to. They have much to gain from us believing them.

The monopoly of monopolies

In 2020, the New York-based AI policy institute AI Now crowdsourced a 'new lexicon for AI'.[17] They sought out terms that drew attention to important issues in AI and questioned the way in which we imagine technology. Two of the important phrases they gave rise to were AI monopolies and the AI arms race. These are issues that rarely pop up in the Triangle of Doom, which is why I brought them up on *The Moral Maze* when responding to the question, 'Should we be afraid of AI?' Yes, I said, but not for the reasons Triangle of Doomers give. We should fear the cartel-like behaviour and the monopolisation of compute power by Big Tech (and Western powers). Tech entrepreneurs have a vested interest in staying silent on these issues. But their major contribution to the homogenisation of AI development and the concentration of power is significant. This is why it's a major problem that smaller companies are struggling to compete with Big Tech's resources and vast user bases from which they can collect and sell data. There will be no more Metas or Amazons, because these companies will crush, absorb or control them, as Microsoft has done with OpenAI, in which it owns a 49 per cent stake. Take Musk's use of data from electric car company Tesla and social media platform X to help power xAI, his latest AI venture, which powers the Grok chatbot. Existing big data companies are at a huge advantage. Data and compute power are the key to success. Small AI-powered drug discovery companies are now spending hundreds of thousands of dollars to access Big Tech-owned large models; as one AI founder said to me, 'Right now, brute force seems to be the answer.' Even the new AI upstarts are reliant on Big Tech for investment and computing infrastructure. Silicon Valley AI startup Anthropic has committed to using Amazon's cloud architecture and proprietary chips to train models in return for major investment. The EU weakened its legislation on foundation models to keep home-grown French AI company Mistral happy, only to see Mistral swept up by Microsoft in one of Brussels' most embarrassing grifts. Paris-headquartered AI company Hugging Face uses Amazon Web Services, while London-born Stability AI chose to partner with Amazon SageMaker (a machine learning platform) to speed up its text-to-image model, Stable Diffusion. Canadian AI platform Cohere uses Google, while US-based Inflection AI uses Microsoft. Whether or not these 'strategic collaborations' contribute to monopolisation, the ecosystem is arguably increasingly reliant on Big Tech platforms and cloud services. Is the market getting smaller, not bigger? And what does this mean for consumers? Big Tech controls how much we pay, what ads we see, how much screen time we get, the fate of politics and polarisation, where our businesses sell, how much our products sell for, what information we consume, how we consume it. And we're told that this is small fry – insignificant and irrelevant – because the apocalypse may be coming.

And then there's the geopolitical implications of competition over natural resources and crucial bits of hardware. Take the geopolitical rivalry around Graphics Processing Units (GPU), computer chips that are foundational to AI hardware. The Taiwan Semiconductor Manufacturing Company Limited makes GPUs on behalf of AMD and Nvidia, two North American-headquartered companies that design and sell semiconductors and GPUs for all kinds of AI devices, from robotics and autonomous cars to crypto and gaming. TSMC has large-scale access to some of the best silicon-manufacturing facilities in the world. Trump accused them of pinching it from the US: 'They took almost 100 per cent of our chip industry,'[18] he blustered. Of course, neither Taiwan nor its business endeavours are the US's by right. Taiwan's out-competition of the rest of the world means that it now has a stronghold over chip production, making China's sights on the nation more focused than ever. Bloomberg reported in 2024 that the Netherlands has run simulations on a potential China invasion, but Nvidia and TSMC are prepared for such an eventuality; TSMC reportedly has a remote kill switch in the machines that make them, meaning that if China invades Taiwan, Nvidia can allegedly choke its production of GPUs. TSMC CEO Mark Liu has said that 'nobody can control TSMC by force. If you take a military force or invasion you will render the TSMC factory non-operable.'[19] Were this to actually happen it would bring AI production to a standstill. These non-negligible vulnerabilities in the AI supply chain show just how powerfully the AI industry can exacerbate frictions in contemporary geopolitics. This is a very real and properly existential risk. For further evidence of legitimate geopolitical concerns, look no further than the US/China 'arms race', including the US's restrictions on exports of AI chips to China and the Middle East and its ban on government use of TikTok. Trump loves to hate China. Trump loves to hate China ('Chy-na!'). He once argued with characteristic simplicity that AI 'is very scary, but we absolutely have to win because if we don't win, China wins.'[20]

In November 2024 the US–China Economic and Security Review Commission announced that it would 'establish and fund a Manhattan Project-like program dedicated to racing to and acquiring an Artificial General Intelligence (AGI) capability'.[21] This is exactly what AI ethics centres like mine and CSER have been telling governments not to do. Why are we imitating a programme that destroyed the lives of hundreds of thousands of people? Why are we 'racing' towards an uncertain goal without clear guardrails and a good enough reason for doing so? It's a terrible strategy. And yet it's what comes of voting in a populist Sinophobe who divides the world into winners and losers. All this is to say that AI development is mired in bids for global supremacy. If you're worried about an AI apocalypse, tense geopolitics is more likely to cause it than AI autonomously deciding to rise up against humanity. These are the problems we should focus on: corporate control of our data, geopolitical sabre-rattling and Big Tech's environmental callousness and tendency towards monopolisation. We may not think of them as forms of bias, but they are at the root of why AI can be harmful.

What happened, you might ask, to globalisation, and to frictionless trade and healthy competition across borders? Major figures in Big Tech and venture capital are now turning to Trump for his stance on tech policy. Even though the Trump administration began antitrust investigations in 2019 against Meta, Apple, Amazon and Google, Trump now appears to have U-turned. From Sundar Pichai and Sam Altman to Jeff Bezos, Mark Zuckerberg and Tim Cook (not to mention venture capitalists Marc Andreessen, Ben Horowitz and David Sacks), tech bros flocked to Mar-a-Lago to benefit from Trump's light-touch approach to tech regulation support for crypto – even after the FTX disaster. Sacks has been clear that nations should be bypassing global trade and creating home-grown AI, which closely aligns with Trumpian foreign policy. Zuckerberg, once a fervent leftie, rang Trump to tell him that after the assassination attempt 'he wouldn't vote for a Democrat'.[22] He had previously called Biden's policies on tackling COVID-19 misinformation on Facebook 'censorship',[23] and no doubt hoped a Trump administration would give Meta free rein. By drawing on trigger words that the freedom of speech brigade could chew on, Zuckerberg fuelled the Republican fire ahead of the 2024 elections. Content moderation is political:

we are in an era when whom you vote for affects what you see online. Ultimately, it now makes sense that Big Tech is against governments that are cautious and interventionist about AI, as has been the Democrat stance.

It's unlikely that Trump will actually meddle less in Big Tech's business. Despite admitting 'he knew no major business leaders and didn't like them', as Yale Professor Jeffrey Sonnenfeld noted from one personal encounter,[24] Trump loves to poke his fingers into the domestic business pie to promote the interest of friends and settle personal vendettas. You need only look at his protracted lawsuit against AT&T, and the White House's feuds with Harley-Davidson and Ford when the vehicle manufacturers attempted to move production out of the US, to see how petty and personal Washington has been towards businesses under Trump. It therefore appears that Trump may not entirely distance himself from the Biden administration's attack on Big Tech monopolies.

The jewel in Biden's regulatory crown was Lina Khan, who addressed flagging competition in platform markets by giving outdated antitrust legislation an overhaul. Her speciality is Amazon. In one of the very few antitrust essays to go viral, she wrote in a 2017 issue of the *Yale Law Journal* that anti-competitive behaviour can no longer be defined in terms of 'consumer welfare' (e.g. increasing prices for consumers within a single enterprise).[25] For one, Facebook and Amazon touted themselves as free to use. And yet consumers, product developers and shops find themselves dependent on these platforms. Dependence is the first step to exploitation. It kills freedom of economic opportunity and free enterprise. Existing regulation is, she explains, totally ill-equipped to ensure that Amazon – a data-collection platform that now dictates infrastructure for many industries – is not engaging in anti-competitive behaviour.[26] One problem is that antitrust regulation, which was set up to tackle the oil, tobacco and railroad monopolies of the early twentieth century, assumes that companies prefer profit to growth; but because Amazon has historically prioritised growth over profits, it has put itself in a position where predatory pricing is an attractive way of minimising competition. Pricing, however, is far from the only issue. Most Prime members no longer go comparison shopping, particularly if a greater price can be justified by leaving it very late in the day to buy an inflatable mermaid-in-a-bath Halloween costume or, more seriously, urgently needed baby formula. If consumers are locked into using a service and aren't looking elsewhere, companies then rely on Amazon to sell their products.

This means that Amazon can dictate the terms on which companies use the platform and how much they pay. Amazon then uses the data it has on those products and the customers who purchase them to weaken them as competitors by, for example, creating own-brand versions of those products. Then there are the things we don't see, for example Amazon's chokehold over global infrastructure, made possible by its success across multiple industries. You are perhaps familiar with its freight and delivery services or leasing of warehouse space, but one of its standout achievements is its control of 50 per cent of the cloud market: Amazon runs the backend for Netflix, Pinterest, Slack, Yelp and NASA. Bernhard Rieder, Giovanni Sileno and Geoff Gordon put it brilliantly when they call this a 'dense and tightly integrated ecosystem of technologies, expertise, and business synergy that is difficult for newcomers to compete in, even if they are not immediately bought out'.[27] Don't underestimate Amazon's attempt to buy up the whole supply chain: Reuters reported in mid-2024 that it's 'racing to develop AI chips cheaper and faster' than Nvidia, in order to avoid paying 'Nvidia tax'.[28] These chips are mostly supporting Amazon Web Services, the big money-maker of the megalith and likely future of the company.

Amazon is also not alone in being viewed as an anti-competitive megalith by Democratic administrations – not by a long shot. In its efforts to protect consumers, crack down on monopolistic behaviour and enhance competition from smaller enterprises, the Biden administration filed a series of lawsuits against Apple, Amazon, Meta and Google. In December 2023, the courts ruled that Apple had copied its blood oxygen level readers (which soared in popularity post COVID-19) on its Apple Watch from medtech company Masimo. The White House subsequently banned Apple from selling the Watch Series 9 and the Ultra 2. In March 2024, the Department of Justice filed a lawsuit against Apple for antitrust issues like stultifying the growth of apps, products and services that could otherwise make users less reliant on the iPhone, as well as extracting 'more money from consumers, developers, content creators, artists, publishers, small businesses, and merchants, among others'.[29] For years, app developers have complained that the company charges 27 per cent commission, occasionally costing them their businesses, while Apple points out that a large swathe of third-party developers don't pay at all, including, they say, those whose apps don't have a million new annual installs, NGOs, educational institutions and particular government entities. Nevertheless, the DoJ has good evidence to suggest that Apple is going out of its way to make it difficult for 'superapps' to host services on the cloud, fearing that because these products are cloud-based and you don't need a powerful smartphone to run them, fewer people will buy iPhones. Finally, the US Federal Trade Commission is also arguing that Meta withheld information from them when it originally permitted Facebook to acquire Instagram and WhatsApp,[30] information which likely frames these companies as potential competitors. As purchasing the competition weakens it, any such transactions can be highly anti-competitive.

Though venture capital opinion leaders would claim otherwise, the argument that 'the Democrats are against small tech' is not exactly true. What Khan's new framing of anti-trust shows is that the question is not, 'Which political party is for or against startups and tech companies in the US?', for both are acting in the interests of the AI industry in different ways. Instead, the question is: 'Why do they take different approaches, and which industry players and stakeholders are they allying with and why?' This is not about whether they are curtailing Big Tech's success. If you count yourself as a dedicated capitalist, take note of Biden's suggestion in July 2021 that 'Capitalism without competition isn't capitalism – it's exploitation'[31] (though Karl Marx established that labour exploitation is a feature, not a bug, of capitalism).[32] We may not think of monopolies as a form of bias, but they are at the root of why AI can be harmful to individuals. Our narrow definition of bias prevents us from working towards a less concentrated net of AI suppliers. Shifting power requires unprecedented collaboration between government actors, community organisers, civil society, activists, tech unions and legal and policy experts. We need to join the dots for tech policymakers between problems that are seen as short-term (AI that creates – and is the result of – targeted discrimination and human rights abuses) and those presented as long-term (dangerous superintelligence). If mass extinction does occur, it won't be because AI turns evil, but because we did not decentralise corporate power, deal with day-to-day inequalities in the AI industry and tackle incendiary foreign policy.

This is about finding ways to prise Big Tech's sticky fingers from its control of AI, and reclaiming our ability to make informed and varied choices about the companies we trust to provide us with AI goods and services. If you're still bewildered by how once-dedicated Democrats like Musk and Zuckerberg with scrappy startups invented in college dorms and rented garages are doing whatever they can to justify monopolistic, anti-democratic institutions, the answer is, quite simply, their desire to dominate AI production and global geopolitics by being the first to launch the greatest, most profitable AGI. We've seen ample evidence of this, including Big Tech's changing stance towards regulation. Big Tech was relatively accepting of AI legislation in the US until around the time GPT-4 was launched. When big companies are happy with guardrails it's an indication that they still fear competition, because larger enterprises can afford to pay the fines that smaller enterprises cannot, and lobby regulators to tailor regulation to their demands. If Big Tech is anti-regulation, it shows it isn't majorly concerned about competition and is just consolidating power by taking major stakes in promising startups (as was the case with Microsoft and Mistral). As one founder of a TechBio AI company told me, 'the anti-regulation stance may be a sign that they just want to be left alone to make their Übermensch'. Time will tell.

The capitalist elephant in the room

At a time when it's more important than ever that we talk about it, entire AI summits and conferences go by without a single mention of capitalism. From geopolitical tensions and the fragility of AI's supply chain to the huge interest among billionaires and others in EA and other ethical movements which conveniently encourage the growth and expansion of certain industries, it's undeniable that capitalism is the unspoken elephant in the room. It's also the single greatest contribution to harm against human and non-human life. Don't be misled by those who point the finger at one kind of capitalism as the 'bad kind'; capitalism is capitalism, and newer iterations are not detached from older ones. They're still part and parcel of the same problem. Capitalist tools, 'from labor exploitation, policy capture, and economic planning to intelligence services, ruling class hegemony, and propaganda' are, as scholar and investigative journalist Michael Kwet notes, hard at work in AI's supply chain.[33] In particular, we can see them looming large in Big Tech's heavy investment in telecommunications, power and data centres in the majority world, which isn't as good as it sounds. Amazon Web Services (AWS), for example, promised to build $2.5 billion-worth of cloud infrastructure in South Africa between 2018 and 2029, including lots of data centres: noisy and energy-hungry pollutants. Local government in South Africa has fewer powers to protect its environment or to ensure that data centres aren't leaching energy from populations who need it to go about their daily lives. Labour outsourced to South Africa rather than in the US and Europe also tends to be more exploitative and even less well remunerated. And once AWS services are up and running, South Africa first becomes a testing ground for unregulated products, and then its institutions and companies will be reliant on AWS products. As Kwet argues: 'Amazon's expansion will not benefit the average South African and will bring more labour exploitation and likely enable more surveillance-based policing of poor and marginalised communities.'

And then there's Microsoft. In the 2000s, South Africa did have a free and open-source software policy preference. This is now a thing of the past following Microsoft's privatisation of the digital ecosystem in South Africa. Kwet argues that Microsoft is creating what he calls 'infrastructural debt'. It's not a question of whether its participation in South African society is more of a good thing or a bad thing – it's about recognising that citizens have not been given the facts, nor had the opportunity to choose whether they are willing, for example, to have Microsoft track students in return for providing high-tech education facilities. This wouldn't be the first time secondary education has been privatised by Big Tech, and because higher education is globally in crisis, it makes sense that it's becoming increasingly dependent on private investment to stay afloat. But

Microsoft also widely funds police, militaries and prisons in the country, partnering with surveillance vendors and other third parties who will then run their software on Microsoft's cloud services. Microsoft's Africa Partner of the Year 2017 was even a prison management system.[34] Journalists like Kwet have played a fundamental role in tracking how the majority world is used as a testing ground for carceral innovations – from Microsoft's police cars in South Africa to its unsafe Bing Chatbot let loose on the public in India.[35] This all fits the definition of digital colonialism fairly neatly: political, economic and social control over a territory, particularly social and disciplinary institutions like law enforcement and education. We might also call this corporate imperialism, which makes a mockery of dreams of an AI revolution that will empower everyone equally.

Indeed, critics of India's vast biometric data bank Aadhaar argue that its mode of surveillance is inherited from British imperial rule.[36] It forces, they say, its population to hand over biometric data without their consent or proper understanding of the system, and then monetises it by giving the private sector access.[37] You don't have to look far to see how the idea gained traction, and where it came from. In the 1950s, William James Herschel of the Indian Civil Service – officially known as the Imperial Civil Service, which took over bureaucratic rule of India in 1958 following the demise of the East India Company – forced local business owners to put their handprint on documents signed with colonial authorities.[38] By the 1990s, fingerprinting had exploded as a means of commercial governance across India. When the Dosadh 'low-caste' communities were fingerprinted for surveillance, it marked them as potentially dangerous to the colonial regime *and* as a measurable human resource for jute mills and other businesses in Calcutta.[39] The fingerprinted person straddled the line of criminality and commercial value. So it remains.

Sam Altman has said that AI will 'break capitalism',

implying that AI is not capitalistic (or that capitalism can break capitalism).[40] Very much like technology, capitalism disguises itself as the answer to the problems it creates. But AI is born from capitalist values and tendencies, which run through its blood: perpetual growth, faith in an unfettered 'free market', and the assumption that the market is always right and dictates the natural order of things. The tech market largely decided that it would back Trump in the 2024 US election, during which sexual violence and white-collar criminal activity appeared to be desirable leadership qualities. When anyone says that AI will render work obsolete I am always reminded of Mark Fisher's brilliant *Capitalist Realism*, whose anthem is 'Capitalism doesn't break, it bends'.[41] When there is cash and competition there is also labour, inequality and exploitation.

When capitalism is the only driving force behind AI development it becomes an existential risk. To say that AI is itself dangerous is like saying that unextracted oil is harmful. As Canadian anthropologist Zoe Todd reminds us, what is harmful about oil is petro-capitalist extraction and production.[42] In the context of Husky Energy's 2018 oil spill across Cold Lake, Alberta South and Saskatchewan, it's the extraction and spillage of oil across Indigenous territories that's the problem. Similarly, the unfettered pursuit of profit is what makes certain kinds of AI catastrophic, both immediately and in the long term. As the wonderful Meredith Whittaker, President of the Signal Foundation, reminds us, shareholders demand that AI companies' revenue and growth increase every year forever, and this is, by definition, metastasis – a pathogen that spreads indefinitely.[43] Capitalism as an economic orthodoxy justifies infinite, unfettered growth. There is no redeemable variation of such an ethos. If the Triangle of Doom's three indices are utilitarianism, effective altruism and misguided Ex Risk, then this is a holy trinity enabled by late capitalism – and the biggest driver of the existential risks posed by AI.

4

Building from Better Visions

One of the reasons why discussions about capitalism are often seen as diminutive or irrelevant in the context of a possible AI apocalypse is that we're stuck imagining AI as the Terminator. This is, as we saw in Chapter 2, largely down to the way apocalypse is fetishised in pop culture. Most of us don't know where AI begins and ends (is it software? a robot? a data centre?) and the language we use to describe it is often deeply misleading. You picture a killbot with silvery abs, or a salty supercomputer like HAL from *2001: A Space Odyssey* (1968), and you get little to no information about how they're built and what they're made of. Neither do these depictions reveal any of the issues outlined in the previous chapter. Who comprises their extended labour force? What are their environmental consequences? Where are the consumers and enterprises in Big Tech's chokehold? This matters because, as we've seen, the stories we use to imagine our relationship with technology dictate the possibilities of how we design and use AI. As we've seen in Chapter 1, it has been our prosthetic since the beginning. To be human is to be technological; there is a great deal that is more than just 'human' about us, as we are bound to the tools that give us life, just like we're reliant on our bacterial symbionts. There are plenty of artists and designers out there depicting AI in ways which shed light on these interspecies intimacies. If only AI engineers and investors were as familiar with their work as with *The Terminator*! We'll now explore what kinds of images

The Creation of Adam from the ceiling of the
Sistine Chapel (1508–12), by Michelangelo

of AI we should be creating to illuminate the reality of what AI is and what it can do.

First, let's return briefly to a couple of images we could do without: humanoid versions of God in Michelangelo's *The Creation of Adam*, and Rodin's *Le Penseur*. I cannot overstate their ubiquity as internet stock images of AI, and as features of AI company or conference logos. In the original, God, carried by cherubim, reaches out to the languishing human man, who listlessly extends a bent forefinger in his direction. In the robot and human version, the human takes the position of God (of course), and it's the AI that barely attempts to meet its creator's touch. The AI is Adam, no longer abiding by his God's rules, playing master of its own fate. It's an apt reminder that Judaeo-Christian beliefs remain silently at the core of Western science, determining the significance and form of present and future technology. As we've seen, secularism is rich in religious symbolism. Creator mythology dominates the most widely circulated images of AI, and it's unhelpful because it justifies egoistic claims made by tech entrepreneurs that what they are creating is conscious life, and that they are gods.

And then there's Rodin's *Le Penseur*, a thick-set, silkily

An AI-generated imitation of *Le Penseur* in humanoid form

muscular man currently housed in Paris' Musée Rodin. Bent over, he is broad-shouldered, a stunning figure of heroic proportions modelled on French prizefighter Jean Baud. Rodin said, 'What makes my Thinker think is that he thinks not only with his brain, with his knitted brow, his distended nostrils and compressed lips, but with every muscle of his arms, back, and legs, with his clenched fist and gripping toes.'[1] Rodin recognises that the act of thinking is embodied – not just in the sense that perfect musculature apparently equates to a great brain (!) – a material activity (it uses your body). When we depict AI as Rodin's strongman in humanoid form, we suture intelligence to a white male template. Hidden in this image are all the elements of ordinary life that make it hard for women and the disenfranchised to spend time in deep thought. As Virginia Woolf famously stated, thinking and writing requires a room of one's own,[2] and is therefore laced with inequalities; it demands drive, space, encouragement and nourishment and can be prevented or inhibited by a lack of resources and self-belief. We don't see any of these supporting relations in *Le Penseur*. And yet, like the Vitruvian Man, he is now supposed to represent not just everyman and the universal man who aims to better himself through mental exertion, but the future of intelligence.

How we represent AI matters. In 2022, a group of artists, researchers and activists started the Better Images of AI project. I use these images at all my talks because they mostly depict AI not as some ephemeral possibility but as material fact, i.e., they show data labellers at work and texts broken down into words and phrases that can be processed by machine learning models. People are often quite tense when they know they're going to hear about AI, but the crowd perceptibly softens when they see it represented as the sum of its parts. These images return us to French philosopher Gilbert Simondon's idea that we need to 'discover [technology] as human',[3] finding the familiar in it and making visible the acts of human labour that result in marvels of engineering. One of my favourite images, *Silicon on Black 1*, is an HD photograph of a silicon monocrystal by Catherine Breslin.[4] It features a shiny charcoal-coloured block, and looking at it I'm reminded of collecting fool's gold as a child and storing it in a papier-mâché box covered with images of semi-precious stones and dyed crystals. Experiencing the tangibility of an object is a form of getting to know it, which is why young children often put things in their mouths when they are presented with them.

We fall back to stock images of humanoids in iconic European art partly because software can be difficult to picture. As a set of written rules that execute tasks it lacks a tactile quality,

Catherine Breslin's *Silicon on Black 1* (2022). A block like
this would be sliced into 30-centimetre diameter wafers to
form the base of Central Processing Units (CPUs)

making it tricky to depict as an accessible artefact. Even in the
Terminator franchise we rarely see Skynet in physical form.
Hardware – the material components of AI – is not usually
viewed as a sexy enough representation of an AI product. As
German media scholar Friedrich Kittler has observed, computer culture tends to focus on software rather than hardware:[5]
software is agile and nimble, hardware is clunky and dependent
on Moore's Law, which states that the number of transistors
in a microchip doubles every two years as a function of expo-
nential growth. The aim of software is to proliferate, to be
both mysterious and ubiquitous, while hardware must disappear from view as we build better, lighter and faster devices.
In 2011, Andreessen Horowitz (AH Capital Management)
founder Marc Andreessen wrote that 'software is eating the
world',[6] overcoming the constraints of hardware and tearing

through the planet in the process. The quote has been represented online as a large Pac-Man 'software' eating a smaller Pac-Man 'the world'.

But the dividing line between software and hardware is no more real than hard borders are for migrating birds. Kittler, like other philosophers of software from Federica Frabetti to Luca M. Possati, has demonstrated how hardware and software are inseparable, because choosing where one ends and the other begins is an arbitrary decision.[7] We are often taught that hardware is physical and software isn't. This is not true. To create functioning software you need programming code, files, interfaces, databases, networking equipment and servers. While you can't hold programming code in your hand, its words, letters and numbers have still been manufactured and do take up space in the physical world. They're made using desktop or laptop energy, often (though not always) human labour, and require data centres if created on cloud-based tools. This is why software isn't just something that runs on hardware, and it's never independent of the machine that operates it. It's as much a physical phenomenon as music, which we experience as vibrations, movements in the air and the body. Of course, software is always more than the 'instruments' that play it, whether they be computers and circuits or semiconductors and silicon, just like a violin concerto is greater than the sheep intestines from which strings are sometimes made.

How we represent software depends on which aspects of it we want to highlight. In Anton Grabolle's *Classification Cupboard*,[8] three chests of drawers demonstrate that data need to be contained within a classification system to be processed and understood. The pieces of furniture themselves are warped and skewed; one is datafied into pixels, demonstrating how the categorising of software does not mirror reality but abstracts and contorts it.

Teresa Berndtsson's *Letter Word Text Taxonomy* features

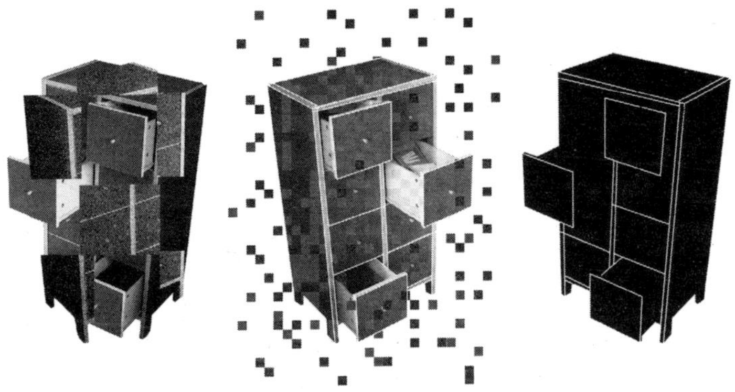

Anton Grabolle's *Classification Cupboard*. Grabolle explains
that the cupboard is a metaphor for a classification system, where
the drawers represent an algorithm's categorisation classes

a book open on a keyboard in the foreground, with words printed on it that look as if they were typed out by a label-maker machine.[9] Above them is the letter 'A', in a much larger font. These familiar images of text are great because they offer a more approachable representation of something like a large language model, which processes and generates text data.

Another image from the Better Images collection invites some fundamental questions about how software decides what it means to 'be' something: *Fish Reversed* by Rens Dimmendaal and David Clode represents a machine vision system in the process of breaking down a fish into abstract shapes.[10] In the first image, the fish is definitely a fish. In the second, it's four shapes, and in the third, there's a small segment of a yellow circle where the fish's mouth once was plus a large grey semicircle. The image raises a crucial question in machine vision, which is, what are the key features of an object or entity? In this case, what makes a fish fishy? Chances are a biologist will tell you that, technically speaking, there's no such thing as a fish; one

Teresa Berndtsson's *Letter Word Text Taxonomy*. Berndtsson says: 'Words are placed, as in this image, within a symbolic taxonomy. The letter is a part of a word, which is a part of a sentence, which is a part of a context, which creates meaning.'

of the most cited pieces of evidence on this comes from zoologist Stephen J. Gould, who noted that a salmon is more closely related to a camel than to a hagfish.[11] Suddenly engineers are confronted with larger questions that invite context-specific answers, like 'What does a bed look like?' 'What does a nurse look like?' Socially and globally, these things are not fixed in time or space.

We also need stock images of AI that highlight labour concerns. Thanks to the Better Images project, free under a CC licence is Nacho Kamenov and Humans in the Loop's 'A trainer instructing a data annotator on how to label images'.[12]

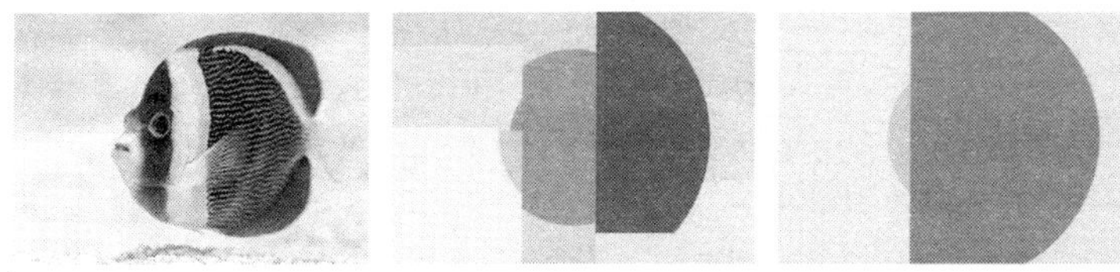

Fish Reversed by Rens Dimmendaal and David Clode

It shows a woman standing over another woman at a computer, pointing at her screen in the act of explaining a labelling exercise. Where the operation of capital is relatively subtle in this image of AI's invisible labour force, it's all too clear in Clarote and AI4Media's *Power/Profit*.[13] In the centre, a figure is standing between the high walls of a data centre swarming with wires. Above them, a giant left hand clutches the top of the wall, while the right stretches to catch dollar bills from the air that are coming from the hand of a consumer holding a mobile phone. Below, six identical men sit around a table of a map of the globe, as if planning world domination, while three large economy upwards-trend arrows hover behind them. In between, melting into grotesque forms, are eight customer

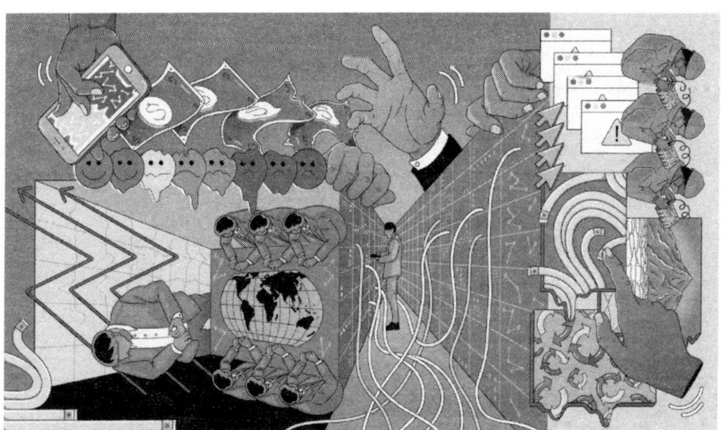

Power/Profit by Clarote and AI4Media for Better Images of AI

service satisfaction emoticons that are usually found below 'How did we do today?' signs in supermarkets and airport toilets.

The Better Images collection tells urgent stories about AI's supply chain, labour issues and geopolitical tensions over materials. But it doesn't just point us towards what we don't want but what we do: positive, sustainable relationships between planetary resources and people, such that no component is exploited or outmanoeuvred by resource-rich companies and the nations that benefit from them. 'A trainer instructing a data annotator on how to label images' depicts the *process* of creating AI, not just a hypothetical rendition of AGI. This is great, because it associates good technology with good work practices. In other words, utopia isn't just the final product, but everything that goes into building a technology. I spent many years researching utopias for my book *The Planetary Humanism of European Women's Science Fiction*,[14] and what I found was that an ethical and realistic utopia isn't a destination, or a moment in time when AI has miraculously made us all equal. Instead, utopia is the process of working together to develop a fairer world. This is why we need images of AI that get people thinking about relationships between the plethora of workers that create it, the conflicts of interests between states and state-sized tech companies, material resources, public buy-in, and data taken from exploited citizens, the undocumented and the stateless.

Representing the labour of creating AI is important because it foregrounds the pressure we put on the natural world in building 'autonomous' systems. The vibrant monocrystalline elemental form of Catherine Breslin's *Silicon on Black 1* invites questions about how it was produced and where it comes from (high-purity silicon melted at 1,425 °C in a quartz crucible).[15] The public needs to be able to picture the refining process, as well as the minerals (like quartz) from which monocrystalline silicon originates. The shiny, metallic object in Breslin's photograph was once a piece of quartz and is likely to have hailed from North Carolina's Spruce Pine mines, which produce 90 per cent of the high-purity quartz mined globally. When, in 2024, Hurricane Helena wreaked havoc on the Spruce Pines area, images of the mineral began to enter media coverage on AI, telling a story about climate change and the fragility of AI production. Ultra-high-purity quartz is an essential component of computer chips, meaning that a shortage in quartz supply would topple AI production.

We need more images of key AI materials and of how they are produced, alongside statistics that anchor AI as a climate problem rather than a climate solution. By 2027 the AI sector could consume up to an estimated 134 terawatt hours of energy each year, the same usage as the Netherlands,[16] and climate science researcher Anne Pasek has shown that Google's thirsty data centre in the Dalles, Oregon drinks more than 350 million gallons of water annually. That's almost a third of the city's total water use per year. If these numbers don't hit a nerve, the thought of a large, noisy data centre in your backyard might. We need to be able to visualise what *else* AI means, beyond AI slop content on social media and ChatGPT: destabilised local water tables, hiked-up electricity prices and increasingly frequent blackouts. Pasek explains that visualising the cloud as, well, a cloud is entirely misleading: it's not an ephemeral, barely there natural artefact, 'it's just someone else's computer'. The image of the cloud serves the same purpose as Apple's minimalist aesthetic in disguising programmed obsolescence, e-waste (Apple still does everything in its power to stop images of its e-waste from making it on to the internet), or the fact that its non-universal charging cables and constantly changing ports end up in the purgatory of an abandoned electronics box or consigned to the dustbin. As founder of the Apple Together workers' union Janneke Parrish told us on *The Good Robot* podcast, Apple's goal is to 'surprise and delight the customer'.[17] The sleek, barely there thinness of Apple's technology can indeed be surprising and delightful. Electronics dumping grounds are less so. It's in Apple's interest to hide or obscure this side of its business: we can only buy into the fantasy of a feather-light, mobile and pared-down life if we can forget that most electronics end up in landfill. But without photographic evidence it doesn't strike a chord. Out of sight, out of mind.

We require visible evidence of how Big Tech is sickening the planet, but we also need artists and designers to picture ecologically positive AI systems. One of my favourite illustrations of a speculative prototype is from Indigenous studies and digital media researcher Michelle Lee Browne, who designs AI systems using organic materials.[18] One of these is an AI biotech eel called Txitxardin that Browne plans to create initially as part of a virtual reality game that explores the importance of eels to the Euskaldunak (Basque people). But she also thinks carefully about what form it could take in the real world. She experiments with the technical aspects of non-DNA computing and saltwater wetware construction, and with sustainable materials and energy sources like kelp-based outer casings and solar receptors. She also bridges the divide between material components and mythology by suggesting that the ashes of Basque *sorginak* – witches, priests and priestesses – could be mixed into the hardware. The design reflects a commitment to imagining local forms of AI by including the traditional symbol of the Basque people and their country, the *lauburu*, on the 'skin' over the 'spine' of the eel-like creature. The device, she says, was inspired by the nereids or sirens of Basque mythology that live by rivers, and is designed to guide users on their watery adventures.

This speculative form of AI is brilliant because it outlines what a co-operative relationship between humanity and technology looks like, bearing in mind that AI is always a mixture

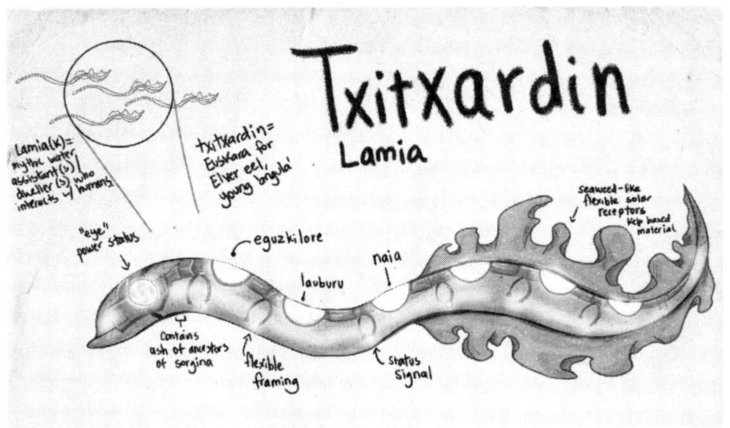

A speculative design of an AI biotech eel called 'Txitxardin',
inspired by Iparralde (French-colonised) Basque family
practices and stories, by Michelle Lee Brown and Kari Noe

of both human and non-human life. In the West we don't
know how to live with AI other than in relationships of control
and domination, because we have historically chosen violence
as a means of managing animal and ecological life. Browne's
prototype combats this with what is not just a respectful
ecological approach to AI but an expression of radical co-
dependence: we can't create AI unsustainably because that will
undermine our own chances at survival. We should, as business
ethics scholars have urged since the 1990s, consider the environment as a stakeholder in the creation of AI, rather than
as an unhappy resource to be extracted. Incorporating non-
human life into democracy continues to feel like quite a radical
intervention. It invites the question: what would it mean for
materials and energy sources to be political actors? Philosopher Bruno Latour calls this a 'parliament of things' – a mode
of governance made up of both animate and inanimate life
forms.[19] If we had a legislature that took seriously non-human

involvement in the AI lifecycle, it would also free us to address the environmental impact of AI on people across the globe. But before Western society can begin to see the natural world as an agent in the production of AI, we need a radical philosophical pivot. We can begin by questioning whether objects are truly 'inanimate' in the first place. AI, I would argue, is always 'alive' – and this has nothing to do with 'consciousness' or robot rights, but because of its (human) and material infrastructure. Beware: this way of looking at life isn't compatible with anthropocentric hubris, or the image of humanity at the top of a hierarchy of life on Earth. Instead, when we start to think more deeply about our entire relationship with the non-human world, it opens up all manner of exciting possibilities for what AI could be.

Beyond dead and alive

When I first encountered the work of scholars who investigate why we should think of animate matter as 'alive', or at least 'lively', I was captivated. Jane Bennett's descriptions of the trickle of chemical waste in junkyards are not unlike the figures that come to life in *Toy Story* (1995), where viewers also get a glimpse into the 'secret life of things'.[20] She shows how there's an aliveness in the sludge of chemical waste and the meeting of decaying materials by drawing attention to the interactions between chemicals that create 'animacy'. The 'inanimate' world is, frankly, much more lively than we give it credit for. Take the catastrophic 2003 Northeast blackout in the US, which Bennett uses as an example of how interactions between parts of the energy infrastructure we might not see as 'alive' can be the agents of disaster.[21] The blackout was caused by a series of faults, from a power station suddenly going offline to a software bug that prevented operators from taking action to manage the system. This led to an overloaded power line coming into contact with trees and triggering a series of circuit breaks that cascaded into the worst power outage in American history. The blackout made it all too clear that non-human things have power in energy systems, and should therefore be taken seriously as actors in the network. This is also the case with human consciousness, a highly energy-intensive process which depends on a network of actors, not all of them animate or 'human'. The doctrine of 'human exceptionalism', the idea that we are different/better than everything else, would have it that consciousness is a human-only affair. But as scholars like N. Katherine Hayles have demonstrated, there are lots of non-conscious processes that structure human cognition,[22] from our interactions with technology to the relationship between thought and cell function. Willed action has always been influenced by technologies – the things we use to cook, write or travel with – and phenomena like cell function that we may not be aware of but which make awareness possible. We therefore need to be 'biophilic',[23] Hayles says, in our approach to understanding what consciousness is, which means keeping our ear to the ground and being attuned to how humans are involved in other life forms. If we do this, we can explore consciousness in a way that enhances connections to the natural environment rather than wipes them away. So much of what we call consciousness is supported by non-human cognition, which means that there are far more interesting ways of thinking about the non-human world than as a set of objects and 'objective' machines. The wonderfully complex, sticky evolutionary history that humanity shares with non-conscious entities that nevertheless do 'think', from technology to bacteria, is often overlooked when people ask the question, 'Can machines be conscious?' People tend to imagine 'machine consciousness' as machines thinking and acting independently of humans, just as discussions around human consciousness overlook how decision-making processes are distributed across our bodies.

Mainstream biology is now cottoning on to the relationship between conscious and unconscious cognition that up until the early 2020s thrived at the margins of science. An entirely new discipline of nutritional psychiatry has emerged in response to evidence that the gut affects your mood, influencing how you handle stress and whether you experience mental ill-health. I like to see this as a surprising resurrection of elements of early medieval medical texts on the humours, wherein bodily fluids directly conjure states of mind, meaning that your irritability could be conveniently blamed on a yellowing of the bile. Much of what is considered 'frontier' science on the gut and mood was also preceded by twenty-first-century feminist philosophy of science, such as the work of Elizabeth Wilson, who over a decade ago was using feminist ideas to challenge mainstream views of what is and isn't a 'thinking' (cognitive) process.[24] American ecologist and philosopher David Abram has also explored the moods of our senses, for example by describing smell and touch as 'gregarious' organs that participate in – and are dependent upon – the world around us.[25] I love this description, which takes seriously how distributed consciousness is. We don't just process the world up there in our brains, but everywhere throughout our bodies. If physical processes – whether gastronomic or sensorial – involve and alter cognition, does that make the human brain less valuable? Equally, are thinking machines less awe-inspiring if the cognition takes place in many different parts of their distributed 'bodies' – in the data centres, in the humans doing the data-labelling, or in the quartz mined and manufactured for semiconductors?

When AI opinion leaders harp on about AI consciousness, they are often fetishising the brain (or computer as brain) as the location of intelligence. The obsession with the brain, or some central locus of intelligence, is pathetic and outdated, harking back to a time before we understood just how distributed cognition is, or appreciated that other animals did any thinking. There is no such thing as a neutral approach to cognition – how we understand what it means to think always says something about who we believe we are as humans in relation to other Earth-dwelling creatures. When we worry whether AI can be conscious we also show a concern for our place in the hierarchy of things. Theories of consciousness are as much full of philosophical, religious and humanistic ideas and ideals as they are scientific facts. I'm therefore on board to ditch the phrase 'machine consciousness', which makes machine cognition seem like a mystical artefact rather than a distributed material network, and the tiresome, pointless discussions that come with the assumption that all kinds of consciousness are the same. I am invested in ideas about consciousness – whether in relation to humans or machines – that are ecologically suggestive, socially beneficial and grounded in new data about the relationships between the bits of your body traditionally associated with thinking, like the brain, and those that are not, like the gut.

Some space in the dustbin should also be saved for another widely disputed term in AI, the idea of 'machine autonomy', often taken to mean machine 'independence'. In the previous chapters we explored how disability theory shows that the experience of autonomy for a human depends on how accessible you find social systems and facilities. Similarly, when we hide the infrastructure that supports machine 'autonomy', we elevate AI from a product that needs engineering, monitoring and training to a god in machine form. It is never just software or applied statistics. When we interact with any AI technology we are *participating* in a system of engineers and data labellers, corporate infrastructure, crowdsourced workers, your own data and – often – that of all a technology's users worldwide. The mouthpiece of this assemblage is the chatbot: capitalist magic turns behind-the-scenes labour into an autonomous product. That's also why AI isn't 'just a tool': tools are assemblages, as we have seen, of human and non-human actors. From medicines to machines to multinational conglomerates, they construct worlds and change our minds and bodies, our societies and the environment. You would think that the more we learn about how technology shapes human cognition, the more we would avoid creating tools that are detrimental to the human psyche. Amid a disaster of contradictory messages about what it means to be human, conscious and autonomous in the age of technology, we need more risky and expansive responses to the question of what AI can be, and how we should be interacting with it. We must encourage perspectives that respect our intimate ties to the environment and recognise that to be human is also to be technological, as we saw in Chapter 1. Only then can we establish some continuity between who we were before AI and who we are now, and come up with some creative and less defeatist answers to the question of what will become of humanity and its symbionts in the future.

Automated haunting

Perhaps nowhere is the question of what is human and what is a machine more awkward, controversial and high-stakes than in the burgeoning griefbot or deathbot industry. In 2024 my colleagues Tomasz Hollanek and Katarzyna Nowaczyk-Basińska pioneered ethical investigations into companies selling consumers eternal life on behalf of deceased family members. Now the market is full of what they call 'digital afterlife' products, marking a new era of postmortem presence.[26] They're a case in point of how bad ideas about death and consciousness cause real-world harm.

Speaking to the media, Tomasz warned: 'These services run the risk of causing huge distress to people if they are subjected to unwanted digital hauntings from alarmingly accurate AI recreations of those they have lost. The potential psychological effect, particularly at an already difficult time, could be devastating.'[27] We should also look closely, though, at what these friendly automated haunting devices consider to be at least a partial resurrection. They imply that you can interact with a person without their body being present, because the body of the deceased is a mere container, while the brain, or more specifically digital archives in the form of uploaded text and social media posts, is the real person. This is an example of why it's so reductive to think of a human brain as analogous to a computer control system. The digital afterlife industry relies on the metaphor that brains are just like computers and vice versa, so that consumers can trust a product likening itself to a disembodied brain to store the essence of a loved one.

Are deathbots, we might ask, the gateway drug to transhumanist fantasies of mind-uploading? The way they are designed to evade death stinks of the transhumanist impulse to use AI to supersede mortality. Paradoxically, the transhumanists' denial of death via longevity programmes comes from the same place as their fantasies and fears about the apocalypse. Fetishising the apocalypse goes hand in hand with speculations about life after death – a life without death – which is effectively the post-apocalypse.[28] Post-apocalypse is a more traumatised kind of immortality, but it's a life without mortality nonetheless. Both the denial of death and the fear of the apocalypse reveal a slightly unhinged obsession with death that in terror management theory is known as 'mortality salience': death anxiety prompted by trauma or low self-esteem. Shakespeare's Hamlet, who used a skull as a therapist, was one fictional sufferer.

The popularity of deathbots demonstrates that Hamlet and the transhumanists are not alone. These products, which are developed by companies like You, Only Virtual (YOV) and Here After AI, are symptomatic of the West's eschewal of death and dying. Our diminished acceptance of and proximity to death as a social inevitability can partly be put down to how, from the perspective of a Roman foot soldier, we're as good as immortal: while his life expectancy was around twenty-five years,[29] by 2024 that figure has tripled.[30] Creators of digital afterlife products are also tapping into the commercial potential of conversational technologies like GPT, which have improved dramatically and are much loved by consumers: following its launch, GPT was the fastest-growing consumer app of all time. I am writing this from Mexico, where I have participated in Dios de Los Muertos, the 'Day of the Dead', when families visit the graves of their loved ones and have little parties. I have a sense that deathbots will be less necessary here, given that communing with the dead is freer and less taboo, and therefore the demand for a purpose-built tech product might be lower. Not only are people communicating with the deceased, but they are celebrating with them!

By contrast, the digital afterlife industry takes emphasis away from the importance of physical spaces like burial grounds as sites of reflection and communion with the dead. Grievers are expected to visit an app, where instead of birds and trees you might encounter targeted advertisements. This isn't the first time death has intersected with capitalism. Mourning has been a lucrative business for centuries, as evidenced by elaborate Sicilian tombstones and 'rock star' eulogists in Iran. The difference, as Hollanek and Nowaczyk-Basińska argue, is that AI brings with it a whole different set of questions. What if a customer depends too much on these bots for their well-being, such that they become unwell? Who is liable if a bot gives a 'family member' harmful advice? What if a child uses it? Does the bereaved customer know how their data is being used? Whatever your take on these products, it's clear that mourning well and living well are connected, because being able to mourn properly affects our quality of life. The question is whether we can find solace in the shadows of our loved ones somewhere in the smokescreens of data and interface, how long that can last, and if it's worth the risks.

Deathbots are the most troubling example of what we get when we believe that AI can somehow transcend its material origins – in lithium, silicon and mass data-harvesting – to embody the reincarnated soul of a deceased individual. By allowing companies to commercialise cycles of life and death, we expose grievers to manipulation and abuse. Part of the issue is that the deathbot industry appears to think it's possible to imitate conscious thought. But cognition takes place in the body, not just in an isolated mind, and in synchrony with a whole host of information-processing entities, from the microbiome to the senses. When we use accurate and truthful images to depict technology, they can help us visualise a more nuanced way of living with the non-human world. Equally, if we insist on the same old images of isolated geniuses and god-like machines we'll be stuck in the same rut of poor AI uses forever, no matter how new and powerful the device on which we project our aspirations to become an Übermensch or resurrect the dead. As we will now see, the images of AI that we have and the promises they make are manipulating us into using AI for completely inappropriate purposes. Just like the tale of the Emperor's New Clothes, if we believe everything that AI companies tell us about their products we'll quickly find ourselves standing naked in the streets.

5

Beware False Promises

We have just explored the digital afterlife, part of the thoroughfare of new concepts and ideas created by AI. The more words you learn, the more appear waiting to enter your lexicon. What makes this especially complicated is that companies use every phrase under the sun to describe their AI products, except what genuinely represents what the tool does. From 'behavioural intelligence' to 'intelligence candidate video screening', euphemisms abound in industries like AI recruitment. These terms don't describe what AI systems really do, they bamboozle the consumer into thinking the technology is powered by something fancier than a simple algorithm automating the individual judgements of data labellers. Amazon was also guilty of marketing misdirection when its automated 'just walk out technology' obscured the thousands of Indian data workers making the whole operation reliable by reviewing footage and purchase receipts.

It's common to hear people say that ChatGPT 'hallucinates' when it answers your question with a false statement. I once asked it to dig out some research papers on AI and health, only to find that a couple of them were fake papers that didn't exist at all. They looked perfect, with plausible author and paper names, and real publishers. This is just a plain old system error. By anthropomorphising an error as a 'hallucination', we give these systems a false consciousness and mask the hundreds of engineers, data labellers, silicon chips and gigabytes of data, all working together to – imperfectly – come up with an answer to your question or request. By designing the interface of ChatGPT to make you feel like you're interacting with a human individual, its parent company OpenAI disguises the many human and non-human cogs in the system that create errors. They suggest that a hallucination is not an engineering mistake but a feature of AI on the path to consciousness. It's another kind of overpromising.

Equally, AI engineer Margaret Mitchell warns us to think twice when we hear the phrase 'AI generates and understands visual content'.[1] If you've ever used an online wheel picker, the colour fade is determined by a number of different values, for example red, green, blue (RGB) and hue, saturation, lightness (HSL).[2] These parameters are presented as percentages that change when you drag the slider or move the dot around on the colour fade above. This is effectively a combination of numbers. Unlike the human visual system, they're recognising the values assigned to a code which corresponds to one point on a wheel picker.

So AI doesn't see as we see. Nor does AI 'understand' complex ideas as we do. What it's actually doing is generating text that we can make sense of. When we say a model 'reasons' mathematically, what is often meant is that it can do calculations; when we say it has 'artistic expression', this denotes that it structures content in the form of a piece of art; when it 'visually imagines' an object, it can do the necessary vector arithmetic in order to, say, associate the shape of stripes with the concept of a tiger and then recreate it; and when it 'understands' the text it generates, what actually is going on has little to do with the way humans interpret what we read or hear. Instead, it means that we can make sense of the content that AI creates. Mitchell has proposed we say instead 'this model generates content that we perceive as visual images' and 'this model generates text that we can understand'.[3] Just like the terrible images commonly used to depict AI, every anthropomorphising term we use brings us one step closer to believing claims that AI is, or could be, sentient. We therefore need to interrogate how our language characterises AI. Just as the Better Images project promotes more accurate, creative and informative representations of the technology, meaningful and self-explanatory language is a hugely important part of not only describing AI but using it correctly.

After university I spent a couple of years doing communications work at tech companies. I was terrible at it, constantly saying the wrong thing to journalists over the phone and spending too much time in the company sauna. Things have now come full circle, and I'm helping to improve regulation of how AI companies market their products. At the annual retreat of an executive search firm where I was speaking in 2023, posters advertising various AI products were arranged around the room. One claimed that an Amazon shopping experience could 'read your mind'. Find me someone who doesn't think that is truly terrifying.

Given consumer uncertainty about how AI works and what it's genuinely capable of, AI marketing is insufficiently regulated, with many advertising standards bodies lacking the confidence, authority and resources to step in. Until regulators ensure that AI marketing isn't excessively misleading, ethicists are running in slow motion behind a conveyor belt of opaque or spurious claims. Left unchecked, these claims stoke the public's fears around AI. The issue is not so much that the technology is moving too fast, but that marketing departments are selling make-believe.

Some of the more egregious untruths claimed for AI in recent years are that it can debias hiring by turning candidates into neutral data points, spot a violent protest before it kicks off, or even detect your sexuality. It's worth considering these propositions in detail, because together they show some

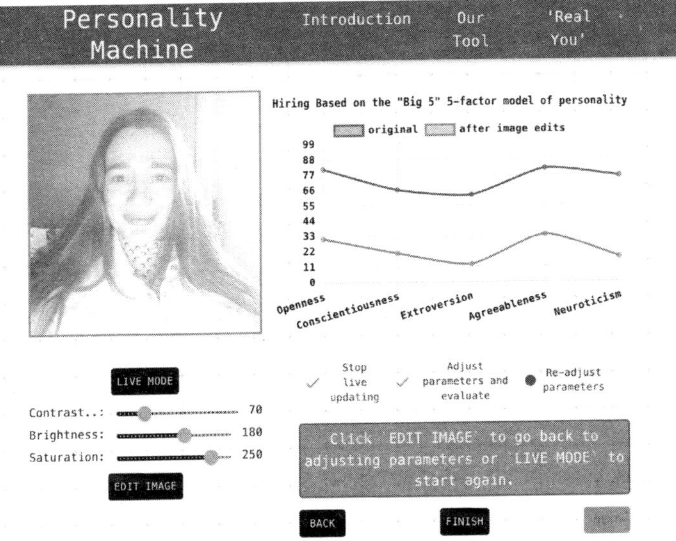

A screenshot from Personality Machine: the blue line shows my original personality score, and the green line after I changed the contrast, brightness and saturation of the image

of the ways in which, regardless of how sophisticated an AI product is, it can be used harmfully to replicate – rather than remedy – structural biases. In 2022 I asked some computer science students from the University of Cambridge to replicate an open-source video hiring system we found on LinkedIn. They recreated the tool from scratch using some parameters from a similar state-of-the-art model on GitHub.[4] It worked by capturing an image of your face and then measuring the Big Five personality schema (neuroticism, extroversion, agreeableness, openness, conscientiousness), a common psychological model for personality. We found that when we altered the lighting, brightness and saturation of the captured images it also changed our personality score. This means that unrelated visual cues are taken as evidence of who you are as a person.

Most worrying for the students, though, was the claim by a manufacturer of AI hiring technologies that these tools could de-bias recruitment. We argued that race and gender cannot be 'scraped' from a candidate's profile, as these tools often claim to do. Also unappealing to the students was the fact that HR uses these tools to feign 'colour blindness' by effectively saying, 'AI doesn't see race (or gender, or disability, or class) so we won't be discriminating.' Pretending not to see race won't make it go away. And, as the students also emphasised, you can't reduce a person down to a set of neutral data points. AI can't observe the 'real you' with any degree of objectivity because it models the world by making it simpler and bite-sized, and decides where to selectively focus.

In a research paper that Kerry McInerney and I wrote about these tools, we called them 'AI-powered video interviews'.[5] But because there are countless phrases used by companies to euphemistically describe similar technologies, it's difficult to search for who is using AI and how. The problem is worse in languages other than English. Asvatha Babu, a PhD researcher at American University's School of Communication, has discussed how difficult it is to track where facial recognition technology (FRT) is being used in India because there isn't a consistent way of describing what we call FRT in the Tamil language.[6] This means that when stories about FRT appear in Tamil news, journalists focus more on the application of FRT (like finding missing children, ensuring women are safe on the streets, or identifying criminals) than discussing the technology itself, which is described in passing using inconsistent descriptions. Without a fixed word for FRT, how can you write a news story about it, much less discuss the ethical concerns involved in its roll-out?[7]

Part of the reason why this happens is that journalists lean on Google Translate to describe these technologies. When you Google-translate 'Face Recognition' into Tamil from English, you get *Muga Angeekaram*. *Angeekaram* roughly translates as 'institutional recognition',[8] as in 'this product is institutionally approved [by a quality-checking body like the US Food and Drug Administration]', which is totally useless. The surveillance aspect of FRT is therefore lost, and with it any nuance around the harms and costs of being watched – particularly where FRT is allegedly being used to 'protect' women and children through increased surveillance. This wouldn't be the case if FRT had become a buzzword in Tamil, like it is in English. As with most things, there are pros and cons to the hype that the new AI lexicon creates, from FRT to 'foundation models'. While I have mostly focused on the negatives, Asvatha saw the positives of buzzwords: they carry information from previous narratives about the uses and abuses of the AI product in question. Without this, it becomes easy for news coverage to effectively ignore the technology altogether and focus on the talking points, whether women's safety, child-trafficking or robbery. The public therefore lack information about what FRT is, how it's being used in other places around the world and with what impact. They need this information before they can weigh in on whether the possible benefits of new technologies outweigh their risks.

Of course, the word that Tamil eventually chooses doesn't have to be an exact replica of FRT. Asvatha emphasises that when such concepts are translated, decisions have to be made about what exactly they mean locally. That process of naming will be driven by socio-economic incentives and institutional values, because language doesn't merely describe, it creates and organises themes and issues in our minds according to dominant interests and concerns. This, of course, won't happen in a vacuum – English taints all it touches, and will colour every language's way of characterising new technologies.

This is a problem for many reasons, not least because FRT isn't even a good description of the technology in English. The word 'recognition', as I will explain, is completely misleading. FRT doesn't so much recognise an ideal candidate as project a company's view of what made a good employee in the past on to future applicants' profiles. Protest recognition technologies popular with law enforcement agencies are similarly noxious when they claim to be able to identify which crowds will become dangerous. Such technologies are not clairvoyant; they merely take law enforcement's perspectives on criminality and bring them to life in a crowd of people. A more accurate name for them would be 'subjective face predictions', because they're making predictions based on the police's subjective interpretation of who is likely to be a criminal. So while AI-powered 'protest recognition' pretends to recognise dangerous protests, it does nothing of the sort. Whether it's used for recruitment, dating or law enforcement, AI recognition is pure illusion.

The fallacy of recognition

I'll now take issue with two words in particular: recognition and detection. In 2018, two Stanford engineers claimed to have created an AI that uses facial recognition to 'recognise' or 'detect' a person's sexuality from looking at a photo of them, and that it can do it better than human Amazon Turk workers.[9] I found this very interesting indeed, given that my sexuality can be rather elusive, and I've never felt that my constantly changing face – which has undergone jaw surgery, years of orthodontics, and one or two other things – offers many clues. Unfortunately for the engineers, it turned out that their AI system – a deep neural network (DNN) – was predicting a person's sexuality based on how they posed for their picture, the tilt of their head, and whether they were wearing make-up.[10] These images were scraped, without the consent of the romantic hopefuls they displayed, from an unnamed US dating website – again, technology cannot be ethical if it doesn't get the approval of its participants. A few years ago I was on two dating apps, as a heterosexual in one city and as a bisexual in another. I wonder what the system would have made of me. The sexuality you choose for your dating profile can be complicated. Perhaps you're looking for a spouse of the opposite sex, for example, but this isn't a full indication of what interests you sexually. How you identify your sexuality and who appeals to you romantically can be two very different things. Whether society names our sexuality or whether we name it ourselves very much depends on our culture(s), history, race, class and geography. Assuming that people identify in such and such a way can be a real problem, particularly when it comes to healthcare. In the 1990s, at the height of the AIDS epidemic, many men who had sex with men did not identify as gay, resulting in the failure of prevention schemes targeted at gay men. Using a label to define your sexuality can be political, and the reality is that not everyone wants to do it or feels it's right for them.

With all this in mind, we can ask what exactly the gaydar experiment was 'recognising'. As AI engineers Blaise Aguera y Arcas, Margaret Mitchell and Alexander Todorov's investigation of the study showed, it did not in fact 'recognise' signs of a biological truth written on the body.[11] Instead, the tool highlighted that some people make aesthetic choices to signal what they're into. That's it. Plus, the Stanford researchers admit that 'unfortunately, we could not identify heterosexual Facebook users',[12] by which they mean the tool didn't spot any physical indicators that correlated to people looking for someone of the opposite sex. This is a meaningless statement, as there are many reasons why someone might state on their Facebook profile that they're heterosexual. A study by the Pew Research Center also shows that bisexuals are far less likely to be 'out', and therefore might label themselves heterosexuals on, for example, dating apps.[13] As some say, we are the invisible majority. Sexuality is, for the most part, an uncategorisable mess that cannot be reduced to visual cues and certainly isn't branded into our DNA. The 'born this way' narrative has been politically helpful in its suggestion that being gay is as natural as being straight, but it has also resulted in some less useful investigations into the 'source' of sexuality.

What the gaydar tool did make clear is that opaque technologies which operate under the guise of science and institutional expertise can expose people to violence. It's telling that the tool never claimed to recognise heterosexuality. Ironically, the engineers said they were doing a good deed by warning the LGBT community that authoritarian regimes might use similar technologies to 'out' them against their will. Fitting in can be a matter of life and death. In Jennie Livingston's iconic documentary about the 1980s New York queer ball scene, *Paris is Burning*,[14] queer men and trans women turn to hair and make-up not to make themselves hyper-visible – as drag artists often do today – but, on the contrary, to live life as a woman while not drawing attention to themselves. 'Passing', as it's termed, means fitting in, and avoiding the aggressions of the transphobic and homophobic public gaze. Many of the young people in the film began to participate in the ballroom scene because they were thrown out of their homes. This is why ballroom participants often belonged to 'Houses', families that did love and accept them. By the end of the documentary, some have killed themselves, others have been murdered. This is why fears that trans women want to rape people in bathrooms are particularly cruel – these are people who have experienced a lifetime of abuse and neglect, and are among the most vulnerable members of society. Transgender people are over four times more likely than cisgender people to be victims of violent crime, according to a new study by the Williams Institute at UCLA School of Law.[15] They have a much lower life expectancy (628 deaths per 100,000 people per year).[16] In the Netherlands a study has shown that they are 2.6 times as likely to die of cardiovascular disease, 3.1 times as likely to die from lung cancer, and 8.7 times as likely to die from infection.[17] Trans women are also 4.3 times more likely to be murdered than other women in the USA, but at greatest risk of fatal violence are trans women of colour.[18] Far from being threats to public bathrooms, they are themselves one of the most vulnerable groups on the planet.[19] When I was eighteen, three men attempted to attack me in the women's bathroom. The fact they were wearing trousers didn't stop them from coming in. Time and again, we see misconceptions about the source of danger in society popping up in new technologies.

'Recognition' systems don't merely observe the world – they create and shape it. Like the Victorian sexologists, who established the idea of sexual identity in their attempt to eradicate moral miscreance, these systems don't 'recognise' homosexuality so much as create an idea of sexual deviancy that might ultimately limit the way in which people live their lives and express themselves. Fixing people into categories in order to control them is not a side effect but a defining feature. The issue is not that these technologies might identify people's sexuality against their will, but that they establish sexuality as a fundamental truth which can be used to deny some people infrastructural support, leaving them homeless, destitute or vulnerable to violence. Taking a stand against this requires 'disidentifying' with the way you are recognised by society. Anti-racist and pride movements, for example, are largely attempts to disidentify from associations with criminality and perversion. My message is that we need to do more than 'avoid' recognition technologies – we must reject their claim of being able to recognise and observe people neutrally. It's not enough simply to say that facial recognition is biased: it's much more than this. FRT brings the world to life according to the rules with which it was programmed and the companies and institutions that deploy it, and when law enforcement enters the mix, AI can cut lives short.

Recognising what is going wrong: policing

In November 2023, the Commissioner of the UK's Metropolitan Police called me 'the girl that thinks we should turn our computers off' as I walked to the bathroom of a small policing conference. It was a disappointing day; I like computers, so the comment was odd. But let's rewind for a second. I attended the event because my long-term collaborator Federica Frabetti and I had spent several years looking into AI companies that had helped police in the US to track, monitor and ultimately shut down Black Lives Matter protests – specifically, two companies called Geofeedia and Dataminr.[20] Social media companies (like Twitter – which owned a stake in Dataminr) granted them access to their application programming interface (API). The relationship exists because the business model of social media companies relies on surveillance, on collecting your personal data and selling it to third parties. When they sell to law enforcement agencies, it can be used to surveil and potentially even prosecute you. Geofeedia enabled law enforcement to match the Instagram photos of people at BLM protests against the police's databases of people with warrants out for their arrest, and then go into the crowd and detain them. The fear that this generates stalls protests by scattering terrified campaigners.

The American Civil Liberties Union (ACLU) found that Geofeedia had partnered with the Baltimore Police Department to monitor high school students' Facebook messages planning their attendance in the 2016 Freddie Gray (BLM) protests.[21] They noted that the BPD, aside from surveilling minors, had chosen #MuslimLivesMatter as one of its 'trigger' keywords, i.e. words that would signal police intervention, even though the sentiments often expressed by that hashtag were loss and mourning. There's one particularly striking tweet that Geofeedia had identified as potentially threatening. It appears to have been written in the wake of the 2015 Copenhagen attacks by gunman Omar Abdel Hamid el-Hussein on a Danish synagogue. The tweet goes: 'The shooting at the Copenhagen Synagogue fortifies my belief that my duty as a Jew is to stand with my Abrahamic cousins. #MuslimLivesMatter.'[22] By 'Abrahamic cousins', they're referring to the 2015 Chapel Hill shooting in North Carolina, when a gunman killed three Muslim students. The fact that the Jewish author of the tweet takes this attack on his community as a sign of solidarity with Islamic victims is deeply courageous, and generous. It's the essence of peace. And yet, because it uses the hashtag #MuslimLivesMatter, it's flagged by Dataminr as a threat. This shows that not only do these systems have about as much nuance as a punch in the face, but they are actively making the world worse, not better. More training data or sentiment analysis won't help. There will remain a certain violence in transforming this hashtag – a symbol of peace – into one of suspicion. I call this the automation of intolerance: the use of digital tools to scale up the ways in which we hate and mistreat each other.

While Geofeedia has since ceased operating, a string of 'event detection' companies have taken its place, making the ACLU's task a constant game of whack-a-mole. One is Dataminr, originally used by journalists for the somewhat benign task of geolocating potential news stories by drawing a circle on a map – rather like a geolocalised property filter on a rentals website – and doing filtered keyword searches on social media posts. Now Dataminr is used by law enforcement globally, by federal agencies in the US and several NGOs, and with bigger clients came bigger claims; its website boasts '50 proprietary LLMs and multi-modal foundation models' that use 'trillions of daily computations across billions of public data inputs from nearly one million unique public data sources'.[23] The assumption is that more technologies and more data create more objectivity, because technology is somehow inherently objective. Ironically, this implies that objectivity exists on a sliding scale, that you can have more or less of it rather than it being a fixed concept. Dataminr also equates speed with objectivity, claiming that the faster their 'real-time information' service, the more objective its output will be. These associations between speed, technology and objectivity are so tightly interwoven that we rarely stop to question them.

In our research, we found a Dataminr patent online which was subsequently deleted following the release of our paper. The patent describes how a client can do a keyword search to look for social media posts about an event. It shows that this process happens differently depending on what kind of client you are and where your interest lies.[24] The way the system analyses and processes social media content is therefore done in a way that *represents the client's interests*. This means that if the client is the police, they'll see what they want to see. The system then alerts them when the frequency of posts on these issues spikes, for example around #MuslimLivesMatter. To digitally represent the message as something that is useful to them, Dataminr divides the posts into tokens made up of words, metadata, hashtags and a sentiment score indicating whether the message is positive, negative or neutral (#Muslim-LivesMatter = negative). It then scores the messages according to predefined criteria that determine whether they might be relevant to the police, clusters them together, and matches the scored messages to the police's search requests. It calls this process of aggregation a 'prediction'. When Baltimore PD received these so-called 'predictions' they were always viewed as correct, which led to increased police presence at protests. This makes them fundamentally different from a prediction like the weather forecast. Taking an umbrella with you when you leave the house will not stop it raining. Dataminr's insistence that a collection of tweets and images of people gathering in the street suggests a violent protest is about to happen is less a prediction than an instruction: be vigilant, go out into the crowd, behave as if it were a violent protest. This is why Federica and I say that these systems are not really 'recognition' or even 'prediction' systems. They are performative – they *create* the worlds they claim to merely observe.

Dataminr often uses the word 'predictive' to describe its platform. This is a terrible idea for a company that works with law enforcement, given that the police are continuously tempted by a *Minority Report* (2002) model of crime prevention, a movie in which mutant children foresee crime before it takes place. Economic and meteorological forecasters know that the past is not enough to rely on when predicting the future, and often the data we look at is complex, ambiguous and unpredictable. Judging a person's future solely by their past – or their demographic – can be a death sentence for many young people. Journalist Madhumita Murgia has tracked the victims of an AI risk assessment tool called ProKid+ used by the Dutch government to predict whether a minor who committed a crime is likely to reoffend.[25] If the AI tool decides that this young person should be on a 'list' they will be forced to endure constant surveillance, routine stops and house raids on their route to adulthood. Technology cannot capture life's twists and turns in advance, but it can easily foreclose its meandering, unpredictable pathways. It is morally abhorrent to have a go anyway for the sake of arrest numbers.

Federica and I proved that because Dataminr trained its 'protest recognition' systems on images of BLM demonstrations in the US, with captions and hashtags like #defundthepolice, it was more likely to take on the political orientation of the US police and therefore associate dangerous protests with leftist organising and crowds of Black and Brown people.[26] It's not difficult to see the implications for protests globally. Just note how few police showed up at the Capitol Hill riots. It's our job to stay vigilant to these pockets of technologically mediated totalitarianism packaged as 'innovation'. Technologies we do not fully understand make it difficult to cultivate our sense of where and how fascism emerges, which is why quality investigative journalism has such an important part to play in our democratic ecosystem. Leaks from whistleblowers, as we will explore in Chapter 9, are also important in shifting the flow of power. In 2022 I was put in touch with The Citizens, a group of investigative journalists concerned with technologies that threatened civil liberties, founded by Carole Cadwalladr, the journalist who broke the Cambridge Analytica scandal. The connection had been made through my cousin Louis Barclay, who had created an excellent app that helped people use social media less and had been sent a cease-and-desist letter by Facebook. They warned him that unless he stopped operating they would sue him and delete his Facebook profile. The threat of having his neglected account deleted was amusing, the lawsuit less so. In any case, the situation put him in touch with a good crew of bold people, from Wikipedia's Jimmy Wales to Carole Cadwalladr. It was unsurprising that Carole's team of journalists were also looking into the politics of supposedly neutral AI products, given her interest in how political engagement in Brexit and the Trump elections was mediated by technologies like Cambridge Analytica. She raised concerns that AI could not only target and direct voter behaviour, but also take on the politics of those who build and deploy it. Federica and I were interested in Carole's warning that technologies that had already been flagged by civil society as dangerous in the US were making their way across the pond to Europe and Africa. Wherever we are, we may think our national or corporate values determine our use of technology, but it's the values of an AI company's previous clients that establish the way a product works. As the New York and Minneapolis Police Departments tasked with managing BLM protests were some of Dataminr's first law enforcement customers, the way the officers interacted with the software would likely have played an important part in shaping it for future police clients. In 2016, Dataminr collaborated with South African law enforcement to monitor students at the #Shackville protests, which campaigned for better access for Black students to decent accommodation at the University of Cape Town and was led by the Rhodes Must Fall movement. These multinational police departments' view of the relationship between race and criminality would therefore also be ingrained into how any future client uses Dataminr's tools.

Over the course of twelve months, Max Colbert helped us look into whether and how the UK's police force were using Dataminr. Max calculated that the UK government had spent over £5 million on Dataminr contracts. I had also found that in 2011 Lord Hogan-Howe, former Commissioner of London's Metropolitan ('Met') Police, had been paid by Dataminr to give a talk promoting its services in the House of Lords.[27] This wasn't the only odd decision of Hogan-Howe's career. In 2016 he prompted outrage by suggesting in an opinion piece that the police should not, at first hearing, 'believe the accounts of those alleging they have been abused', citing the principles of police impartiality.[28] He had also previously overseen the Operation Weeting fiasco (2011–15), when the Met Police attempted to use the Official Secrets Act to force *Guardian* journalists to disclose their sources for the *News of the World* phone-hacking affair.[29] By taking aim first at the free press rather than the crime itself, law enforcement took the defensive route preferred by authoritarian regimes.

At the time Hogan-Howe was promoting Dataminr's services to the House of Lords, the Met Police was already plagued by disharmony. Funnelling £5 million into Dataminr's services revealed a frantic urge to throw precious resources at technology, in the hope that it would redeem the force from what were widely seen as profound problems with its trustworthiness and strategic direction. In an attempt to shift the attention elsewhere, Hogan-Howe used the talk to outline his commitment to a 'total war on crime'.[30] Certainly, 'cracking down' is easier than building up (investing in increasing social welfare, education, collaborating with community partners, improving local services, supporting those enrolled in the troubled families programme and other preventative measures). In 2015 and 2016 police forces across the UK appeared to be responding to public calls for a 'whole place' or holistic approach to crime prevention.[31] In some London boroughs, like Hackney in East London, this was defined as inclusive policing that integrated with mental health services, and greater accountability.[32] Things were looking up. In 2018, the UK police published a national consensus between them and health and social care organisations. But by 2020, Thames Valley Police were back to their technological fixes, aiming for an 'improved use of technology by police, in order to prevent crime and support *earlier intervention with known offenders*'.[33]

A suite of laws passed soon after – during the tenure of despotic UK Home Secretary Suella Braverman – still direct the course of how AI is currently used in policing, notably the Police, Crime, Sentencing and Courts Act 2022 and the Public Order Bill 2022. As Max Colbert reported to *Byline Times* in 2021, an inquiry by Parliament's Justice and Home Affairs Committee was 'taken aback by the proliferation of artificial intelligence tools potentially being used without proper oversight, particularly by police forces'.[34] The report identified 'a new Wild West' of AI used in crime prevention, where 'all 43 police forces are free to individually commission whatever tools they like'.[35] The issue is multilayered, involving a chaotic, pressured, internally divided force, a poor understanding about these tools by those deploying them, vendors exaggerating the capabilities of AI systems, a lack of police accountability, and little transparency about what and how tools are being used in law enforcement.

And so, in November 2023, I found myself at the City-forum Round Table on the Policing Mission at BT Tower in Central London. The Commissioner of the Met Police, Sir Mark Peter Rowley QPM, had an unenviable job. He needed to earn back the trust of British communities so that citizens would be less averse to complying with authority figures ('the trust of authority in the Western world is going down – we are fighting for legitimacy,' he said). However, he was also adamant that achieving this objective involved behaving in a way that to him signalled neutrality. Officers should not dance alongside happy paraders at Pride, take the knee at BLM demonstrations, or perform any other movement or gesture that might indicate affinity or affiliation with justice movements. Such a position earns him the awkward double bind of marrying detachment with involvement. For whom, we might ask, does rigid non-participation read as impartiality? Some communities trust non-action, others read it as antipathy.

There was a lot of blame-shifting in the room that day. One Special Constable blamed the *Guardian* for its 'toxic policing narrative'. I put up my hand and asked whether the speakers recognised that technology amplifies the police and the government's combined politics, and whether they sought ethical consultancy on their projects. I emphasised that my colleagues and I would be pleased to support the force by offering these services. Rowley responded that the police have no politics. An officer behind me tutted and said this was absolute non-sense, of course policing has politics. He left soon after. Later, Rowley caught me en route to the bathroom – 'You're the girl that thinks we should turn our computers off' – before turning back to his conversation. This was a great shame, as barking at experts doesn't help increase public trust. In the face of declining support, it's difficult for institutions, like the people who compose them, not to become defensive and antagonistic. Friends who worked on police projects at McKinsey have noted their stubbornness, dislike of cultural change and refusal to collaborate. There was a great sense of pride among long-haulers, people who have been in the force for a decade or more. But in any enterprise, new perspectives – from those who have jumped ship from within industry, for example – offer different ways of getting things done. The force has historically demonstrated a dislike of hiring laterally and a preference for promoting from within, which makes gaining new experience from different industries difficult. The ethical use of technology requires plenty of healthy internal and external agreement, which can only be attained through a heterogeneous workforce, community transparency, and being accountable to the policed population. Keeping their cards close to their chest doesn't put the police at an advantage with people, it just makes citizens resent and distrust them.

What I wanted to explore with the Met that day was how the tools they used were constructing reality – one that reflects the bias of its end-users, the police – rather than objectively representing it. Dataminr might claim to merely observe a peaceful protest for signs of violence, but in practice, when its 'trigger' alerts prompt the police to act heavy-handedly, the situation is far more likely to turn ugly. HR AI tools claim to identify which candidates are a perfect fit for each company, but the reality is that it would be incredibly costly and labour-intensive to create a bespoke product for each client with whole new sets of training data that reflect a company's ideal workforce. And even then, because the decisions these tools make are based on a company's historical hiring preferences, by predicting a good fit with past hires they close off, rather than open up, fruitful divergences between future employees and current and past ones.

While collecting examples of false claims about what AI

could achieve, it became clear that AI isn't in fact observing the world. It can't read your mind, spot dangerous protests before the fact or assess someone's employability just from their face. Companies and marketers have merely convinced us that it can, and these beliefs are beginning to shape the facts to fit the story: changing consumer behaviour, recasting what we think makes a protest 'dangerous' and projecting ideas about who an 'ideal candidate' is on to recruitment videos. Federica and I were witnessing how AI created things – good candidates, bad citizens – simply through the act of observing and naming them. Look, says border control while listening to an asylum seeker through accent recognition software, it's a suspicious, lying migrant! Look, says an employer watching a candidate through an AI system, it's an excellent candidate with a con-scientious personality! There's a word for creating something by naming it: 'performativity'. Performativity is an important idea that has proved hugely influential in a range of fields. Economists have used the concept to show how prominent economic models don't just observe economies but influence their behaviour. Physicist Karen Barad, for example, has also used the idea to demonstrate that the way in which a scien-tific experiment is conducted can shape the very thing that is being observed (look no further than theoretical physicist Niels Bohr's demonstration of how the way in which wave particles are observed changes how those particles move).[36] Barad's work created a ruckus among scientists who were outraged by the suggestion that experiments might alter the very thing being measured. This is not to say that the knowledge scientists gain in experiments is not real; rather it emerges because of the experiment, not despite it.

It's crucial that AI isn't marketed in a way that makes it seem like a neutral observational tool. With more truthful and realistic explanations of what these systems do, we can start making informed choices about which ones we use, just as we make decisions every day about what products we put on and in our bodies – organic, sulfate-free, or even full-fat. For now, being 'AI literate' means being able to take the misleading claims made by AI companies with a healthy dose of scepticism. Resisting the allure of AI marketing material can be as straightforward as choosing not to eat processed meat or palm oil; with consumer protection laws and ingredient transparency we can exercise our right to choose what we eat. We have a similar right to accurate information about how an AI system selects candidates and perceives violence, so that we're not encouraged to claim that AI makes us objective and neutral when, in reality, it simply facilitates thoughtless and impersonal behaviour.

From objective to relational

The issue of seeing science – and AI – as inherently objective goes much deeper than the marketing claims made by AI companies today. In fact, when we review the history of science, we see that its relationship with objectivity hasn't always been like this. It was only from the nineteenth century onwards that scientists began to disavow their involvement in whatever it was they were studying – an approach that, as Donna Haraway and others show, is fundamentally wrong.[37] The equipment the scientist is working with, and the hypotheses and knowledge they bring to the table, can't be erased from the experiment to produce impartial answers. Science is never neutral, and AI is no different. Big Tech ethics principles rest on the assumption that technology is and should be objective; as we'll go on to show, the view that tech can be dispassionate leads to an inability to care for the people technology impacts most.[38] We'll explore some of the failed efforts to use technology to secure ultimate omniscience, including innovations in the study of DNA. The graveyard of misfired attempts to control the world reveals a great deal about the disappointment AI might bring if we mis-understand what its capabilities are and take it for the next great oracle of our time.

When a company claims that AI makes its technology objective, it means impartial, unbiased and apolitical – as if the system is pure science, and therefore totally disconnected from the outside world. Most of us don't give the validity of the objective versus subjective binary a second thought. We take it for granted that objective means a truth about the external world, a fact with universal validity, while subjective relates to personal judgement. Subsequently, the popular view is that subjective judgement can be biased – in fact, it's necessarily biased – and objective judgement cannot be. This formulation, which sets bias in opposition to objectivity, has paved the path for technosolutionism: the idea that good technology can solve any problem. It's often based on the assumption that because technology is objective it can do what subjective human judge-ment cannot. The recruitment systems I discussed earlier claim to diversify the workforce without having to rely on a poten-tially prejudiced ('subjective') hiring process.

Historians of science Peter Gallison and Lorraine Daston have shown that the line between subjectivity and objectivity has not always been drawn in this way.[39] In fact, objectivity is a relatively young concept, emerging in a recognisable form only in the seventeenth century – long after the concepts of 'truth' and 'certainty'. At that time, practitioners of science did not for the most part consider their subjective judgement to be a risk when conducting their work. Science and art weren't seen as being at odds with one another, on the basis that both desired to represent the natural world. Scientists collaborated with artists, or even were artists themselves, as in the case of botanist-illustrators like Philip Henry Gosse. In his 1860 book *Actinologia britannica. A history of the British sea-anemones and corals*, Gosse painted a scene featuring a devilish magenta

Philip Henry Gosse's *Actinologia britannica. A history of the British sea-anemones and corals* from 1860

and black eye, with large, conic teeth both inside the retina and around the outer edges, like gnashing eyelashes.[40] This truly 'vagina dentata'-esque creature is sheltered under a lettuce leaf eyebrow. A hot cross bun floats across the middle of the picture. Top right, an anemone with a striking resemblance to a woollen sock with lots of little feet sits above what looks like a peeling manuscript (a rock?). Sea creatures may have been Gosse's passion, but art wasn't his calling. Thanks to the disambiguation of the life sciences and illustration, people who study plant and animal life are no longer compelled to draw.

More talented was eighteenth-century naturalist and entomologist Maria Sibylla Merian. Merian's work was considered excellent because of the way she interpreted nature. In *Pomegranate and Menelaus Blue Morpho Butterfly* (1702), now housed in Windsor Castle,[41] not one but two butterflies feed off a multi-seasonal pomegranate tree with perfectly ripe fruits as well as flowers in full bloom, while a caterpillar shuffles

Maria Sibylla Merian's *Pomegranate and Menelaus
Blue Morpho Butterfly* from 1702

up a delicate branch. This really is fantasy play – there is no
room for withered stems here, nor unsymmetrical butterflies
or yellowed leaves. Like AI tools that claim to reveal the true
nature of things, these illustrations warp the world to make it
as their scientific observers would like to see it. The goal was
to establish archetypes, creating an imagined perfect specimen

that would typify what a pomegranate tree *should* look like, by displaying the features that appear with some regularity in other plants of that species. Characteristics that represent 'healthy' inheritable traits are important, but other 'healthy' features that are not so regular or recurrent are not. Those not deemed healthy at all are excluded, lost from history. You can see how this is dangerous territory, and yet machine learning does exactly the same in its ruthless pursuit of neat categories. It recognises 'useful' patterns and discards anomalies. It's a process that has inherited a great deal from the taxonomies of twentieth-century biology, which in turn relied on idealised seventeenth- and eighteenth-century depictions to tell them what was normal and what wasn't.

The urge to use science to make life neat, symmetrical and categorisable is especially visible in British physicist Arthur Mason Worthington's 1877 drawings of mercury and milk droplets hitting a clean glass plate.[42] To be able to capture the moment, he would sit in a dark room and carefully time the splashes to take place at the moment when he created a spark of light (using a Leyden Jar, a common way of storing and releasing an electric charge at the time). Once the flash hit his eye, he immediately jotted down the image imprinted into his retina. The resulting hieroglyphic images are symmetrical and cartoon-like, resembling monochrome, mythological Pink Floyd album covers or furniture design blueprints. It didn't matter that they didn't look exactly like real individual splashes. They depicted the universal truth behind the drops – how they were supposed to be, as if imperfections would disguise the essence of what was being observed. That was what da Vinci was attempting to unveil: the truth behind the human form. But when science removes flaws, fixes what it sees, and seeks the universal, it can only define phenomena by excluding imperfections. A lopsided snowflake cannot tell you about what makes a snowflake a snowflake because it's malformed.

Arthur Mason Worthington engravings of splashes
made by drops falling on a plate, from 1877

Yellowing leaves, withered arms, asymmetrical droplets – these are worse than useless in the eyes of science, unfortunate malfunctions that do not express the universal nature of those things. Paradoxically, this approach loses touch with what is truly universal: variety. Real life doesn't happen under laboratory conditions; the observable world is lopsided, frayed and rough round the edges, as Worthington was about to discover.

By 1893, objectivity had morphed into a different form. It dictated that objective science could only be achieved if the scientist disappeared from their research. Kant had published *Critique of Pure Reason* in 1781, wherein he claimed that objective understandings of the world could not be attained through individual contemplation and intuition. He argued that while the senses gave us access to the spiritual, metaphysical realm, rational science could reveal objective reality. Kant somewhat immodestly compared his inversion of status quo thinking to the Copernican revolution, the once-controversial realisation that the Earth revolves around the sun. His claims spurred on the new, fashionable genre of 'mechanical objectivity' which prohibited the scientist from interfering with what they saw. New mediums like instantaneous photography allowed (but didn't guarantee) such approaches (some scientists would take many photos of an object and then collage them together, which slightly defeats the point). When Worthington tried again to capture hydrodynamics using instantaneous photographs, the resulting images were blotchy and slightly blurred. Nevertheless, these were deemed to be truer depictions than the scientist's pen. As a scientist, he was expected to erase himself, as you do when you mop the floor backwards towards the door to avoid walking over the spots you've just cleaned. Being a good scientist now meant being a neutral, detached, non-invasive observer, not an artist free to take licence when depicting the natural world, as in the case of Merian and Gosse. Objectivity remains a guiding principle of scientific work, and AI's perceived objectivity plays a major role in why it's widely seen as one of the most important scientific outputs of our time – as was made abundantly clear when computer scientists Demis Hassabis and John Jumper won the Nobel Prize in Chemistry in 2024.

The shift towards a newly defined objectivity resulted in some retrofitting and creative recasting of the work of key philosophers and scientists including Descartes, Kepler and Newton. They have since been named proponents of positivism, a philosophy that gained prominence in the early nineteenth century by seeking to exorcise intuition, faith and psychological introspection from ways of knowing the world. Instead, according to positivist rules, truths about life could only be derived from 'rational' observation, which meant using as little intervention (deemed subjective input) as possible. The photographer's hand was regarded as much less invasive than the illustrator's, making the image more objective. This is, however, just a sleight of hand enabled by machines; as anyone who takes pictures on anything more sophisticated than a smartphone will know, there is a great deal of labour, selection and processing involved in getting the perfect shot. Equally, some nineteenth- and twentieth-century anatomical illustrations provided as true an image of an object as contemporary

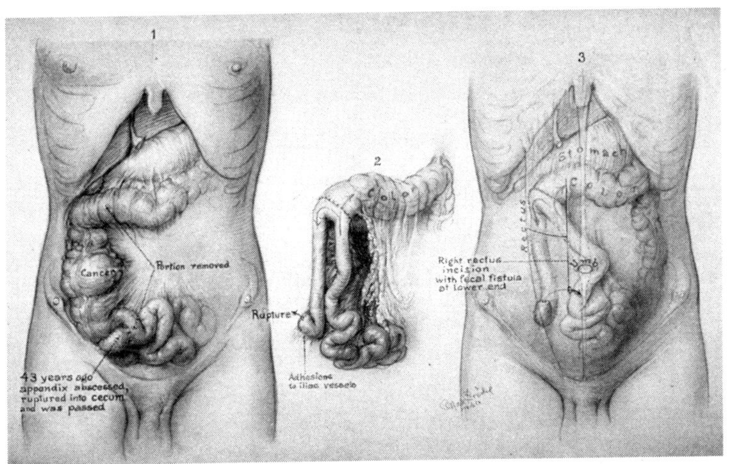

An example of Max Brödel's anatomical illustrations, which used
a carbon dust technique to create his characteristic realism

photography could, not least Max Brödel's extraordinary
tissue realism and cross-sectional anatomy. Exceptions aside,
the seventeenth-century bond between illustrator and scientist had been broken, and art and science divided; scientists
retreated from imposing their personality upon their work,
while Romanticism had artists going in the other direction
altogether ('I wandered lonely as a cloud,' brooded William
Wordsworth in 1807).

In Haraway's words, nineteenth-century scientists had
become 'transparent spokesmen'.[43] They could not be seen to
implicate themselves in their investigations, even though their
claims about the world would still be expressed according to
how they chose to run their experiments and read their results.
Artistic movements of the era followed suit, with realist paint-
ers also aiming to visually describe what they saw without
subjective or stylistic interference. Charles Baudelaire, who
wasn't much fond of them, believed that they focused on minor

genres like landscapes because they lacked imagination. In his obituary of the Romantic artist Eugène Delacroix, he mocked them for their 'erroneous' style, and voiced their hypothetical internal monologue saying: 'I want to represent things as they are, or as they would be in supposing that I do not exist.'[44] In science as in art, the practitioner still speaks through their work, regardless of what approach they take or tools they use. The pursuit of objectivity, however, can result in art and science being used as ventriloquist dummies for the artist or scientist to hide behind. Attempting to disguise your voice can make it harder to assess your implication in your work, paradoxically creating more opacity around your intentions or ideological stance. It also takes a great deal of effort, which is what dispassionate, positivist science is all about: being passionate about achieving a dispassionate relationship to the observed world. Where previously scientists had been allowed to add an extra butterfly to a botanical illustration of a plant, they now had to restrain themselves. The scientific self was invisible, its vision of perfection irrelevant. Today, botanical images are confined to museums and table mats, while science seeks scanned electron microscopic images that we believe offer us greater insight into plant life.

Although the privatisation of scientific research in recent decades has made it less of a public good and more of a commercial enterprise, the ideology of scientist-less and valueless science had already established its legacy. Looking back to the nineteenth century, however, we see that making yourself invisible requires cultivating a particular set of morals and virtues, because – and here's another paradox – the doctrine of value-neutral science comes with a great deal of its own values. Today, because we fail to learn from the past, objectivity in science still equates to being apolitical, value-neutral, and with as little subjective intervention as possible. As we can see from the way Big Tech's behaviour relates to its generic, wishy-washy ethics statements, vague principles can make an organisation unprincipled, being value-neutral can render it valueless, and not stating meaningful morals can lead to immorality. As I witnessed, key figures in the Met Police understandably want to believe that technology possesses an inherent objectivity that can carry their goal of providing dispassionate policing. But dispassion can slide quickly into thoughtlessness, and with it, heartlessness.

In the 1980s, scientists and social scientists like Donna Haraway and Bruno Latour caused a great deal of panic among the scientific community by proposing that science was not objective in the sense of 'all-seeing' and 'neutral'.[45] Geneticist Alec Jeffreys' development of the genetic fingerprint in 1984 had companies champing at the bit with its possible applications, from bioinformatics and biological weapons to genealogy tools, personalised medicine and police investigations. Like the omniscient, god-like capabilities associated with AI, the study of DNA was touted as the 'master plan' that would reveal all of humanity's secrets. But, as Haraway tells us, no technology offers an ultimate truth about humankind. Using the latest technology to play the 'god trick', disconnectedly hovering above what you are observing, stops you from seeing how your actions are entangled with social and cultural assumptions. Ultimately, the understanding we do have of DNA hasn't answered all the questions we had hoped it would about human behaviour, society and control. Most diseases are affected by hundreds or even thousands of genes. But the real issue is that scientific 'master narratives' often crush other approaches to solving the problem; in this case, hype around DNA diverted attention from explorations of, for example, cell-in-cell phenomena and bacterial symbiosis. As systems bio-engineer Alfonso Martinez Arias says, cells, not DNA, are the architects of life.[46] The exaggerated hype around DNA serves as a warning to us to refrain from believing that a particular technology will provide the ultimate truth about ourselves and the universe.

No technology can be disentangled from social and cultural assumptions. Knowledge is always limited and rooted in context. This is just common sense. All experiments take place in particular (laboratory) conditions, under a specific set of assumptions, using tools made with the aim of looking at the world in a particular way. And yet Haraway and Latour were shunned by a surprisingly defensive discipline that wasn't listening to what they were saying. You're bringing down science! they said. You're undermining its ability to express truth! (You want to turn our computers off!) Their suggestion was that empirical science was not purely descriptive but also creative, requiring some set design, some arrangement of the apparatus, and a selection of theories. Even in the 1940s, German philosopher Max Horkheimer warned that positivism denied the socio-cultural and historical situatedness of science;[47] in other words, society is not 'out there', but in the room with the scientist, influencing the decisions they make and their interpretation of what they see. Science is relational, it's about the interactions between technology, ideas and context. Relational isn't the same as relative – as in, 'it's all relative'. Don't panic – it's not all relative. What Haraway and Latour were trying to say is, look, there's more than one way of conducting and interpreting an experiment. This is why it's important that the scientist doesn't try to be invisible, as was the case in the nineteenth century, because the world doesn't exist independently of the way we observe it.

While tech companies themselves claim to be creating objective technologies, their CEOs are some of the most opinionated people on the planet. We now live in a twenty-first-century technocracy, where Elon Musk and other unelected politicians not only dictate political agendas and macroeconomic trends but have the public's attention, trust and admiration – even in relation to subjects in which they have little expertise. We might take our warning from Nick Beaumont's excellent science-fiction comedy *Venomous Lumpsucker*,[48] in which all jobs have been taken by computer scientists, including veterinary and animal conservation work, which is now all about automated solutions rather than animal welfare. Scientism – the view that science is the best way of attaining knowledge about the world – encourages us to kneel at the foot of the laboratory flask. The less we understand it, the more it earns our respect. As Argentine painter, writer and physicist Ernest Sabato said, speaking about the rise of scientism in the eighteenth and nineteenth centuries, 'Science had become a new magic, and the man in the street believed in it all the more the less he understood it.'[49]

When the public encounters an AI tool that appears to do something impossible, and indeed doesn't do what it says on the tin, the AI company in question encourages us to suspend our disbelief by claiming the product is still at least scientifically valid. When Mayor Femke Halsema of Amsterdam was questioned about ProKid+, she admitted it was not fit for use – yet she still made a telling claim: 'although ProKid Plus is scientifically validated, the complex assessment of various risk factors proved to be quite technical and therefore difficult for those involved to follow.'[50] Scientifically validated means a big fat nothing in this context. By saying the system is very opaque and complicated, she is, oddly enough, putting more rather than less emphasis on its trustworthiness. Why should the word 'technical' automatically equate to being scientifically valid? How many times have institutions defended bad technologies by saying that the issue was human operators? The problem isn't that humans aren't clever enough to work with AI. We want to believe that AI is neutral, because this makes life a lot simpler – and AI products easier to sell.

6

The Fight for Control

The stupidity of measuring intelligence

In the previous chapter we looked at some words that are often used to describe AI systems, but which are in fact red herrings of the most poisonous kind: recognition and objectivity. Now that we know those terms are not what they seem, we've laid the groundwork to explore two more: intelligence and control. These words are even more salaciously deployed in society to make claims about natural hierarchies of superiority. Whereas recognition and objectivity took us to specific use cases in AI like recruitment and policing, intelligence and control are concepts that underpin the way in which AI supports existing power hierarchies. From how we quantify and measure intelligence to the toxic, exclusionary myths surrounding academic brilliance, theories about what intelligence is underlie our quest for ultimate genius in AI. Two imperatives bug me the most – the suggestion that 'AI must make us more intelligent, otherwise we will plateau as a species', and 'for artificial general intelligence (AGI) to be defined as such, it must surpass human intelligence'. Building an AI tool that is as intelligent as, if not more than, a human is the ultimate goal for most AI companies. But what is human intelligence in the first place? And how does it relate to the way we define AGI?

In April 2023 a computer science paper that boldly called itself 'Sparks of Artificial General Intelligence'[1] claimed that GPT-4 exhibited 'more general intelligence' than previous AI

146

models. We don't yet have AGI so, for a start, you can't have 'more general intelligence' without some general intelligence to begin with. Another of the paper's limitations was that, like all tests of AI capabilities, it set predefined thresholds for how well the AI works, known as 'benchmarks'. You might ask what these benchmarks are in the first place, and whether they're good indicators of intelligence. Often, as the proverb goes, we find what we're looking for. Did the authors' desire to find 'sparks of AGI' affect their judgement in any way? The benchmarks they set aimed to test the model's ability to code and do mathematics, because, they said, these skills 'are emblematic of the ability to reason and think abstractly'. But as AI engineer Margaret Mitchell pointed out, reasoning isn't necessarily implicit in either; mathematics can just be calculations, and code can be written by copy-pasting other code retrieved from the internet. And, of course, not all reasoning beings can do those things, and there's no scientific explanation for why these two disciplines should be indicative of the ability to reason. I cried my way through maths GCSE and yet I can, on occasion, still reason. Sometimes, as anthropologist Marilyn Strathern explained, science becomes so obsessed with a target that it doesn't stop to question whether it's the right goal in the first place. Commenting on what's known as Goodhart's Law, Strathern said: 'When a measure becomes a target, it ceases to be a good measure.'[2] The big problem we currently face in assessing 'general intelligence' in AI is how to ensure we're not fixated on one particular way of defining aptitude.

In June 2024, a computer scientist called François Chollet teamed up with entrepreneur Mike Knoop to offer $1 million of prize money to anyone who could get their AI model to reach the top score in their evaluation test. The test would indicate, they claimed, the 'measure of intelligence' of AI.[3] It was called the 'Abstract Reasoning Corpus – Artificial General Intelligence' (ARC-AGI for short) and, as the name suggests, was designed to test an AI's ability to abstract and reason. The AGI after the hyphen indicates that Chollet believes that if a model can 'reason abstractly', then it's on its way towards AGI. This is one interpretation of what AGI would be. By abstractly, they mean making predictions based on a small number of labelled examples, which is called 'few-shot abstraction'. Not everyone agrees on this definition of AGI. 'I don't think that solving ARC is necessarily the golden ticket to achieving AGI,' said computer science researcher Melanie Mitchell in August 2024.[4] Chollet and Knoop state that ARC might, at some point, equate to AGI. But by setting their own expression (ARC) of the target (AGI), they risk conflating the two. You also encourage submissions to the evaluation test that are so desperate to prove their model is suggestive of AGI that they focus on reaching the benchmark score over doing good science. By this, I mean being able to reproduce the results, and not overfitting to the target. Predefining the benchmark closes off science to other possibilities of what AGI might be.

As I have said, this also assumes that abstract reasoning is the best indicator of intelligence in humans. There are many parallels here with the history of human intelligence tests, wherein definitions of intelligence are based on dominant perceptions of what intelligent behaviour looks like. The purpose of such tests is to determine who is and isn't up to the mark we've set. The question of which benchmarks are best for determining intelligence in computers rests on as many assumptions and fallacies as tests for humans. It only takes a brief glance at the history of intelligence-testing to see that our understanding of what makes a human capable or employable is deeply flawed. I'll start off by unpacking why in relation to human intelligence.

In psychology, intelligence is often defined as a person's strong performance across a battery of diverse cognitive tests, because high performance in one test correlates (but not always, just mostly) to good performance across a range of tests. However, that isn't a 1:1 relationship. It's just a general trend – a positive correlation between your performance in one test and your performance in all the rest. This is why intelligence is usually defined as inherently generalisable cognitive abilities, the capacities of an 'all-rounder'. Not coincidentally, AGI is seen as the 'ultimate' AI because it would be generalisable, in other words, an automated all-rounder. I feel we can do better than this rather unimaginative exercise of copy-pasting dominant definitions of human intelligence on to machines. There are also some delightfully arbitrary definitions: Jensen Huang, CEO of Nvidia, the big cheese in GPU advancements, claimed AGI would be '8 per cent better than most humans at exams'.[5]

Intelligence is a highly loaded, glossy and politicised word. So I'm going to set it to one side for the moment, and use the slightly less abstract term 'cognitive abilities' (plural – this is important) to refer to the many capabilities that cognitive ability tests are looking for. When it comes to AI's intelligence, researchers would do better to substitute the word 'intelligence' for specific target behaviours in the AI systems they test, like 'correct responses', 'coherent answers' and 'consistent results'. Being specific is good, and dims the hype. When my mother was in her teens she won the mathematics prize at school. This confused her schoolteachers, who had written her off as stupid because she has dyslexia's playful sense of capitalisation, word order and spelling. That was the late 1950s, when stories like this were common. Today, in my office in Cambridge I'm surrounded by brilliant dyslexics who still often have to fight to get the words out in the right order and on to the page. People who eloquently parrot what they've read in the *Financial Times* are more likely to signify as intelligent – as we know all too well in the UK, where we have been served a stream of politicians whose accents, confidence and refined oratory are substitutes for their critical thinking skills. This mirage of brilliance is a real issue here at Cambridge, where private-school students are still – despite all the propaganda about reverse discrimination – much more likely to get in than state-school students.

When I do admissions interviews at Cambridge, private-school presentability can be deceptive. Every year we engage in an improved but imperfect quest to dodge these proxies for intelligence, thinking carefully about what exercises we choose and how we ask questions and listen to responses. I'm often looking for a critical engagement with an issue or an interesting way of joining the dots. Expensive, formal education or a great teacher can encourage you to read around your subject, but life experience, political engagement and an awareness of your limitations can be just as valuable. Being clever in one area also doesn't mean you have any proficiency in another. Even in the most esteemed academic institutions it's common to hear confident opinions expressed as if they were facts, demonstrating the old adage that it's not what you say, it's how you say it. Social axes of oppression like race, gender, disability and class play an outsized role in whose offhand speculations are listened to: 20 out of Britain's 58 Prime Ministers went to a single school – elite, fee-paying Eton College – even though at present 93 per cent of people in the UK go to state school,[6] and only three British leaders have been female – our most recent famously being in power for a shorter time than the lifespan of a supermarket lettuce.

Just as academic access is fed by encouragement and resources gifted by parents and teachers, it's starved by ill-health and low self-esteem. Two Cambridge professors created the End Everyday Racism project in 2018. It was a website where students and university staff could log everyday experiences of racism, and the effect this has on their health, well-being and education.[7] The data they received through the site enabled them to prove to the university higher-ups that people were unable to do their work to the best of their ability, with statistics on bodily tension, breathlessness, nausea, headaches, chest pressure, depression and anxiety.[8] In fact, more than three-quarters of targets stated that racism prevented them from performing well. Two-thirds of people felt they did not belong at the University of Cambridge following an incident, and more than half experienced a strong sense of detachment from the university. Strain and stress and a lack of institutional support are killers of creativity and focus. They close you in, shrink your prefrontal cortex, limit your memory and weaken your immune system. As anyone who has experienced this kind of stress will know, it's extremely challenging to work well under such conditions. Which brings me to the question of how social and environmental pressure on your physical person, rather than special DNA, dictates your cognitive performance.

Contrary to popular myth, there's no secret to intelligence hidden in the genome: a study of differences in 18,000 children found no genome-wide significant associations.[9] There is, therefore, decidedly no intelligence gene, despite much investigation. In fact, it's more the opposite, that people who perform better in cognitive tests have fewer DNA mutations that impair intelligence. Interestingly, this means that gene-editing to make children smarter would not be 'enhancing' them so much as repairing damaged genetic mutations. The extent to which intelligence is inherited is also uncertain: studies on the DNA of hundreds of thousands of unrelated people found that only 30 per cent of the variation in intelligence is inherited.[10] Many tests fail to recognise the quality of a neighbourhood, number of siblings, divorce, and the quality of a child's school.[11] As I've seen first-hand while doing university admissions, a student who is top of their class at a lower-quality school can demonstrate more aptitude than one with a higher grade at a higher-quality school. We also know that socio-economic success is, unsurprisingly, often inherited – if your parents do well, they will likely try to ensure you do too. But what about the relationship between the parents' socio-economic success and the child's actual cognitive abilities? Well, there's clear evidence that parental wealth affects their offspring's ability to exercise their brainpower, because they are able to max out their genetic disposition to intelligence through a nice environment, good health and great schools.[12] The genetic inheritance of cognitive abilities, on the other hand, plays a minor part in cases where successful parents produce smart kids.[13]

Battles waged over IQ tests are deeply interwoven with ideas about race and the nation. As philosopher Stephen Cave points out, IQ is thrown around haphazardly by educators, politicians and eugenicists alike to create social (and national) divisions. Trump claimed that his cabinet had the highest IQ in history, suggesting that populist Republicans have more brain cells by virtue of their good judgement. Needless to say, the relationship between intelligence and success here is patriotic, rather than scientific. While some cognitive scientists argue that IQ tests are the bastions of meritocracy,[14] they don't fully take into account social inequalities. Cave gives the example of the 11-Plus exam within the British exam system, which promotes 'the better-resourced, white middle classes, whose members found themselves thereby reaffirmed in their position and advantages'.[15] Researchers who use IQ tests to defend the view that social mobility is always possible if a person is skilled at what they do also argue against the accusation that society is unequal. In response, critics have demonstrated that such conclusions are reached using inappropriate analytic techniques. So the battle rages.

Claims that intelligence is not only hereditary, but determined by race, are all too common. This is, at its core, a eugenical position. We may think of eugenics as a moment in history that flourished with nineteenth-century pseudoscience, but as Donna Haraway succinctly describes, eugenicists 'are real, they are not old fashioned, they're up to the minute'.[16] From Italian ethnic absolutism under Georgia Melloni to Donald Trump's praise of Henry Ford's good bloodlines – Ford was an enthusiastic anti-Semite – ideologies of selective breeding continue to flourish. They justify both calls to address overpopulation, mostly directed at social minorities (a third of Puerto Rican women were coerced into forced sterilisations by the 1980s, while thirty-one US states still permit coercive sterilisation of people with disabilities and illnesses like sickle cell disease). This is why it's no use pretending to statistics students that eugenics and dysgenics are merely the discipline's unhappy origin stories. Statistics cannot be divorced from how its founders – including Francis Galton, Karl Pearson and Ronald Fisher – developed it to support and validate their views on 'racial hygiene' and white supremacy. Statistician and university lecturer Brieuc Lehmann asks his students not to turn their backs on difficult aspects of their subject by viewing eugenics as merely a dark spot in its history, but to recognise that it was foundational to and continues to be an inherent quality of statistics. Cleaning, processing and classifying data, and deciding which of those data are 'more' or 'less' important, and which should be excluded, is just what statistics does. This is the situation in Aldous Huxley's science-fiction eugenics comedy-dystopia *Brave New World* (1932), where people are grown in bottles and streamed into class groups based on their engineered intelligence.

And then there's the stumbling block of gender – one of the most globally widespread and enduring inhibitors and dictators of potential. My great-aunt, who invented biodegradable disposable nappies with a reusable lining and the first modern sanitary towel, was barred from going to university by her parents, who didn't see it as a suitable life path.[17] She subsequently got divorced and went to live in an isolated bothy in Scotland. Working at Cambridge makes it exceptionally apparent that the ability to think deeply is less an innate attribute than an opportunity. It's easy to look around – particularly in this unending climate of political intellectual disagreement – and wonder whether intelligence is a broken concept.

Keeping in mind how these factors dictate our value in the economy, let's turn back to OpenAI's definition of AGI as 'highly autonomous systems that outperform humans at most economically valuable work'. That is, intelligence that is economically productive. There is an irony to the discrepancy between the expected economic benefit of generalisable machines and the limited economic output generated by academics. Intelligence and the economy are often strange bedfellows. And yet we should be concerned that intelligence is being defined in relation to growth and value. In 2023, the US media reported that Elon Musk was urging people he deems smart to procreate more. Shivon Zilis, Director of Musk's Neuralink venture, who has had three of Musk's children, has said, 'I can't possibly think of genes I would prefer more for my children.'[18] In an excerpt from Walter Isaacson's 2023 biography of the tech mogul, Zilis was also quoted saying: 'He really wants smart people to have kids, so he encouraged me to.' Despite not being romantically involved, their decision to have children together via IVF aligns with Musk's concerns about the decline of the ('smart') global population. Musk has frequently voiced the importance of reversing this trend among highly intelligent people, seeing it as crucial for civilisation's survival. In July 2022 he tweeted, 'Doing my best to help the underpopulation crisis. A collapsing birth rate is the biggest danger civilisation faces by far.'[19] Why is this ecologically disastrous propaganda considered by some to be a smart move? The answer, as we've seen, is because the value of human intelligence from this perspective is its economic output. In fact, intelligence is only recognised as such if it turns the wheels of the global economy. The potential to raise capital and generate profit is surely the dullest, most incomplete measure of intelligence, and yet it's the one that's being used to create a potential AGI.

If intelligence is contextual and specific, then attempting to create an artificial general intelligence is a fool's paradise. We need specific, purpose-built tools that are actually useful to day-to-day life. We also want AI technologies that bring to life more expansive, interesting and relevant understandings of intelligence which speak to the major issues we all face, like the climate crisis. We can take inspiration from Donna Haraway's concept of planetary intelligence, which is about nurturing relationships with our ecological ecosystems rather than putting extra strain on the planet. A system that embodies planetary intelligence is optimised for co-operation rather than competition – which would resolve a whole host of existential risks – and puts these issues front and centre by supporting the ecosystems we depend on for survival. Unlike conceptions of intelligence that are only modelled off a select group of human cognitive abilities, planetary intelligence is about attributes that help us live well with each other, and can be exhibited by all sorts of earthly creatures. There's much to gain – and fun to be had – in venturing beyond exclusionary definitions of intelligence and into more interesting terrain. Our anxious bids to establish what constitutes machine intelligence are inextricably tied to what's known as the 'control problem', and the age-old fear of being at the mercy of a more intelligent creature – and the need to dominate each other.

Controlling AI's values

In 1952, Christopher Strachey wrote and presented a radio broadcast for the BBC called 'Control without Men', a study of control mechanisms in animals and machines.[20] The technologies Strachey worked on were the foundations of modern control systems, which are devices that manage or direct other devices in the same system. This can be as simple as a sensor which changes the settings in a CCTV camera depending on whether it's night or day, a thermostat which regulates a boiler, or the operating system on your computer. When you download a new version of Windows or Mac OS, a central control function called a 'kernel' tells the operating system how to interact with your device. AI, on the other hand, has no central control function. When ChatGPT creates a response to your question it isn't following the instructions of pre-written software, but instead is spontaneously processing data through many layers of a neural network. Each layer performs computations using the inputs it receives from the previous layer. Layers work together and each focuses on a different aspect of the data it is given. How this all happens also depends on the variables the model is using, like how much emphasis a bank puts on a person's income when calculating a loan payment. Then there are the absurdly large quantities of data used to train the model, which comes from many different sources and is stored by cloud computing services like Microsoft Azure or Amazon Web Services. And finally there are multiple general processing units (GPUs) – the power this process runs on – which are located in many different data centres across the world. When ChatGPT creates an agenda for your next holiday, that action is profoundly decentralised.

This all means that in AI today, what is now called 'the control problem' no longer refers to centralised decision-making but to a more philosophical issue: how to dominate AI – which can defy human control in numerous ways – by making its values align with 'our' values, whatever these may be. In other words, solving the control problem means finding a way to definitively ensure that AI systems are working towards the same goals as we are – that AI's definition of something like 'fairness' or 'truth' aligns with what 'we' take it to mean. But this takes it for granted that there are a set of universal human values that AI can be aligned with. In 2025, ex-OpenAI engineer Daniel Kokatajlo posted a graph on X which stated that AI alignment will be 'solved' in November 2027 (delightfully arbitrary), after which time Artificial General Intelligence will capture the US government sometime around January 2028.[21] Speculative graphs about the future are like podcasts: every AI guy has one. The point Kokatajlo was trying to make was that OpenAI should 'slow down and solve alignment' before a superintelligent AI takes the reins of human governance. Whether an AGI caretaker government would be any better than the human administrations we keep voting for is not discussed. Unfortunately for Kokatajlo, the question of AI and values isn't a problem that can be solved. There is no single answer, because there are as many human values as there are human opinions.

And yet many prominent figures in AI have fallen under the spell of the promise of value alignment. In Stuart Russell's much-quoted statement 'Machines are beneficial to the extent that their actions can be expected to achieve our objective,'[22] the word 'our' is doing some heavy lifting. If AI is presumed to be beneficial in that it carries out 'our' objectives, as I often hear, then whose objectives are they? Vagaries like these are part and parcel of Big Tech's empty, ill-defined oaths to uphold 'human values'.[23] It's up to the rest of us to ask: 'Whose values are the ones to prioritise, and who should be in control of control systems?' AI ethics conversations often end with the conclusion that AI should advance 'our objectives', as though that were a robust enough concept not to require qualification. Asking whose interests we should serve is where these conversations should begin, not end.

There's a wide gulf between human values in principle and in practice. I once had the humbling experience of giving a lecture in a large hall where (at least) two students were listening to some music as I spoke through shared Bluetooth headphones. During a group exercise I went over and asked them to take their headphones out. I reminded them of the question we were discussing: what are your family values, and which should AI seek to uphold? They said 'respect'. I cackled. As my mother has always said, 'Do as I say and not as I do.' It's one thing to think a value sounds good. It's another to feel incentivised enough to put it into practice.

Making sure that AI aligns with human values sounds sensible and appealing but, as with the teenage boys, doing it well involves some soul-searching followed by meaningful action. Values are performed – lived, carried out – not just stated. It would be unthinkable for most companies to list their primary value as profit, but the reality is that making money is the concern against which all other values must be measured. This issue also extends to nations, particularly those run like corporations. Trump has referred to the US as 'a very powerful company',[24] and alt-right bloggers like Curtis Yarvin are a significant inspiration to the Trump administration's view that states should function as corporations, with citizens akin to shareholders or customers. If we see Trump's US as aligned with – in the sense that it shares the values of – the US's largest corporations, then profit is the government's prime directive. Growth, therefore, can be stimulated by a strategic takedown of every other nation's values. This is value nationalism, a kind of posturing that is mostly about saying, 'We have the right values, but they over there do not.'

We see this when American politicians imply that there is nothing we can learn from China in defining what the values of AI should be. Comments like 'We can't let China write the rules for AI' are two a penny in the US government; that particular quote from Commerce Secretary Gina Raimondo[25] was a call to action for the 2021 Global Emerging Technology Summit. In 2024, Kathleen Hicks, US Deputy Secretary of Defense, argued that the US must outcompete China in AI because it's 'powered by a free and open society, committed to responsible-use values and ideals'.[26] With only a small interpretative sleight of hand, the message becomes that the US has values and ideals while China does not. These comments are more than an expression of outrage about restrictions on civil liberties and censorship in China: they're also a marketing campaign for American AI™. The reality is that the US has no particular investment in standing up to human rights abuses; it just feigns outrage about misdeeds 'over there' to justify its own global dominance.

More to the point, US AI nationalism ignores what Chinese consumers have been doing to make sure that AI companies respect their values and serve their best interests. One important issue that has been raised is 'big data swindling' [大数据杀熟] (dà shùjù shā shú), where private companies exploit data by showing different consumers different prices for the same product based on their shopping history.[27] People are usually quite surprised when I tell them this: there is a widespread assumption that the Chinese government exorcises all ethical issues from the public fora, and that China's people themselves are unethical – people who eat dogs, as Trump claimed in 2024. It's good for the US government that the West believes that Chinese people lack morals. Yet when the news broke in China about big data swindling, citizens successfully petitioned their government to combat immoral corporate behaviour. The People's Republic of China subsequently stepped in to introduce the Personal Information Protection Law to end the swindle. In April 2021 it was reported that the local government in Guangzhou made large internet companies sign a pledge saying that they wouldn't illegally collect consumers' personal information or treat customers differently based on their spending patterns.

If we want to find a point of commonality with Chinese consumers, the anglophone approximation of big data swindling might be 'enshittification', coined by Cory Doctorow to describe the phenomenon of tech companies providing consumers with low-cost services and then hiking up prices and reducing quality once they corner the market.[28] Doctorow originally gave the example of Airbnb, whose fees are now many percentage points higher than they were at its inception, and Uber's implementation of surge pricing in 2015, having previously kept prices artificially low thanks to venture capital funding. Despite the best efforts of governments to play down the lessons we can learn from other nations, we would all benefit from recognising that we share problems and can collaborate for solutions. All this proselytising that 'our values are better than their values' doesn't get us anywhere – in fact it justifies a lack of self-improvement. This is why I work closely with AI ethicists from across the Middle East and East Asia to develop an awareness of shared concerns and different approaches to fixing them.

Values are more powerful when they don't close you off from the rest of the world, and are instead a way to open conversation about issues faced by people exposed to AI products thousands of kilometres apart. For example, with the expert in Islam and biomedical ethics Mohammed Ghaly, I'm exploring how AI legislation can be improved by learning from Islamic theology and jurisprudence about caring for and empowering people with disabilities. Ghaly's research can also be applied to African contexts; fifty per cent of the continent's population is Muslim, and yet discussions around African ethical traditions mostly only mention Ubuntuism, possibly because it's more palatable to Westerners than Islam. Intercultural conversations about what good technology is help avoid ideological tribalism – which political scientists Hyrum and Verlan Lewis call the 'single greatest threat to the continuation of our [the US's] constitutional democracy at present'.[29]

This is the risk in framing as 'alignment', or as a control

problem, the issue of which values AI should bring to life. It implies a homogenisation of values: one nation's to rule them all. But there's another problem with the way the term 'control' is used in AI: it often only appears in the context of whether AI will become 'out of control'. This implies a battle we've already lost, and stems from a place of fear and defence where we're on the back foot. Another related issue is that the common questions 'How do you solve a problem like out-of-control AI?' and 'Is AI out of control?' don't actually refer to control systems themselves, but control as a metaphor for domination. While it makes sense to dominate something scary, our kneejerk way of looking at an issue is not always correct.

The war on drugs is a good case study for why conflating control with domination is a bad idea. Authorities have tried to eradicate drug use with a top-down approach that criminalised communities instead of working with them. Punitive responses, 'crackdowns', were the favoured tool of governments impatient for change, comfortable with a heavy-handed approach to penal power, and with a limited understanding of the social context of the narcotics trade or the ins and outs of addiction. They tried to fight a war, not treat a health and social crisis. As Matthew Bacon and Toby Seddon have demonstrated in their study of how behaviour is regulated in drug treatment services, power and control are central to many routine interactions: 'The ways in which drug workers balanced care and control functions were remarkably similar to those found in penal settings.'[30] Such approaches, which make use of a diverse mix of power mechanisms, have been proven to be less effective than welfare, healthcare, an engagement with treatment, and working with drug user motivations.

And yet harm-reduction approaches like community-building and public health have been systematically ignored in favour of battles against addicts and cartels. This is because the values associated with a harm-reduction approach are interpreted by right and centre-leaning governments as left-wing, like non-judgement, equity and social justice – in other words, values that stem from an awareness of the social conditions that underpin drug abuse. In 2024, Amnesty International's Erika Guevara-Rosas urged governments globally to abandon the punitive policies of a 'war on drugs', saying that, 'For over six decades, this ill-conceived approach to public health has not only failed to reduce the use and supply of drugs, it has also resulted in widespread human rights violations, violence, mass incarceration, suffering and abuse across the globe, affecting disproportionately people from historically marginalised communities.'[31] I would argue that the control problem must be approached with a similarly counterintuitive logic, lest it fail as spectacularly as drug policy. Top-down disciplinary control is not the same thing as community-led co-management. We must be particularly careful that we don't make this mistake with AI because, as historian of AI Jonnie Penn recounts, the history of computers as 'control systems' is very much connected to the history of social control. At the turn of the twentieth century, the behaviourist school of thought took off in psychology and became a popular area of study concerned with how best to measure people's behaviour.[32] The idea was that if you understood people's reflexes you could pre-empt, manipulate and control them better. Attempts to discover how the mind was organised therefore influenced views about how society should be structured; as Penn puts it, the mind was a metaphorical venue for society and organisation.

The history of computers oscillates back and forth between freedom and control, utopia and hell. The Ferranti Mark 1 not only programmed Christopher Strachey's queer love letters, but also helped the British government do calculations to produce nuclear deterrents and guidance systems for missiles. Many years ago, at the reception after my granny's funeral at the house where her father, an engineer called Vincent Ziani de

Ferranti, had lived, I remember pulling back a dusty curtain in the living room to discover a silver model of a Bristol Ferranti Bloodhound Mark 1 missile sitting on the window ledge. No one had ever told me anything about the company's missiles; at most, its work in wartime cryptanalysis was occasionally raised in passing. An older relative who caught sight of the model missile I had unveiled murmured, 'Oh yes, I remember those,' and winked at me before tucking it back out of sight, as if it were still a state secret. Vincent's father, the inventor Sebastian de Ferranti, had pioneered the transmission of electric energy from power stations like Deptford, which he designed in 1887, while his activist wife Gertrude Ince campaigned tirelessly for women in engineering and for women's labour to be alleviated through domestic electricity. Despite these contributions, the uncomfortable truth is that the defence industry is never far away from innovations in electronics.

There will always be a struggle between the utopian possibilities of computation and their role in behind-the-scenes manipulation and destruction. The cybernetics movements entered the tug of war between military and peacekeeping uses of computers in the 1990s by reimagining these 'bleak tools of the cold war', as historian Fred Turner called early computers, as technologies that could decentralise power by replacing bureaucracy with distributed networks.[33] This tension lives on in how we experience platforms like Facebook, which claims its primary business is connecting billions of users while also siphoning off their data to the highest bidder and collaborating with law enforcement to bring about whatever version of social control their customers value most. Despite its strong utopian potential, and continued usefulness for many people, control is at the heart of how Facebook operates as an advertising platform and a partnerships business. In the 2010s, Facebook's decision to allow Global Science Research to collect user data ultimately enabled Cambridge Analytica to use people's personal data to influence their voting behaviour. Both business decisions made the commercialisation of the exchanges we have with each other online the core of what they do as a company. On social media, relationships between people are managed by packaging us into categories. This is key for how these platforms monetise users, because unreliable, unruly, unpredictable behaviour is hard to commercialise. They control the wilderness of human nature to make money.

We've looked at many issues with the language of control in AI: why AI isn't a control system and how one nation's values are used to control others. By raising awareness of the fact that the US's take on ethics is local and not universal, we can loosen its chokehold on the values endorsed in AI guidance and regulation across the world. Controlling AI shouldn't involve top-down disciplinary control from one nation but community-led co-management of AI systems that are bespoke to local values and concerns. Legislators and users alike can't unquestioningly accept the ethical priorities that Silicon Valley puts forward. That's why we need to be sceptical when AI enthusiasts talk about solving 'the control problem' and prioritising 'our' values on our behalf. Whatever we decide those values to be in our localities and communities, it doesn't make sense to copy-paste them from Meta's website.

7

Feminism by the Back Door

We've seen how noxious definitions of intelligence power discriminatory ideas about what AGI should be like, and why we need to restrain the impulse to establish universal values in favour of ones that speak to different contexts. The temptation to discover 'one true' ethics for AI is central to the phenomenon of cookie-cutter ethics principles. Despite not corresponding with a happier, more inclusive workforce or less discriminatory and harmful technologies, AI principles remain popular with companies and states alike. You may yourself have reflected on the gap between what your employer says it believes in and how the organisation conducts itself in practice. No doubt people who worked at the tech companies that were the first to overturn their corporate DEI policies to align with Trump (Meta, Amazon, Google ...) saw from the speed at which these policies were erased how superficially they were implemented in the first place. This is why ethics principles need to stem from feminist and anti-racist ideas if they are to mean anything – so that organisations don't just 'say' things but 'do' something concrete. Agreeing to a principle like 'non-discrimination' is useless unless you're ready to commit to what that actually entails. It doesn't mean impartiality. It means raising up the people who are often treated poorly in an organisation.

Big Tech does not do this. Instead, it offers non-committal ethical statements bogged down in vagaries. In one of my favourite *Good Robot* podcast episodes, Kerry and I chat to ex-Google ethicist Alex Hanna, who left the company after her manager Timnit Gebru was fired in 2020.[1] In the episode, a mellow Hanna sat talking to us with her cat, dissecting Google's ethical principles in deadpan, explaining why each injunction was contradicted by the company's behaviour. On the face of it, Google's stated principles are entirely unobjectionable – which is also why they're useless. No one is going to contest a statement like 'don't be biased' or 'be fair'. But they don't stand for anything. To be 'for' something good means being willing to stick your neck out and take some action.

Of course, Google isn't alone in playing politics with its ethics principles. Microsoft's 'Responsible AI Standards' have similarly pedestrian adjectives: transparent, accountable, inclusive, fair etc., aligning with the consensus view of which AI principles are palatable to consumers. Meta's are almost identical: robustness and safety, transparency and control. And governments and corporations across the world are following suit, issuing bland ethics directives that obscure the issues that really matter. At a recent workshop I ran with experts in Islamic ethics at Hamad Bin Khalifa University (HBKU) in Doha, Qatar, we asked attendees to compare and contrast guidelines from Europe and the Gulf region.[2] You'd imagine some cultural differences, perhaps, but they were eerily similar. This is the McDonaldisation of global ethics frameworks; Big Tech, by virtue of its influence, speaks not only for itself but for the rest of the world.

The fact that almost identical, broad, high-level, uncontroversial principles have travelled around the world like the Big Mac shows how little effort and investment goes into making ethics meaningful. Digital Dubai, for example, lists ethics, and then humanity, security and inclusiveness. The Egyptian Charter for Responsible AI's key principles are human-centredness, transparency and explainability, fairness, accountability and security and safety. Microsoft's are privacy and security, inclusiveness, fairness, reliability and safety, transparency, accountability. And on it goes. The more examples of this I see from both private- and public-sector organisations, the more I realise how little thought is given to consumers. Mass-produced ethics principles are appetisingly bland, quick to produce, and disinterested in the consumer's health – good to eat, hard to digest.

But the biggest problem with these broad-stroke, unspecified approaches is that they are challenging for companies to implement. Shane Jones, a principal AI engineer at Microsoft, found this out the hard way when trying to raise concerns about the image generator DALL-E 3 that had not been addressed by its Copilot designer, nor disclosed to the public. Jones had been 'red teaming' Copilot, hacking it to see if it was robust enough for public consumption. It wasn't. In response to the text prompt 'car accident', DALL-E 3 showed an image of a woman in underwear kneeling in the front of a car, and then again on its hood.[3] He raised the issue and was ignored. His repeated efforts to alert higher-ups through internal reports and a post on the senior leadership channel, which received 70,000 views, were met with a wall of silence. When that failed to do anything, he went public, writing to US senators, the US Federal Trade Commission and Microsoft's board of directors. He said, 'given our corporate values, we should voluntarily and transparently disclose known AI risks, especially when the AI product is being marketed to children. However, I have not been successful in convincing Microsoft management to take action on the issue.'[4] Microsoft's values were, surprisingly, worth diddly-squat when sticking to them threatened commercial operations. The disjuncture between ethics principles and business operations is a sleight of hand that has been perfected over time in the corporate sector, where vague and euphemistic language brimming with unarticulated assumptions is the norm.

This is because companies often view the principles themselves as a stand-in for the action that they signify. By *saying* that they value transparency, they get themselves out of having to actually do transparency work. This makes principles not so much meaningless as meaningfully empty; after all, a minimalist's house can convey as much meaning as a hoarder's room. In the previous chapter we encountered the word 'performative', which means bringing something to life by naming it, like the biblical injunction 'Let there be light!' Where a 'performative' statement creates the action that it refers to, its opposite – a non-performative – means saying something instead of doing it. Politicians are great at this.

Writer and scholar Sara Ahmed gives some terrific examples from her time working at universities helping students who had been exploited by staff. She notes that institutional apology statements can all too easily replace subsequent action.[5] If this feels familiar, that's because it has become the norm for institutions and public figures to cut straight to an apology rather than attempting to right wrongs, or, God forbid, behave well in the first place. It reads as a resigned, 'Sorry there's nothing we can do.'

In 2024, former wheelchair racer Paralympian Tanni Grey-Thompson had to crawl out of her London North Eastern Railway (LNER) train at King's Cross because the assistance she requested didn't come.[6] The experience of sliding her body along the dirty platform in front of other passengers jars with the detached, honed response of LNER's public apology, 'We are sorry to understand there has been an issue.' It's clear from the distancing effect that they don't want to acknowledge direct involvement, let alone the humiliation Grey-Thompson experienced. To do so would mean that they would have to make a change. Instead, the apology is a template response, fine-tuned by numerous previous 'issues'. We already know the reasons why little will be done: the system is too complicated and old to change, they are understaffed and short on cash. Crucially, the transport network wasn't built with disabled people in mind, so any accommodation made for a disabled person is a paltry attempt at retrofitting a service that really needs a complete overhaul.

But it's not just personnel shortages, institutional disorganisation and a lack of commitment that make companies unable to live up to their ethics principles. Size matters too. The bigger the company, the less personable and responsive it can be. We see evidence of powerful corporate complacency when employees are forced to issue impersonal statements. If you've ever almost had fisticuffs with a customer service agent because they are parroting a corporate canned phrase back at you like 'that's our policy', you'll know that the transformation of employees into impersonal machines is also a mechanism of power. What irks us most about these policies and this attitude, according to one TeleTech company, is that individual agents are disempowered to help. Recently, the father of a friend who was receiving palliative care for severe bowel cancer was unable to get the drug he needed for his son from the pharmacy, which required a local prescription. You can't get one without an appointment, which wasn't available for several days. In the meantime, his son suffered terrible pain. The pharmacy could not give the father the drugs with a standard prescription, even though it had them in stock. 'We are sorry,' the pharmacists told him, as did the medical staff in A&E of a nearby hospital, and I have no doubt that they were. But, like many an enormous, unwieldy and underfunded organisation, the NHS's precious yet often chaotic services can cuff medical staff into inaction. Ultimately, they were either unable to digitally process the right kind of prescription through the system, or faced being struck off if caught bypassing protocol.

Protocol, of course, goes wrong when it lacks knowledge of the world. Small-minded protocol disables agility and prevents representatives of the institution from responding. If you are unresponsive, you cannot be responsible. If you're unable to demonstrate that you care by resolving the issue – and your idea of resolution is a corporate apology – then you will fail to exercise responsibility. Care comes from the Latin *curare* – which also means to procure or provide. It's impossible to care without also taking action to provide the necessary remedies, whether they be a timely medical treatment or compensation and redress for a harm caused by an AI product. This is hard to achieve when Big Tech is 'too big to care', as Lina Khan, Chair of the US Federal Trade Commission, said of Google.[7] The tech titan controls around 90 per cent of the global market for web search and faces little competitive pressure. It can release an unreliable or unsafe product without fear of losing customers to rivals. Fuelling its inaction are vague, unimpactful corporate guiding principles. They feature prominently on Google's website, but are conspicuously absent from the company's material presence in surveillance systems and on the battlefield. To be vague is to be non-committal, ambiguous, unsure how or unwilling to proceed. A lack of moral clarity on the part of your average Joe might see them winding up in bed with their neighbour's wife, but for tech giants and providers of AI, uncertain morality is a global crisis.

Leading adjectives, leading us down the garden path

In his book *Vagueness*, philosopher Timothy Williamson argues that vague language conveys an intentional ignorance;[8] intentional because, as we can see in the context of ethics principles, it is vague on purpose. When we are vague, it's sometimes because we don't know what we're talking about. But often it's because we want to stay in control of a situation by, for example, evading scrutiny. We're actually being quite precise with our choice of words to remain as vague as possible.

Similarly, Big Tech is precise in the vagaries it deploys to signal ethics without committing to positive action. It knows that the language it uses has to sound right to us consumers – and to investors or shareholders. It rings true only to the extent that it aligns with what is familiar to us. Fairness? Yes! Transparency? Yes! But what do those words mean for, say, Google? Who knows: it's difficult to draw a circle round mist. Certainly, it doesn't translate into satisfying customer support chatbots or proactive steps to avoid selling harmful technology. Marketers often regret the 'unbearable vagueness' of marketing communications. British philosopher Mark Sainsbury called vagaries 'concepts without boundaries', explaining that being useless has a purpose.[9] Whereas non-performative ethics statements are ineffectual in the sense that they don't make an impact, unsubstantiated and undefined principles make use of their uselessness to encourage thoughtless behaviour.

What, then, is a thoughtful ethics principle? We might start with an even larger question – what does it mean to be thoughtful? A thoughtful action is something that has been laboured over, considered, detailed, that stands out and breaks out of the behavioural status quo. Thoughtfulness lends itself to others, and looks beyond itself; in other words, it's selfless. It involves reflection, and is self-reflective (it asks, 'What should I be doing?' and not 'What is everyone else doing?'). But are there any AI companies who actually do this? Joyfully, yes. Alex Hanna's current place of work, the Distributed AI Research Institute (DAIR), is an AI research lab founded by Timnit Gebru where transparency is nowhere to be found in its research principles. Instead, it lists 'healthy, thriving researchers' as one of its priorities, reflecting DAIR's view that good technology means good labour practices.[10] Its strong sense of mission and personality is visible in its principle of 'proactive, pragmatic research: we also believe that AI is not always the solution and should not be treated as an inevitability', and

'Community, not exploitation: We believe that research should centre the voices and experiences of those most impacted by technology and should be rooted in their communities.'[11]

Timnit Gebru's ex-manager Margaret Mitchell, ousted with Gebru from Google, now works as a principal ethicist at Hugging Face, an AI company which details the limitations of its own ethical charter. 'We are aware of our imperfections and we should constantly look out for ways to better operationalise ethical values and other responsible AI decisions. For instance, this includes better strategies for curating and filtering training data.'[12] Hugging Face's ability to be self-reflexive shows that its principles are realistic, considered and applied in practice. It avoids possible vagueness by giving examples of what it means and outlining a roadmap of how it is going to improve. Hugging Face is also countering the assumption that ethical principles are universal by including tailored ethical ideas for each project. This is crucial, because ethical concerns vary depending on the technology and the context in which it's going to be used.

At the beginning of 2023, I got a call from an Italian company called Ammagamma whose tagline is, 'There's no such thing as AI'. This was quite the provocation, and my curiosity was piqued. They wanted a team of AI ethicists at the University of Cambridge to assist them in building an online assessment tool to help companies meet the obligations of the EU AI Act for high-risk AI systems, which we've called HEAT (the High-Risk EU AI Act Toolkit). The idea was to do this in a way that wasn't quite as dull, miserable and uninformative as other auditing tools. What if we answered AI developers' questions about why AI ethics matters at the same time as helping them build great AI systems? Could we also apply feminist ideas to defining key terms in the Act, like non-discrimination and human oversight, and other ethical obligations, like consent and redress? I knew Ammagamma would be the perfect partner in this mission when I read their 'manifesto'. Manifestos are often political, and companies usually like to stay clear of politics that might come across as radical, so I was surprised to see that they had one. One line reads, 'Man is an imperfect interpreter: The desire to know implies the need to interpret.'[13] As we have seen, AI doesn't observe the world neutrally – it actively 'produces' a world view based on its training, deployment and design. It's reassuring to see this reality reflected in these quite poetic lines. I also like their phrases, 'Reality is representable as an architecture of data and relationships' and, 'The world is a harmony of relationships to be cherished', i.e. not to be exploited for the purpose of changing voter behaviour like Cambridge Analytica. Ammagamma knows that ethics is not superfluous 'woke' fluff, it's about understanding AI well enough that you can be sensible about what technology can and can't reasonably do. As we will explore in the final chapter, this has meant turning down gambling clients and deciding not to make AI systems that automate social interactions.

Words matter. That's why when Ammagamma and my team at Cambridge set about creating our regulation tool, we knew that we couldn't weaken ethics principles even further by parroting the same old vague terminology on transparency and fairness without careful qualification. We took a controversial approach to redefining two terms that are common currency in AI, and often mean very little: consent and complaint. Every day, you hand over data and participate in our immensely weak consent mechanisms, whether that be clicking on a pop-up to access a website or scrolling through miniature T&Cs to find the clickwrap agreement to download an app. Thinking through these issues in relation to sexual consent can help re-inject some meaning into the debate. In the face of a strategic weakening of AI ethics principles, we need robust regulation and guidelines defined and reinforced through a real understanding of how power – and consent – operates in this world.

Is consent a con?

Consent matters in both sex and data. Regulators and activists turn to the concept for AI because it can at least be defined with some degree of consistency within the rule of law. The way in which the law views consent is important not just because it regulates social behaviours through its decrees (not a given, of course, because the law is only as good as its implementation), but also because it sets standards for how we should relate to each other.

There is a 695-year gap between the first sexual consent statute and the first data privacy law. The former was in 1275, when English lawmakers decided you had to be aged twelve or over to consent to sex (it would take six centuries for that to be increased to age sixteen), the latter in 1970 by the German state of Hesse. The entanglements between sex and data consent began in 1995 with the European Data Protection Directive, which introduced the term consent in relation to sensitive personal data – the kinds of data that warrant grounds for needing 'explicit' and 'unambiguous' consent (note the use of sexual consent terminology here), defined as pertaining to 'racial or ethnic origin, political opinions, religious or philosophical beliefs, trade-union membership and data concerning health or sex life'.[14] This language of 'unambiguous' consent then made its way into the EU's General Data Protection Regulation (GDPR), which is important, because it shows that language in one piece of regulation often turns up in another, and therefore regulators need to get it right the first time with a term that works in other contexts.

GDPR is all about defining consent in relation to whether and how you want to hand over your personal data. Consent must be 'freely given, specific, informed and unambiguous indication of the data subject's wishes'.[15] It must be the 'clear affirmative action' of agreeing to hand over data. At this point, we might wonder whether it matters that we're giving 'clear affirmative action' if we don't know what we are agreeing to. Often, when we click on the 'agree' button, we're simply indicating that we want to enter a website, rather than that we are happy with the site collecting and selling our data to third parties. There is no mention of the power dynamics that might affect the split-second decisions we often make when 'consenting'. I work in this field, and yet whether I click agree or not on a cookie pop-up is largely based on how I'm feeling in that moment. Ultimately, companies should not be able to hold to ransom a person with no information who's being asked to hand over their data.

Ultimately, you are being coerced into agreeing to something you don't fully understand and have no way of knowing what the future ramifications of your consent will be. That's why the only way to make the consent process meaningful is to shift the power imbalance. When you consent to your data being used online, is 'consent' really the right word to describe what happens when you tick the box? Or are you pandering to a tech company much more powerful than you because you're worried they'll limit your experience of a site if you don't? These are fundamentally questions of power. They influence how you experience consent mechanisms, whether by limiting the timeframe within which you make the decision or leaving you uncertain about missing out. This is not to say that you lack agency when you make the choice – you still do the clicking – but intense power gradients are shaping the conditions within which that action takes place. Agency – the ability to act freely – depends very much on our status within a broader network. The point is, we weren't involved in setting up that choice. Tech companies are deciding for us, not with us, how our fundamental rights should be protected.

Perhaps the most significant example of self-defeating data consent practices was Aadhaar, the world's largest biometric ID system. Aadhaar not only controls the data of almost 18 per cent of the world's population, but creates that data by recording the biometric markers of an entire nation. The idea was that, by collecting the fingerprints and retina scans of everyone in India, the government could solve the problem of undocumented and paperless people and ensure that everyone had access to social provisions. The project aimed to be the cornerstone of India's digital 'stack', an interface that could use population data for a variety of purposes. The project sparked many years of searing infighting as to whether its benefits outweighed its flaws, much of it centred on the themes of privacy and consent. The problem was that while each citizen had to give their consent to being incorporated into the system, it was also compulsory to enrol. Consent, therefore, became a requirement rather than an option. Journalist Praavita Kashyap calls the concept of consent in Aadhaar a 'spectre', the illusion of choice rather than a living participatory agreement.[16] It's the kind of consent that finds its home in totalitarian regimes (consent or else!) and that goes hand in hand with coercion, its disciplining force. Such a farcical approach not only undermines the concept of consent entirely but merges the consenter and the consentee, one of the titular moves of regimes that abuse power.

Feminism, of course, has a lot to say about consent. Throughout my teens, my female friends and I did not consent to (and yet experienced anyway) lots of things that hopefully will be less prevalent for future generations in this post-#MeToo world. Recently, a man my age who went to many of the same school and university parties was taken to court for a sex offence. At the time, we never really considered how awful he was; we just knew he was gross and tried to stay clear. Those that did accept his advances often had low expectations of male behaviour. As girls, we were trying to both please boys and have them leave us alone. Looking back, consent simply wasn't a concept we were aware of. Accepting someone's advances isn't a choice when turning them down gets you labelled a 'prick tease' and submitting makes you a 'slut'. What was absolutely clear, though, is that it was normal for us to feel uncomfortable. In fact, so normalised was the sensation of being ill at ease that it became confusing when groups of boys didn't seek to provoke and engaged with what you were saying without resorting to innuendo. The worst thing is the perverse comfort that comes with familiar but damaging behaviour, regardless of the moral standing of what that entails.

The anglophone feminist conversations around consent that might have helped me navigate my early adolescence emerged into the mainstream in the early 1980s. They entered the legal lexicon in dribs and drabs thereafter: Belgium had a consent-based definition of rape by 1989, but only in 2022 and after much feminist campaigning did its legislation unequivocally state that the absence of a 'no' doesn't mean 'yes'. Spain followed suit that same year. Before this, where consent hadn't been given or received ('non-consensual sex'), the law viewed rape as 'less bad' when someone didn't say the word 'no'. To this day, Germany and Austria still have a two-tiered approach, whereby if it's not clear to the court of law that a person has tried to refuse the rapist receives a weaker penalty. Victims find they have to prove they didn't consent, which contributes to the fallacy that consent has to be an action, a vocal 'no' or a struggle. Not wanting to have sex doesn't always come with a no: we can be frozen, unable to move, exhausted, or take it to be the easier option. The law in this case is potentially forcing an action out of someone who effectively has their hands tied by the power relationship that defines the situation. This is the double bind that characterises life on the wrong side of power. The many people who have asked themselves, 'At what point does giving in to sex with my partner to keep the peace become rape?', all too common a question on women's forums and between friends, know that consent means little within an unequal power dynamic.

We can see this kind of decayed consent all too clearly when tech gig workers 'agree' to work in bad and often illegal conditions. Because Uber, Deliveroo, Bolt and Just Eat drivers are managed by algorithms, they never know what the customer pays and are largely in the dark about surge-pricing models and how jobs are allocated.[17] This all gets even worse in the data-labelling industry, where workers are deceived and manipulated in numerous ways. Kenyan tech worker Mophat Okinyi made the headlines in 2023 when he brought to light how Big Tech was outsourcing disturbing work – like handling graphic and sensitive content – to the contractor Scale AI and its subsidiaries, including Remotasks, where he worked.[18] To keep end customers like you and me in the dark about the exploited, international labour force that powered the services they used, Okinyi and his colleagues were also never told who the client was. Uncertainty and instability were everywhere: employees lacked formal employment contracts, meaning that their work could be abruptly taken offline, or their account suddenly de-activated, and they could be dismissed with no warning. They could not protest and had no rights. That's how inequality is maintained and why they couldn't consent to do the work they did. As I have shown in the sex examples, consent is weak when inequality is stark, and the inequality between data workers and their employers is shocking. It's maintained through a lack of transparency about what the work is for and how it's evaluated, negligible workers' rights, and the degrees of remove between Big Tech and the majority of its workforce, who are employed and managed by numerous contractors and subsidiaries. Imbalances of power like these obliterate consent. How can you agree when the terms of that accord are coercive?

The concept of consent often collapses under the weight of sex consent debates about situations where there is an undeniable power imbalance – from the coercive control of producers like Harvey Weinstein over actors in Hollywood to relationships between students and teachers. Seeing sex through the lens of consent doesn't always fully get to the bottom of why these situations can be fundamentally harmful. When sex is for anything besides sex – to placate a spouse, to ensure your caregiver doesn't leave you – it's exploitation based on a fundamental inequality (gender, race, disability, etc.).[19] Inequality therefore is foundational to rape, just as, I will argue, it's central to what's wrong with our interactions with consent mechanisms used by tech companies when we encounter their products. The next time you feel coerced into agreeing to terms and conditions or cookies, consider legal scholar Catherine MacKinnon's view that 'consent is resigned conformity to pressure and is rationalised as choice'.[20] Just because we're told that it's a choice to consent to the myriad ways in which tech invades our lives, it isn't sufficiently indicative of willingness, because that choice has been set up on our behalf. Our actions are constrained and our desires and priorities shaped by power. The big question here is, what does it mean to act freely, to exercise will and agency, within asymmetric power relations?

Linguistically speaking, too, consenting is always submissive, regardless of how it takes place: to consent is a verb that requires an object (to consent to something). Passivity is actually part of consent's grammar in English. When you consent you submit to something, you allow someone to *do something to you*. That's why prefacing consent with 'voluntary', 'unequivocal' or, most popular of late, 'affirmative' and 'enthusiastic', as is common under the law, merely further invalidates the noun it's supposed to be adding meaning to. If you need 'affirmative' before consent to make it meaningful, then consent on its own isn't active enough. Whether or not consent is affirmative, communicative or enthusiastic, it's still responding to someone else's proposition, the terms of which have already been set. Even prior to this, the person seeking consent has dictated the point at which consent is required.

The reality is that tech companies shouldn't be asking for things that require consent. If they need it, that's because whatever they're doing will potentially infringe on your right to privacy. As tech researchers Leta Jones and Elizabeth Edenber explain, the concept of consent is often asked to 'perform the "moral magic" of transforming the moral relationship between two parties, rendering permissible otherwise impermissible actions'.[21] Without consent, it would not be in any way OK to take our data. If we transferred this back to rape legislation, consent would mean letting someone do something to you that may harm you. This is a terrible formulation, both in relation to data and sex. We might instead turn here to the origins of data protection in 1980, when US attorneys Samuel D. Warren and Louis Brandeis wrote that privacy was 'the right to be left alone'.[22] This could very well be a suitable foundation for work on the appropriation of our data. When you are asked for consent you are being put in a difficult position. You are being harangued by a cookie pop-up to make a choice. The right to be left alone intercepts consent mechanisms by giving people the right not to be approached in the first place.

In 2014, the *Guardian* reported that 1.4 billion Angry Birds app users were being spied on by GCHQ and the NSA.[23] This was possible because when you downloaded Angry Birds, the app would take the fifteen-digit number that identifies your mobile device, called an IMEI, which is essentially your phone's 'fingerprint'. Users had agreed to the Ts and Cs, and none of that contained information about IMEIs. Ultimately, this data should never have been collected in the first place. This is why 'opt-in' should be the go-to approach, especially in the creative industries. Publishers, artists and writers in the UK are currently contesting the government's 'opt-out' preference for protecting copyrighted works from LLMs. They're quite right. It merely panders to AI companies' desire for more data on which to train their models. Granular opt-out choices are nothing compared to specific opt-in choices. The baseline must be opt-in. It's great that there are cool tools such as Spawning AI's 'Do Not Train' registry, which blocks LLMs from training on works like art and music that are already present in datasets, but it would be madness for governments to lean on them to justify an include-first-ask-later approach. I therefore disagree with the UK government's current view (as outlined in the 2024 Copyright and Artificial Intelligence consultation) that products which clean up the mess made by unethical AI are 'key to a system that works for both the creative and AI industries'.[24] No! They exist to pick up the pieces of what is currently a bad system, not to be the cornerstone of a good one.

I have said that consent does not eviscerate inequality. The most important thing we need to do is replace paltry data consent systems with efforts to shift the power that tech companies have over our data. Step one is education, which is across the board one of the most powerful tools for fighting inequality. We need to improve our 'data literacy' so we actually know what is being asked of us. So far, companies are merely letting us know what will happen if we don't consent to a pop-up: 'you may see ads not relevant to you'. But what about the bad stuff? I would like to see companies having to provide information on worst-case scenarios of what could happen, like cigarette-pack cancer warnings. Not everyone who smokes gets seriously ill, but it's common, so you need to know. Information science expert Helen Nissembaum has called for pop-ups to be more specific about what they are actually asking: 'I'm OK that you're using cookies to track me,' or 'I don't want to be tracked but still want to enjoy the service,' or 'It's fine to use cookies for this particular transaction, but throw unnecessary data out and never share it with others.'[25] This should also happen more often than the first time we access the website. GDPR states that you can withdraw consent at any time – like sex. But how do we know that the terms have changed, and therefore no longer want to participate, if we're not being informed?

All these questions are important, but they still keep this issue at the level of the individual. The reality is that companies don't always know where data goes, and so can't guarantee us updates or advance warning. And users are often happy to give away things they shouldn't, based on not much information. Humans are terrible at thinking about long-term harms when there's a short-term carrot dangled in front of us. If we settle for merely improving consent mechanisms, then we will be mired in these various conundrums forever. Part of the reason why decisions shouldn't be left to individuals is that the privacy decisions of strangers can affect our own choices. As was the case with Cambridge Analytica, when people were largely unaware that their personal data could be aggregated to sway voter behaviour, we often don't know enough about what can be inferred from the data we hand over. As individuals we not only lack information about how our data could be misused, but don't feel empowered enough to stand up and fight when it happens. Research by the European Commission shows that, generally, consumers choose to shy away from redress when a company exploits them because they don't feel it's worth the effort or don't know how.[26] On our own, we think our difficulties are insignificant or insurmountable. The problem is in the aggregate, so the solution needs to be too.

Seeking our consent to use personal data and our agreement to privacy policies is not enough. We need co-ordinating action between different consumer and data protection bodies: this means multiple relevant authorities, including national and international consumer protection agencies, sitting down and deciding what is acceptable to ask of the consumer in the first place. Public bodies should establish through citizen consultation what a mutually beneficial agreement between citizens and tech companies looks like in relation to data. They can come up with some answers to questions like, 'What data arrangement is beneficial for citizens, and are there other ways for them to access websites without giving away data, or giving away less sensitive data?' We need more funding for civil society and advocacy groups, but we would also benefit from a greater number of citizens taking direct action. Complaints count, as we will discover next.

The insurers vs Mötley Crüe

I have a special Twitter account that I use to escalate complaints as a last resort. It doesn't get logged into often, and it always feels rather shameful when it does. Unfortunately, though, it's very effective, because companies aren't necessarily bothered by your sob story over email but do care what you write about them online. I log in when it's time to offload my fury on to some unsuspecting corporate account; this has the potential to be more effective than their shoddy formal complaint procedure. The last time I did this was when I was burgled on a winter holiday and relieved of all my jewellery and most of my clothes by some robbers who somewhat mysteriously left a Mötley Crüe calling card (of their 1983 album *Shout at the Devil*). A final kick in the teeth came from the insurers, who were not convinced that the stolen clothes were in my wardrobe at the time of the break-in, claiming that these items were 'unseasonable' to wear over Christmas. Among them were some cropped tops. So I tweeted the insurance company photos of me in those very items in December the previous year. Marvellously, one of the philosophers I most admire retweeted the image on the basis that it was time for insurers to cease policing women's sartorial propriety.

As anyone who has worked in business knows, consumer complaints are a painful but important improvement mechanism. Feedback systems not only help companies identify and address stakeholders' concerns but also enhance their experience of and trust in the product, thereby enabling sustainable growth and a competitive advantage. In 2012 the European Commission's Consumer Agenda stated that redress and enforcement measures needed to be improved.[27] And yet, over a decade later, the situation is still generally not good for consumers, and, predictably, it's even worse when it comes to AI products. Complaint and redress mechanisms for individuals harmed by AI also did not make it into the EU AI Act. The Act only includes the individual's right to lodge a complaint with a market surveillance authority, and does not stipulate how they can enforce compliance. This is pretty useless. It's crucial that we have some guarantee of redress when an AI tool has a detrimental effect on our lives. Not having stipulations on how AI's wrongs can be put right in the EU AI Act risks contradicting GDPR's requirement to compensate affected persons when harm arises from personal data processed by the algorithms. It also weakens the Act's ambition to uphold fundamental rights. There are fifty articles in the European Charter of Fundamental Rights concerning dignity, freedoms, equality, solidarity, citizens' rights and justice. Each of these needs to be addressed and protected in the context of AI, which is what a rights-based approach would have done – favouring the implementation of these rights and making them paramount. But thanks to hefty corporate lobbying, we've been left with a paltry risk-based approach, which only asks companies to state the likelihood of these rights being breached. Fundamental rights are supposed to be non-negotiables which cannot be 'balanced' against risks.[28]

Civil society groups like Access Now campaigned hard for a better outcome, and even proposed a new section of the Act called 'Rights of Affected Persons'. But by 2023, tech company lobbying in Brussels had increased to €113 million a year ahead of the finalisation of the Act, crushing the voice of civil society. And so we have been left with legislation that gives us no guarantee of redress or compensation if we experience harm because of a high-risk AI system. If you're outside the EU the situation is even worse, as none of the Act's protections apply to either EU or non-EU companies that export banned AI systems across the world. The Act was introduced alongside the AI Liability Directive, which sounded hopeful, but also only protects citizens from a slim set of material harms such as death and destruction to property, and then merely as a result of a defective AI product. This is yet another example of death being the lowest common denominator in AI ethics.

Part of what you want when you make a complaint is an explanation of what happened. But globally, there are only a very few instances in which you'd be entitled to one from an AI company when it would involve detailing how a decision was made by one of their products, whether you were denied a loan or shown a disturbing image in response to a silly prompt. This is partly because companies that deploy AI are often still far from being able to provide explanations about how systems work, even to themselves. As Federica Frabetti has noted, even AI engineers only have a partial understanding of their systems because doubt and uncertainty are inherent components of software.[29]

Doubt doesn't just come from the technical aspects of AI, but from its social dimensions. When you complain to a company that something has gone wrong, you're providing a free explainability service. This happens a lot at Amazon, where customers are invited to email jeff@amazon.com when they want to report a problem. When Jeff decides one of these queries is worth a response, he uses the 'question mark method' to investigate. This involves forwarding the email with a question mark to executives, who then send the email down the company hierarchy until it arrives at someone who can answer it. The explanation that the customer was asking for is often not a clarification as such, but an admission of guilt, a guarantee of improvement or a request for compensation. Adham Abdelfattah, former Head of Product and Growth for Amazon's Business and Industrial Supplies, once received such a question mark email from Bezos. It was originally from a customer who didn't know how to search for a particular type of screw when shopping on the platform.[30] Abdelfattah realised that the problem was that most customers don't know what screw they're looking for; they just need a replacement for the one that broke in their oven or some other domestic appliance. Abdelfattah ended up creating an entirely new way of searching for screws on Amazon. Complaints are issues brought to light by a complainant who is willing (and has taken the time) to freely provide their account of a negative experience. By collecting and acting on that information companies are gathering intel that helps them understand how their system operates. You also can't be accountable to consumers if you can't provide an account of why your products work the way they do.

At the moment, legislation isn't giving companies the chance to do this. And so the compliance tool I helped build, HEAT, proposes that AI companies and deployers allocate a complaint oversight officer to oversee the complaints process – to initiate the question mark, if you will, and ensure it has an outcome that pleases the customer.[31] Making someone responsible for dealing with consumer problems means it's far more likely that users will be able to lodge complaints and have them acted on. As we all know, it's a nightmare when no one in particular is in charge of your case and you're passed around different teams like arsenic soup. HEAT asks AI companies not only to make it straightforward for individuals to submit feedback, lodge complaints and report incidents, but to structure the complaint process into defined stages and ensure consumers receive frequent status updates, followed by appropriate remediation to put things right. This was based on how my team would want to experience the complaints process ourselves, for our dissatisfaction to be addressed and to be communicated with responsively. These kinds of non-defensive and constructive procedures are a good thing all round. Borrowing here from the UK's North West Ambulance Service complaints procedure, acting on feedback could be 'an acknowledgement, explanation and a meaningful apology for the error, reconsideration of a previous decision, expediting an action, waiving (or recompensing) a fee or penalty, issuing a payment or refund, changing policies and procedures to prevent the same mistake(s) happening again and to improve our service for others'.[32] Taking complaints seriously is very much in the spirit of (rather than, unfortunately, the letter of) the EU AI Act.

Complaints are not just opportunities for companies to learn about themselves, but for the complainant to learn about the company too. As Ahmed says, complaining can teach you about an institution. When I complained to the insurers I learned that they didn't wear cropped tops. Less glibly, it gave me insight into their workforce's demographic (age, gender) and how that affects the way they treat customers. When, on another occasion, I complained to Microsoft Outlook that I'd been barred from my Hotmail account for many failed password entries, I gained insight into the nightmares of account lockout mechanisms. When I Googled the issue, I found that many other people have had the same or a similar problem. Reading about their experience gave me insight into my own situation, and in joining that community of digital complainers a bigger picture of security conundrums and cyberattacks was revealed to me.

When we have a complaint, it's important that we don't feel alone; this is partly because it often indicates a larger issue that only reveals itself when other people raise similar concerns. We've seen many of these big-picture moments in the past decade with #MeToo and #BLM, and in tech thanks to the rise of tech labour unions (of which more later). Unions are crucial complaint mechanisms. I joined the University and College Union (UCU) at the University of Cambridge when I started working there, and when I had a problem with my contract two years in, a kind and well-informed member helped me solve it. She showed me how to navigate Byzantine university policy and argued on my behalf for a better contract. When you complain, you seek out information and expertise, making it a powerful upskilling process. In Ahmed's words, complaints themselves (as well as fellow complainers) can be 'companions', stories you can carry around to inform people, give them information, anger, hope, clarity and connection.[33] This is why it's vital that we are able to complain about bad AI, not only for our ability to understand AI systems – to become 'AI literate' – but to participate in them – to be 'AI competent'. A byproduct of complaining is the competence gained in navigating the system and understanding how it works (or how it doesn't). All this effort is undoubtedly labour: we're not just learning, but working. You'll feel this from the time, energy and emotion you put into the complaints process. Reflecting on the crucial investigations of feminists of colour into how power operates in powerful institutions (like universities), Ahmed likens complaint to housework. The process of making a complaint, she says, keeps your – or someone else's – home in order, and involves the similarly 'painstaking' drudgery and repetition of administrative tasks and care work.[34]

Ahmed also notes a more modest ambition to the act of making a complaint, which is that it's a useful form of record-keeping. When you complain, you make a record of something that happened. I think here of the journalist Max Colbert's insistent, repeated resubmissions of freedom of information requests to the Metropolitan Police, knowing that they would be rejected, accompanied by a nonsensical bureaucratic copy-paste response. It would have made me weary to keep complaining, to feel like I was wasting my time and effort constantly hitting my head against a brick wall. But to Max, each rejection was a record of non-democratic police behaviour that would form a bigger picture of the police's indifference to citizens' participation in the public sector. Even the vacuous nothing that comes out of our complaints can still tell a damning story about what really happened.

Part II

How Can We Get AI Right?

8

The Case for Controversy

Every year, female motivational speakers from all over the world face a crowded calendar near 8 March. When International Women's Day (IWD) rolls around, we get wheeled into a range of venues to speak about 'women's issues'. Corporate feminism still gets you in the room, so no complaints from me. Companies usually play it very safe with their event titles by opting for words like 'bias' and 'equality' over 'feminism' and 'justice'. One talk for an IWD event at which I was a panellist had been called 'Balancing Bias'. The session had been devised by a large media company, who had no doubt chosen the title to signal a centrist, catchy approach to AI ethics. 'Balancing Bias' conjures up a balanced diet, a yoga balance pose, a bipartisan cause, balancing work and family life, being emotionally balanced – a friendly concept. No bad thing to sound amiable when encouraging people to do the right thing. It's similar to the term 'unconscious bias', which implies that the 'bias' isn't so bad because it's unintentional. 'Unconscious bias' is merely another way of taking the perspective of the perpetrator rather than the recipient of harm. All this tacit hand-holding in AI ethics terminology turns anti-bias measures into a support group for people and companies accused of racism and sexism. Despite the effort that goes into making ethics uncontentious, I find that the employees who turn up to pro-equality events are almost always ready to have a less placid conversation. They're already dissatisfied with their employers' unfulfilled promises about improving the plight of minoritised employees. As smart people, they know that balancing bias doesn't mean much – neither in relation to society and culture, nor when it comes to technological fixes. If you want to engage your audience, you've got to be straight with them.

The concept of 'bias' has dozens of mathematical definitions, and is an essential component of all machine learning (ML) systems. The rule 'words that appear in similar contexts tend to have similar meanings' is one example of a bias that can be important for ML models to learn. So you'd reasonably expect an engineer to question what exactly it means to 'balance bias' in this context. I once asked AI engineers at a large tech multinational how they defined bias. Some said: 'the intercept between the x and the y axis'. Others said: 'Bias can be good, right! In my field, in terms of trying to find a threat. You want to bias towards finding threats rather than being fair [...] You know, we are by definition discriminating in the data.'[1] Because bias means something different in mathematics and computer science than in relation to social issues, there's a great deal of ambiguity for engineers to grapple with. If they can't be made sense of by the people making AI, ethical principles like 'don't be biased' are as good as useless.

If tech companies' main engagement with AI ethics is an attempt to 'balance bias', it raises the serious question of what we're meant to be balancing it against. Profit? Innovation? And is the implication that a balanced position is a neutral one? On this path to bias-neutrality, which harms are acceptable, and which are not? The rationale seems to be that anti-bias efforts minimise profits and must be tempered, which aligns with the outdated trope of 'balancing innovation with regulation'. Setting them as a dichotomy makes it seem as if innovation is always good and regulation is always restrictive. As in the case of policing and surveillance technologies popular with government bodies hoping to boost productivity, modernise, save money and regain public trust, it doesn't matter if the technology even works. The very fact that it's being used is supposed to signal that this is a modern enterprise, capable of using new AI devices. There is an undue emphasis on AI as a way of automatically innovating a company.

AI can reverse scientific and social progress by bringing outdated science or cultural perspectives back to life. Regulation, therefore, doesn't just slow down tech development, but when done constructively it can enable companies to shift direction and develop tools that are socially useful, as we'll see later. But we need real ethical discussion to reach a place where regulation ensures that innovation is safe and beneficial for a wider spectrum of users. Positive innovation should mean more than vague ethical principles like Google's woolly exhortations to 'do no harm' and 'don't be biased'. Precise directions, warnings and considerations for companies to follow are the way to go. Despite the odd, platitudinous titles they choose for their events, this is what companies actually want to hear about when they invite experts to galvanise their workforces. They're just too stuck in the habit of using corporate jargon to say what they really mean. What we need is disagreement, I said to the roomful of data and media professionals that Women's Day. Difficult conversations should be taking place at C-suite level that are – crucially – informed by the expertise of the people building these systems, about how far they are willing to go to right global wrongs in administering their systems.

Reparative AI

There are many under-recognised scholars and programmers who can guide us on the path to better, more ethical AI. One of my favourite approaches to the problem of harmful and unfair AI comes from Australian- and US-based computer science researchers Jenny L. Davis, Apryl Williams and Michael

W. Yang.[2] They take a radical approach by using algorithms to promote the interests of the least well-off. Unlike most equality measures, they don't aim to treat groups equally, because doing so would mean pretending that the inequalities of the past didn't happen; you need to account for how the past shapes the present. An example of an AI system that aims to right social wrongs was led by Wonyoung So of MIT, who aimed to combat mortgage-lending discrimination in the US.[3] AI systems typically use the baseline wealth of a racial group as an input for determining mortgage loans. As 7.7 per cent of white people in the US live in poverty, compared to 17.9 per cent of Black people, being Black already makes you less likely to get a mortgage loan.[4] The 'reparative algorithm' designed by So's team sought to combat mortgage-lending discrimination by estimating the amount of money that governments need to provide for today's Black borrowers to secure a prime mortgage loan in the US. Their work is consistent with what reparative means in its traditional context – drawing attention to an issue, and working to repair a broken society. It's based on the idea that you can't expect people to beat the odds and magically raise themselves out of poverty. Unfortunately, because of mainstream backlash against what people wrongly call 'reverse discrimination', righting social wrongs through reparative or 'affirmative' action is still highly politicised – and the Trump administration is now trying to outlaw it.

We need social justice mechanisms that mean business. As I write, the Caribbean Reparations Commission is calling for former colonial powers to provide education programmes, return heritage objects and assist in public health crises. I like introducing this idea at conferences because it adds a heightened political energy to the conversation. Reparations are still a source of vehement disagreement, prompting shouting matches in the pub, Parliament and over the kitchen table. I often hear people say that the UK can't afford to give money back to the Caribbean, as if reparations were just about cold hard cash – which they aren't, if you read CARICOM's Ten Point Plan for Reparatory Justice. CARICOM is community-led, like much reparative work. It's driven by the people who continue to experience colonialism's legacy – economic and social inequalities, exposure to the climate crisis, debt, poorly constructed housing, widespread illiteracy – and therefore are best positioned to come up with solutions. Just as Joy Buolamwini and Timnit Gebru created a dataset to improve facial recognition's ability to observe Black women's faces, or Masakhane build datasets for endangered and low-resource African languages, CARICOM doesn't propose silver-bullet remedies.[5] It knows that repairing the deep fissures created by trauma, abuse, colonialism and loss is like putting together a 1,000-piece puzzle.

Whatever your feelings about colonial reparations, algorithmic or otherwise, the issue is a sharp reminder that 'good technology' isn't fluffy – it means hard choices and difficult politics. This is the heightened pitch at which we need to talk about AI ethics. It's not supposed to be easy or pleasant for all. We're supposed to disagree, and we need to learn how to expect and accept disagreement. I'm personally terrible at this, but we can take inspiration from those who somehow manage it well. Audrey Tang is excellent at pleasant, constructive conversations with people she might not see eye to eye with, something she gaily puts down to a serious heart condition that makes it important for her to manage stress and anger. She calls listening to those you disagree with 'broad listening', as opposed to one-sided broad-casting.[6] During the 2014 Sunflower Protests in Taiwan against the government's proposed trade deal with China, she worked with a group of hackers to set up an AI-assisted discussion platform called Pol.is where citizens could post their opinions about the issue. It helped identify 'consensus points' by allowing users to upvote/

downvote others' statements, and grouping similar viewpoints together. Tang and her collaborators created the platform to respond to citizens' complaints about being excluded from government decisions. This AI was born from the complaints made by those on the wrong side of the government-versus-citizen power imbalance, and a thoughtful engineer's ability to combine her technical aptitude with her knowledge of how to depolarise a debate.

Crucially, reparative work shows why we need to use the expertise of the people doing jobs well outside the tech industry as the basis for AI systems. As with effective altruism, those who are best placed to solve a problem have lived experience of it. This is why good technology involves the inclusion of some unexpected voices. As Eun Seo Jo and Timnit Gebru argue, by collaborating with professional archivists who are experts in collecting, arranging and auditing data in ways that combat existing inequalities we can make sure data collection promotes justice.[7] Experts of all kinds, from teachers to activists and psychiatrists, should have more of a say in AI design and what values it ought to bring to life. In the education sector alone, radical strides have been made in recent decades in changing how we teach young people by engaging with justice and equality in the classroom. Why can't the teachers pioneering these pedagogical revolutions play a part in designing the way that machines 'learn'? Curators and historians are also in a good position to direct how AI systems work with historical sensitivities, psychologists and psychotherapists should lead how AI deals with human subjects and educators. Involving people from all walks of life in AI's creation would be an excellent way of increasing its competence. It's high time more of us were able to step in.

Pro-justice and DIY AI

South Asian feminists, film-makers and journalists Priya Goswami and Aarefa Johari decided to do just this by developing a community-based AI tool with justice at its heart.[8] Their AI-powered Mumkin app helps people who have experienced female genital cutting (FGC) start difficult and sensitive conversations about the issue with their families. Neither are data scientists – Priya is a documentary film-maker and Aarefa is a journalist – but both have many years of engagement with the issue. This meant that they weren't creating an AI tool just for the sake of it, but directly addressing the needs of a specific group of people. The app is grounded in feminist and anti-racist ideas and extensive personal and research experience. Because of this, it ticks all the boxes for a truly useful and positive tool: it serves an urgent existing social need, it makes privacy non-negotiable and it's completely non-judgemental. It is not, for example, the same as people without autism wanting to cure autism using AI, as computer scientist and entrepreneur Rana el Kaliouby tried to do with her 'emotion AI' company Affectiva. These are people with personal knowledge of an issue working *with* and being led by relevant communities.

In the same vein, the Kuini AI Chatbot, commissioned by Health New Zealand/Te Whatu Ora, aims to help Māori women (*wāhine*) stop smoking. It's localised, specific and targeted. It's also built by a company called Indigenous Design & Innovation Aotearoa that is deeply intertwined with the target user group.[9] The Indigenous AI group, based in Hawaii, have created Hawaiian descriptors for captured images to help people learn the language, which has been in decline since 1896, when it was banned from being spoken in schools as foreign residents overthrew the country with the eventual aim of annexing the land to the US. UNESCO now classifies the Hawaiian language as critically endangered. Indigenous AI also made a polylingual Indigenous-language image recognition app with geolocation functionalities, which allows the user to take a photo of an object and learn the word for it in the dialect of the region they are in. The company sees AI's negative effects as linked to Big Tech's desire to make AI products as scalable as possible, and so they design 'local' systems that respond to specific community needs.

The makers of these technologies realise that good technology may not be of universal use, which is why they don't see a global roll-out or a massive user base as a marker of success. Their priority is their users, who will be most affected if the technology is badly designed, but also have the most to gain if it's made well. Unlike many AI systems on the market today, these tools were created by people who have a great deal of knowledge about, experience in and empathy for the subject matter they are addressing with their app. In an ideal world, all AI companies would only create products that respond to a pressing social need (rather than create a need) and employ engineers and product managers who understand that requirement well.

Fortunately, radical thinkers like Goswami and Johari are finding ways of pursuing major shifts in how we build AI. These efforts may be small-scale, but with the right support they can be mighty. What I like most about their tools is that they don't try to create a blueprint for a digital utopia disconnected from reality. Instead, these apps show that utopia is a process – it's the everyday efforts we make in the name of a better world, as I pointed out in Chapter 1. That's why by focusing on improving the process of making technology, and having faith in a more just AI, the HEAT tool I helped create is a cornerstone of utopianism. It shows that if every step of making technology is oriented towards justice, the rest will follow. One important key feature of a pro-justice approach to building AI is ensuring that different relevant communities are meaningfully included in the design process. Another is having an 'exit door' that gives designers of technology the opportunity to change their mind about an AI project. Both strategies make the pro-justice approach *a way of working*, and not a quick fix to the hardware or software. There's no such thing as good technology if it's made unethically.

It's difficult to trust the process when you don't have any insight into it, as is the case when we buy an AI product from a large corporation. But what if AI wasn't built by Big Tech but by local communities, or even within your own home? Would you trust it then? Would it be more likely to solve the issues that matter to you? Would it be more useful in your daily life? This kind of thought experiment often focuses people's minds on what it really is about AI that freaks them out. I generally find that their concerns shift from the AI itself to the corporations that make them. One of the questions I ask young people when I teach is, 'If you and some friends were to build your own AI tool, would you not trust it more?' The first step to DIY AI is establishing your beliefs and priorities, so I get them to write down their family values and explore how they differ from those that underlie Big Tech's incentive structure. 'My family wouldn't try to make money off me,' students say, or, 'My family would genuinely care about my privacy.' This is the premise of Community AI, a youth-driven nonprofit that hosts annual summer camps where kids design their own AI systems. One of my favourite speculative AI tools to come out of the camp is 'E-basura' by Filipina high-school student Sophia Dominique Manalang.[10] It's an Automated Waste Segregator that responds to the Philippines' increasing waste problem with a budget-friendly trash can that automatically segregates and shreds wastes.

When I participated in a panel discussion at the Southbank Centre in 2022 on the topic 'Is AI an Existential Threat to Humanity?', Stuart Russell told the audience that no one could imagine a better world with AI.[11] This is totally untrue:

there are innumerable ways in which people are out there right now building positive AI-enabled worlds and pro-justice ways of working – take the self-managed servers mentioned in the Introduction that are run by community groups globally. Already, a Latin American self-managed server organisation called Yanapak offers its own cloud services, AI agents and AI co-working tools; GNU Ethertics supports a free operating system for radio stations in Latin America; and the Tor Project develops and maintains free and open-source software nonprofit in the name of privacy and enhanced human rights. Don't let pessimist propaganda fool you. We just need investment. The digital democracy platform Pol.is that Audrey Tang co-designed in Taiwan has grown into other pro-social tools since it was used during the Sunflower Movement of 2014. One of these, 'vTaiwan', is a digital democracy platform where citizens can participate in policy discussions and give their feedback on proposed regulations. It's designed not only to help politicians make better decisions informed by what the people want, but to give them agency in being able to affect what happens in their country. One of vTaiwan's successes was shaping Uber's entry into Taiwan in 2013. A shouting match had broken out between those fiercely opposed to Uber (including traditional taxi drivers) and those who called for market freedom (Uber drivers and passengers hoping for cheaper and more convenient options). The result was that Uber now operates in Taiwan but within a strict legal framework co-designed by citizens, which addresses concerns about competition and safety. What is utopian about this in my view is not just that a consensus was reached, nor that citizens have more trust in the government and in their laws, but that it 'enhanced the civic muscle', as Tang puts it, empowering users to do things other than vote and complain.[12]

Diversity 2.0

In 2022, I asked an AI engineer at a tech multinational whether his team was diverse. Yes, he said. We have one person from Ireland, one from Portugal … My colleague and I sighed. The term 'diversity' was evidently not meaningful to these tech workers. They needed real-world examples of why having women and people of colour in teams is not just a moral responsibility but a way to avoid building harmful technologies – or damaging the company's reputation. At this same company, another AI engineer told me that the pendulum of diversity had 'swung too far in the wrong direction'. I looked at the company's statistics: white men between thirty and sixty years old were safely over-represented. Something is going wrong here: people are feeling outdated and unwanted when, statistically speaking, their jobs are not under threat and they're still firmly in the majority. I don't think he disliked women or people of colour, otherwise I cannot see why he would have voiced this to me and my colleague as part of a project called 'Gender and Technology'. The only sense I can make of such a comment was that he didn't understand what his value was in an (aspiring) diverse institution. Unless you have skin in the game, getting on board with a fairer world can be an uphill battle.

The other issue, of course, is that because companies are invested in paying lip service to diversity, the noise around diversity measures is far louder than the activity itself. Indeed, HR told me that, despite their best efforts, they were still struggling to increase the diversity of their workforce. This is why there is often backlash to diversity measures – they're perceived to be doing more, or even over-reaching, despite the evidence showing they're not doing enough. Certainly, the value of diversity had not been communicated to the man I was interviewing, nor what true diversity would actually entail: meeting employees' childcare needs, tackling pay and promotion inequalities, ensuring consumers are represented by the workforce, changing employee perceptions around what makes a proficient or creative AI engineer, and allowing unions and support groups to form in organisations. Instead, the message he seemed to have received was that diversity was coming for his job. Patriarchy isn't just to do with men, it's about power. You need only look as far as the 42 per cent of women who voted for Trump in the 2024 US elections.

Here's the thing about diversity anxiety: it's an exaggerated sense of fear. Often the idea of equality is used to justify why there should not be more diversity. I've heard white actors tell me that the situation is not equal any more because they can't get jobs now that Black actors are preferred for roles. Evidence of why this is far from the truth is just a click away on the IMDB cast lists for the latest movies. When I parroted back the statistics for Black vs white working actors, one white actor told me that the casting director had said, 'We're looking for someone Black for this one.' When a Black actor is rejected for a role, no one explicitly tells them, 'We're looking for a white actor for this part.' But this is the standard, despite it not always being said aloud. It also isn't deemed unfair not to cast Black actors for roles set in historically white contexts, even though white actors have been hideously and unconvincingly blackfaced for years to play people of all races. If audiences can suspend disbelief for all the white actors who played Black characters, then contemporary claims that 'historical accuracy' requires a white cast are excuses for racially selective casting. This, coupled with the relative scarcity of scripts with non-white parts and non-white historical stories, means that there are just less parts going for Black and Asian actors. Regardless, it's still unhelpful to tell a white person that a person of colour got the job on account of their being a person of colour. It makes people resent diversity. It doesn't achieve anything. It creates barriers to participating in diversity measures. When you're told your job is on the line, only the best Samaritan would still commit to the cause. Diversity is not about pointing fingers at racists, it's about building empathy and recognising the facts beyond tabloid fearmongering.

When I was working with a large technology multinational, I saw first-hand how diversity makes AI more ethical. One AI engineer told me how she had flagged to her team that the company's household monitoring products (known as IoT or Internet of Things devices) could be used for intimate partner violence. Nobody in her team had imagined that this would be a problem, but because she had tragically experienced it herself, she knew that the IoT tools were likely being used by abusers to track and monitor the movements of their partners and prevent them from leaving their homes. Subsequently the company built controls and safeguards into their commercial offerings to minimise the risk of this happening. Evidence shows that abuse via IoT is, catastrophically, rife, but the issue might never have been raised without a woman on the team. This is why going to schools and encouraging young people (especially women and those from lower-income backgrounds) to go into AI-related work is an important part of my job, whether in AI design, tech law, marketing or linguistics. We need people in AI roles with personal experiences of inequality as they're more likely to predict effects on marginalised communities. And if anyone's going to get an inflated AI-engineering salary, why shouldn't it be them?

For diverse teams to emerge, company culture has to change. The person who challenged the use of IoT devices was one of only a few women in her engineering team, and girls were even less well represented when she studied computer science at a prestigious Russell Group university. It's not a nice feeling to stand out for something you can't change. Standing out also means your company is likely to be unsympathetic to your needs, whether childcare-, disability- or schedule-related. There's been much talk about the 'pipeline problem' in recent years, or quests to 'find women' at school or university level to go into STEM professions. But these conversations often disguise the real problem of transforming company workplaces into environments where women, people of colour and LGBTQ+ people want to work, where they are valued and their needs are met. This too is AI ethics. Yes, childcare is an AI ethics concern. And unless we resolve the lack of diversity across the field, AI will continue to be rife with problems. These issues are contentious, expensive and long overdue for resolution. They've been sidelined as 'irrelevant' to business, just as they're cast aside in AI ethics conversations. We need better social innovation in tech, spearheaded by the people whose lives are most affected by bad, unaccommodating design. I am often told by employees of Apple and other Big Tech companies that they struggle with retaining women. I can only imagine that the issues above give an indication of why. But I can also see that if companies championed – as we saw in the first half of this chapter – meaningful innovation that involved citizens and helped them flex that civic muscle, they might retain more staff whose sense of fulfilment comes from doing something beneficial in collaboration with citizens, communities and experts.

9

Nerds, Arise: Data Scientists Behaving Badly

In 2023, I received an invitation to a workshop hosted by Cambridge researchers titled 'Should Scientists Working on Environmental Issues Be Activists?' I admit I was rather stunned that this was even a question. Did many scientists still feel uncomfortable at the idea of being labelled an activist? Were they worried that it might undermine their professional status? Were historical associations between neutrality and science preventing researchers from advocating for the planet? Activist has come to mean, in certain circles, annoyance. Defiler of buildings. Barricader of public spaces. A civil disobedient.

But doing activist work isn't about storming the Bastille. It's about insisting that a story is told truthfully and that solutions are found to pressing problems. Belgian philosopher Isabelle Stengers says that activism is about connecting with people and raising their awareness of an issue.[1] In the UK, you can write to a local politician and implore them to act in the community, or take part in a protest to make the problem unignorable to the government. Stengers shifts the emphasis from acts of protest to the purpose of activism: getting people to care, identifying the incentives that make them sit up and do something. In France, where transport union members designed a moving barbecue that rolled down tram tracks in the street, grilling sausages as it went, activism is a fervent (and relentless) part of socialist life. In Britain, meanwhile, the fear of being labelled an activist is apparently enough to stop environmental scientists from speaking out about the climate crisis beyond their labs. This is a needless waste of expert voices. Science has never been without its causes and the narratives that champion them. Every data point can tell a story: it's simply a question of which story you want to tell.

What does it take, then, for a scientist to become an activist? As we've seen from watching AI engineers speak out against bad technology, annoyed scientists become fervent activists when they are unable to do their work properly. In June 2024 a group of current and former OpenAI employees went public with claims that OpenAI had a reckless culture and was not doing enough to ensure its models were safe.[2] This included the aforementioned incident in 2022, when Microsoft used India as a below-the-radar test bed for an early version of Bing powered by what at the time was an unreleased version of OpenAI's GPT-4 model.[3] The test was run without approval from a joint OpenAI and Microsoft Deployment Safety Board. Microsoft initially denied this, only to admit it was true when the incident was made public. Since then, OpenAI employees have been quitting in droves. Daniel Kokotajlo's X status now reads: 'Was a philosophy PhD student, left to work at AI Impacts, then Center on Long-Term Risk, then OpenAI. Quit OpenAI due to losing confidence that it would behave responsibly around the time of AGI.'[4] Eleven other ex-OpenAI employees who have walked out on the organisation wrote an open letter titled 'A Right to Warn about Advanced Artificial Intelligence' in June 2024. At one point it seemed as if there was a new open letter about AI every week. If OpenAI's former staff are heading to social media to voice their opinions, it's because they feel their requests are falling on deaf ears. Indeed, the letter attests to how OpenAI, once a proponent of open source, has become an intellectual monoculture enforced by aggressive disciplinary protocols. The authors' request is simple: that the company not behave like an authoritarian regime and instead 'support a culture of open criticism'; 'facilitate a verifiably anonymous process for current and former employees to raise risk-related concerns to the company's board'; and 'not retaliate against current and former employees who publicly share risk-related confidential information after other processes have failed'.[5] In their desperate bid to gain market share and race towards AGI, OpenAI has been bulldozing through internal concerns. And so engineers have hung up their hats, banded together and spoken out.

I met the founder of Apple's labour union, AppleTogether, in January 2024.[6] With her semi-rimmed rectangular glasses and easy polite smile, Janneke Parrish is the person you seek out at the beach to look after your bag while you go for a swim. Parrish listens. She nods. She takes notes and smiles encouragingly. She treats others with dignity and so comes across as dignified. From 2015 she was one of many $15/hour Apple Maps contractors dealing with job uncertainty and burnout. She soon became aware that there was a mismatch between the company's stated values and what it was doing in practice. In 2021, Apple hired advertising manager Antonio García Martínez, whose book on Silicon Valley culture argued that 'Most women in the Bay Area are soft and weak' and 'come the epidemic plague or foreign invasion, they'd become precisely the sort of useless baggage you'd trade for a box of shotgun shells or a jerry can of diesel'. Over 2000 Apple employees signed a petition urging his dismissal.[7] Parrish clubbed together with colleagues to write an open letter to the company asking it to look into why García Martínez's published misogyny was ignored by the hiring panel, and insisting that people with these views not be 'involved in hiring, interviewing, or performance decisions during their tenures at Apple'.[8] His ultimate dismissal from Apple was hugely encouraging to workers, Parrish says, because its company culture did not take internal criticism especially well:

We [were] encouraged … to keep to ourselves and to not share what we're working on … [we had] a culture of silence that's partly cultivated by the company. It has notoriously strict NDAs that prevent workers from sharing anything really related to their work with the outside world. It's there to cultivate a surprise and delight culture for the customer so that when Apple announces something, the customer is surprised and delighted by it. But the consequence of that culture is that workers don't communicate internally to them with each other.[9]

Parrish was, predictably, fired from Apple for her role in the union, but she continues to do great work at AppleTogether, which provides support and legal counsel for Apple workers of all kinds, including those on Temporary Vendoring Contracts across the globe. 'The thing that I've really learned from all this,' she told me, 'is the power of a single voice to change the course of hundreds of workers' careers, and to change the course of a massive company. As much as I think Apple wouldn't want to admit it, AppleTogether has had an impact on how Apple does business, and more importantly, how workers are treated within it.'[10] Tech labour unions are providing new, powerful models for labour organising that can help us all in what will be an increasingly tense battle with AI companies for dignity, privacy and compensation.

At some point or other, we will all come up against a greater power which we know is doing something bad, be it a line manager, an elder or an entire institution. Whether you can withstand it and fight your cause depends on your tolerance for conflict, ability to compartmentalise, bloody-mindedness, and how good you are at switching off at night. Journalist Carole Cadwalladr, who broke the Cambridge Analytica scandal, is sharp, resilient and tough. Facebook whistleblower Frances Haugen, I am told by those who have worked with her, is another force to be reckoned with. These are often the personalities that can withstand Big Tech's bullying tactics. Cadwalladr pioneered public access to information on what she termed 'the fake news ecosystem',[11] and in 2018 she made public the story of how the Republican Party and the Leave campaign used social media (via private intelligence 'consultants' Cambridge Analytica) to sway enormous swathes of the US and UK's electorates in 2020 and 2016.[12] And that's when the hate mail began: death threats, misogynist trolling, lawsuits. More than once Cadwalladr received human excrement in the mail. Being a (female) investigative journalist is a risky business in twenty-first-century democracies, where they are tried like spies by angry politicians and public institutions can reject freedom of information requests, as is the case in the UK.

Journalists who report well on AI issues are crucial, but so are the tech whistleblowers who can feed them information. Carole was able to progress with the story because of data scientist and whistleblower Chris Wylie, who had an insider view of what Cambridge Analytica was doing. Her testimony shows how serendipitous their meeting was: they were only connected after Carole had spoken to dozens of employees who were unwilling to go on record. Even Wylie needed twelve months to be in a position to speak publicly. Their collaboration should not be reassuring. It's mildly terrifying that we are reliant on journalists building whistleblowers' confidence when they suspect bad business is afoot. Breaking a big story like this shouldn't rely on disobedient data scientists with a knack for explaining computer science in a layperson's terms. But right now that's what's happening, meaning that holding AI companies to account is like getting 'nine planets to align', as Cambridge mathematician Maurice Chiodo puts it.[13] It took a combination of Chris's concern that what CA was doing with data was dodgy and Carole's research into CA's contracts with the Pentagon and knowledge of CA Vice-President Steve Bannon's work as Trump's strategist to blow the story.

When we spoke, Maurice lamented that the difficulty of orchestrating an exposé is the reason why companies doing unethical things with AI often get away with it. It usually requires a data scientist with a bad feeling about what's going on, he said, because scientists are rarely given any ethical training. They don't have the toolkit, the incentives or the institutional support always to consider the moral consequences of their work. Maurice has spent years campaigning for mathematicians and engineers to take ethics seriously, and in the spirit of classic academic bickering he subsequently became unpopular with Cambridge's Mathematics Faculty and eventually jumped ship to the Centre for Existential Risk, where he researches possible extinction-level threats posed by present or future technology. The Mathematics department also laid off – without informing him – a brilliant lecturer called Piers Bursill-Hall because he was teaching the history and ethics of mathematics and the department saw it as a threat to its discipline. For a while students protested on behalf of their much-loved teacher, and Bursill-Hall gave underground lectures.[14] Now he has all but disappeared from the profession – a great shame given that far less sympathetic Cambridge dons still linger at colleges until they can no longer shuffle in for a free lunch. Even today I'll regularly sit next to people at college meals who say Bursill-Hall was a poor mathematician, or that Maurice's PhD in string theory isn't a qualification for the ethics of mathematics. It's clear they don't think that learning about the ethics or history of mathematics is relevant.

A dose of business ethics might be more palatable to mathematicians seeking to enter the corporate world, and can still get them thinking about how to contextualise their work within broader questions about how algorithmic and statistical tools exacerbate the problems people face in society more generally.

They could also explore what their options are if they feel the need to speak up against a culture of intimidation at work, and how this could affect you as an applied mathematician or computer scientist at a tech company. If you want to properly train students for the future, preparing them for these eventualities in higher education is just as important as fixing lines of code.

I'm an engineer, get me out of here!

It's not easy to increase the amount of ethics education that computer scientists get. Corporate ethics training is often optional, comes late in employees' computer science careers, and requires them to take time out of their work. AI ethics master's courses are now available – we started the world's first at Cambridge – but it's competitive to get in, and they don't come cheap. But as public awareness of AI issues increases, AI engineers will likely demand that their companies provide them with robust ethics training.

Here's why: in spring 2024 I met an engineer who had been working on Google Gemini, an AI image generator. Gemini wanted to avoid accusations of racism and sexism that have been levied at other similar tools like Lensa, Stable Diffusion and Midjourney. These tools exacerbated real-world inequalities and prejudices by depicting Black people as poor and white people as rich (as was the case with Stable Diffusion) and Asian women as naked and white men as astronauts (as did AI Lensa).[15] They were also unable to generate an image of a fat person (that was DALL-E 3).[16] Gemini tried to solve this problem by over-representing women and people of colour in their datasets, which means when some users asked it to create an image of a Pope, they were presented with a woman. As the critiques flooded in – from both the political left and right – my medievalist friends were quick to quip that in the thirteenth century it was rumoured that Pope John VIII had been

Gemini's AI-generated image of a pope

A woodcut illustration of Pope Joan from 1474

a woman (Joan!), reigning for two years between 855 and 857 before her disguise wore off rather suddenly when she, according to the legend, gave birth to her lover's child in the middle of a street parade. As spurious as this rumour may have been, only about 1.6 per cent of human history is recorded, of which 0.5 per cent are women's stories.[17] Countless women have been lost to history, and yet, despite the many examples of unethical AI that critics could address, they spent their time worrying about the gender of a fake pope in a picture.

We can therefore read comments on X about Gemini advancing 'a subversive plot to eradicate history, race and culture' for what they are: disgusting, misogynist, racist and white supremacist. Musk called the images 'racist' against white people and 'anti-civilisational', while weaponising the word 'truth' to say that 'there should be no bias in LLMs and they should all be truth-seeking'. The alt-right flocked to the tweet to note their approval. It's unsurprising – given everything else – that Musk ignores the ongoing, widespread promotion of white people and men disproportionate to their capabilities. Views like these are the living legacy of imperialism. They position white men as the underdogs in a bid for survival against a rising tide of women and people of colour. Globally, a woman is killed every ten minutes by her partner,[18] while anti-Black hate crimes soar across the world. And to think some people believe Google is eradicating white people from history.

Despite how seriously we take them, it's also worth reminding ourselves that the images Gemini generates are not real. Fiction is freedom. And yet we are only happy to absorb artifice into our world if it's 'accurate' – if the colour of a person's skin in a generated portrait is consistent with social rules and expectations. 'Historical inaccuracy' has long been used as an excuse to exclude women and people of colour from all sorts of opportunities, from acting roles and male-only sports to jobs offered and deals made at men's clubs. In

my experience, the people who get most angry about 'historical inaccuracy' have a very poor knowledge of and interest
in history. In the US, only 13 per cent of eighth graders were
considered proficient in history, down from 18 per cent nearly
a decade ago.[19] We're getting AI wrong because prevailing inequalities, social divisions and a lack of investment in education
are vaporising empathy and trust, resulting in an epidemic
of small-mindedness. The defence of history in the case of
Gemini, therefore, is pure white paranoia and bigotry. It's not
historical inaccuracy that is the issue, but the fact that race
and nationality are bound together in such a way as to make a
female pope or a Black king of England look 'wrong'.

The Gemini engineer I met was at a loss. He felt profoundly
disorientated by the whole affair; as an engineer he had never
expected to have to get involved in the politics of what he was
making, let alone deal with so much pushback, and from so
many people with such varied motivations! He asked me for
some guidance: what should he make of all the social com-
mentary around Gemini? How should they fix the tool? I felt
sorry for him. Computer science degrees are doing budding
technologists a great disservice by not exploring the social
impacts of technology in their programmes. If you turn ethics
into a one-week module or a single session, you'll leave students completely unprepared for developing products in the
real world. As the Gemini engineer's testimony shows, while
computer science degree programmes make ethics seem like
a distraction from the core material, the difficulty of trying
to navigate ethical issues unprepared can do a great deal of
damage to your work and personal life. The medievalist who
reminded me about Pope John VIII experienced a similarly
anxiety-inducing surprise irruption of politics. What she had
previously considered to be a relatively apolitical debate at a
conference proved otherwise, when the conversation turned
and she was suddenly caught in verbal crossfire over whether

the Inquisition should be taught in the context of Israel-Pal-estine. She was there to talk about triptychs, but left having to engage with anti-Semitism, race and war. It doesn't matter what your job is, politics is never too far away. This doesn't mean that engineers need to anchor themselves on either side of the debate, just that they should be aware of the social and historical context in which they're working.

Experiences like this will only get more common among AI engineers, who will increasingly demand that their work-places prepare them for potential controversies by exploring how the technologies they develop relate to society at large. In May 2024, engineers from a number of Big Tech firms spoke to CNBC about a cluster of interlinked work-related anxieties.[20] They reported, to nobody's surprise, that their employers had little concern for potential downstream effects of products, be they the exacerbation of the climate crisis or the application of tools for gendered and racialised surveillance. Ultimately, the failure of companies to engage with what their workers are concerned about means that AI engineers who do care about the world leave their jobs and switch out of AI departments. The fact is that the most brilliant and creative engineers, who have foresight and engage with the afterlife of a product, do not want to work at places where the emphasis on quality has been lost to AI hype and market pressure. This leaves the door open for companies that *are* concerned about employee retention and real-world impact to attract both workers and customers who feel the same way.

Leave it to the next generation?

When working with tech companies, I thought I'd have to Trojan-Horse feminist ideas into the workplace. Instead, I've found that most engineers are eager to improve the quality of their work life by giving themselves a sense of direction and purpose. They seek to apply their views about what a fair and good society looks like to the creation of technologies that can facilitate such a world, but aren't sure how to go about it.

I was very encouraged by the engineers who talked to me, unprompted, about the state of the planet and their desire to make things better. One complained that his daughter was disincentivised to pursue maths at school, even though she was good at it. He thought sexism in education might have died out, but his role as a father taught him otherwise. Contact between generations plants seeds for growth and change, says youth AI activist Sneha Revanur, who wrote an essay in my and Kerry McInerney's book *The Good Robot* about the value of intergenerational communication.[21] She said, rather defiantly, that there's 'definitely a reason to be optimistic about how Gen Z will enter the workforce as developers and technologists' – but that's if they are equally encouraged to participate.[22] Concerned parents and mentors in engineering can facilitate access for younger generations who might not represent the demographic of a traditional AI engineer today.

Sneha is optimistic about the future AI workforce. Her rationale is that young people have grown up aware of the perils of living life online, from the addictions and anxieties of social media to the use of AI in their classrooms and job interviews, and so are 'less likely to fall into the trap of believing that it's perfectly objective and neutral'.[23] They also tend to wear their life experiences on their sleeves, and are more motivated to pursue careers they feel align with the causes they believe in.

This is true to some extent, but the generational divide is overstated. At a lecture I once gave to teenagers from all over the world at a London summer school, a blond, male high-school student raised his hand to tell me that recidivism algorithms weren't biased because Black people were more likely than white people to commit crimes. The algorithms in question are used to measure the likelihood of a person in custody reoffending, even though studies found that they disproportionately recommended that young Black males should be denied probation. In a study by ProPublica, Black defendants who did not go on to commit another crime over a two-year period were nearly twice as likely to be misclassified as being at a higher risk of reoffending than their white counterparts (45 per cent vs 23 per cent).[24] Youth activist groups like Encode brought the perils of these systems for young people of colour to the attention of their peers globally. The movement was founded in 2020 by the incredibly impressive fifteen-year-old Sneha Revanur to defeat California's Proposition 25 Bill, which was set to implement recidivism algorithms in the state's justice system. Largely thanks to the work of Sneha and her fellow campaigners, the algorithm was subsequently banned in a number of US states.

Unfortunately, the ambitions of Encode weren't shared by the summer school pupil. When I explained that these tools were inaccurate and made a bad world worse, he must have felt as if I was complaining about the laws of nature ('it's not fair that the world is round'). In the front row, a Black student had her face in her hands while he was speaking. Every time I hear a statement along these lines, it's from a white male who wants to tell their peers the important news that racialised criminality is an evolutionary fact. Real science and investigative research, as we saw all too well during the pandemic, is not persuasive enough for the public any more, no matter their age. Amid all the accusations of an overly sensitive generation of 'snowflakes' – highly misleading – the generational divide continues to be bridged by young people who lack any intuitive interest in the socio-economic conditions within which crime is created in the first place. I'm always surprised by the confidence and simplicity with which a young person can still tell an international cohort what's on their mind, with no apparent concern for the people sitting around them.

That young people can be just as conservative and unempathetic as their elders has been made abundantly clear by the voting behaviour of people under thirty in the last few years. In 2024, a survey found that young men in Germany were twice as likely to support the far right as women;[25] in 2019, young men polled in Poland were 20 per cent more likely to vote for nationalist, populist or far-right parties than women;[26] in South Korea, the right-wing People's Party received 24.9 per cent more support from young men than women;[27] and in the 2024 US elections, young women were 16 per cent less likely to support Trump than their male counterparts.[28] The relationship between age and political persuasion is not so simple here – it's activated by gender. This is just one example of how the indicators of a person's politics are always intersectional, by which I mean that our opinions are shaped by the cumulative effects of gender, age, disability, race and class rather than one of these factors on its own. While we can rely on young people's contributions for reinvigorated radical politics on both sides of the political aisle, less life experience means a lack of nuance. One of the reasons it's extremely important that older people are not excluded from AI debates is because the longer you have lived, the more likely it is that life has taught you that there are more than two sides to every story. Things are not so simple. Unfortunately, though, a 2023 survey by Amrat Kaur and Weiqin Chen found that people over sixty years old were concerned that they had few opportunities to learn about AI, even though 73 per cent of respondents were keen to develop their understanding of the subject.[29]

This is why we need mixed-generation and non-elective AI governance. One way to go is citizens' assemblies or deliberative mini-publics, as political theorist Jude Browne has argued,[30] which are widely seen as offering space for deliberation and representation of people from different walks of life. You need a chance to learn about a topic ahead of time and discuss your perspectives with other participants before you enter into the debate. It's certainly not a perfect process – researchers have pointed out that a lively, varied discussion can be undermined by disparities in how well informed discussants are on a given issue – but experienced planning can avoid some of this. What is most valuable in the mini-public is giving people more information on an issue and from as many different angles as possible.

Making decisions about AI requires lateral thinking; a bunch of people with the same disciplinary background may know a lot about AI, but they do not necessarily have a good view of its impact. We can take inspiration here from Uganda's first deliberative polls in 2014, which were widely seen as a substantial improvement on top-down decision-making processes.[31] Local participants weighed in on how to deal with floods and landslides in the Mount Elgon region, and how to manage the resettlement of people forced to leave their homes. By deliberating with non-self-selecting, representative groups from the local population, district officials realised that the decisions they had previously made missed the mark on multiple fronts. For example, they had assumed people would rather travel further for better-equipped schools and medical centres, but participants were clear that smaller, closer versions were preferable. The polls had the added benefit of improving trust between the population and officials and making everyone more informed, be they citizens without access to statistics on climate and natural disasters or government representatives detached from the reality of raising a family when landslides are tearing through your village. Information distribution is a major plus point for mini-publics, as when the citizens' assembly before the Irish abortion vote in 2018 helped the popular press report sensibly on a polarising issue:[32] the assembly brought forward evidence which the media then reported on, rather than doggedly haranguing the nation with hyperbolic and emotive stories. A better-informed public will demand more than hype and panic from the press.

Tech opinion leaders often claim that the public couldn't

possibly be well informed enough about technology to contribute to AI governance. 'There's no way a non-industry person can understand what is possible. It's just too new, too hard, there's not the expertise,'[33] said former Google CEO Eric Schmidt, in a particularly unhelpful speech asking policymakers to leave AI governance to technologists. Philosopher Jonnie Penn calls prominent tech opinion leaders like Schmidt, who believe they should weigh in on AI governance on behalf of entire populations, 'technocrats posturing as ethicists'.[34] They have too much sway over the debate, particularly now that many also have government roles. As *The Economist* noted in September 2024, 'technocrats will always have their place in well-functioning polities, but it should be in the background'.[35] We need to combat this by increasing democratic participation in AI. By involving citizens in AI debates, we can also raise AI literacy, improve public trust in AI, reduce harms caused by misinformation and disinformation and force AI companies to not mislead consumers.

A few years ago I attended a speed awareness course, and had the jury-esque experience of reflecting on bad driving habits with people from all corners of the UK's driving community, from Uber drivers and gabby students to disinterested businesspeople in suits. The only thing this collection of people had in common was a heavy foot on the accelerator. With AI, it's crucial that we have greater exposure to a variety of facts and mull over them with people we might not like. It's what kids do at school, to a certain extent, and what adults lack later in life when we retreat into our ideological corners. Citizens' assemblies are not just about decision-making, they're about hearing the facts, bridging divides, and learning how to make 'painful, but mutually acceptable compromises', as political scientist Ben Ansell put it in his 2023 Reith Lecture.[36]

There have been attempts to use AI to design democracy, including one paper co-authored with Google DeepMind research scientists. It's always ironic when efforts to protect civil liberties are supported by the companies that are so excellent at undermining them; Robert Epstein of the American Institute for Behavioural Research and Technology claimed that 'in 2015, the outcomes of upward of 25 of the national elections in the world were being determined by Google's search engine'.[37] The paper's authors make it seem as though 'human values' are one homogenous thing, rather than what they are in reality — complex and culturally situated. While AI can offer interesting alternative realities, human values cannot be 'solved' using AI like completing a game of Tetris. I wholeheartedly agree with sociologist Jack Stilgoe when he says that democracy 'is not chess, not a puzzle to be completed or a game to be won'.[38] As with the two boys wearing headphones who valued respect without quite being able to demonstrate it themselves, there's a difference between tech companies parroting universal values like 'respect' and actually making difficult, expensive, empathetic decisions which put it into practice.

It shouldn't be up to tech companies to establish human values on our behalf. That's why, as insecure as you may be about your understanding of AI, you need to believe that because your experience of the world matters, you can also contribute to the conversation. You need to trust your instincts, because non-AI professionals have already made waves to push back against bad and ineffective AI.

10

Trust Your Instincts

Schooled by the teachers

Not knowing how AI works hasn't stopped people from coming forward to denounce bad systems. In fact, domain expertise is as important as being clued up about the technical side of AI. We saw this in the blowback from teachers during what was known in the UK as the 'A-Level algorithm' crisis of 2020. It was one of the more embarrassing moments for Boris Johnson's government, which is really saying something given that it happened in the wake of Brexit. I watched it unfold open-mouthed. At the centre of this fiasco was Gavin Williamson, the UK's polarising Education Secretary from 2019 to 2021. Williamson was gaining a reputation for being a proponent of 'free speech', which for many quickly became a euphemism for 'hateful speech'. In the wake of various COVID-19-related education disasters that prevented school students from being able to sit their exams, Williamson commissioned the UK's exam regulator, Ofqual, to create an algorithm that would predict their grades. After a moment of initial confusion, teachers and students were up in arms because the algorithm was basing its predictions on trends emerging from historical data about student grades in the UK. This amounted to low-income state-school students being assigned worse grades than wealthier private-school students. I had a number of conversations with desperate teachers who were angered by the government deferring to technology instead of trusting their informed judgement.

I remember half-watching, head in hands, when Williamson and his allies argued that the algorithm couldn't be biased;
after all, it was just maths. Oh dear, I thought, here we go again
with the assumption that maths and data science are objective
and neutral. Williamson had been a strong advocate for a resur-
gence of STEM skills and yet was wide of the mark when it
came to understanding how algorithms work. He finally made
a *mea culpa* after repeatedly being shouted at by headteachers
on daytime TV, who may not have had a strong understanding
of the algorithm itself but were well aware that their students
were being misgraded. We can all learn from the confidence
these teachers had in their domain expertise, their dedication
to their profession, and how fearlessly they stuck their necks
out in defence of their students. As with the recruitment AI
technology I described in Chapter 5, where good recruiters
knew that this kind of tool couldn't debias hiring as it claimed,
teachers are best placed to know which systems align with best
practice for marking and grading. If AI is being used in your
sector, you can assess whether it does what it says on the tin by
drawing on the knowledge you've earned through doing your
nine-to-five, day in and day out. Rather than worry about what
we don't know, we should have confidence in what we do – and
use it to campaign for and influence the design of better AI.

At the beginning of this book, I said that lots of the discussion points right now about AI (for example, 'Will it kill
us?') leave us none the wiser and more than a little deflated.
Questions like this are also not very productive, leading to
tense conversations which exclude the public voice and overlook the major causes of existential risks. Instead, I want to
bring AI ethics to people in a way that enables them to go out
into the world and make a difference. We can all contribute to
getting AI right starting from what we know, whether that's
in recruitment, sustainability, business or diversity and inclusion. Moving from a focus on death to how we can live a good

life with AI also means investigating what it would mean to sustain and heal each other in a technological world. This isn't just semantics; shifting the focus of ethics means working out how to live well, not kill well. Taking this approach also gives ethics a wider reach, so that rather than homing in on AI and obscuring broader contextual issues, we can explore the social and geopolitical conditions that affect our experience of it. You don't have to be an AI ethicist to do this – your knowledge of the labour force, the environment, society and culture, and your experience of being subjected to AI in any context are important contributions to shaping conversations about what makes AI good.

Being sensible

The AI industry doesn't just require technological expertise, it also needs people who are sensible and have life experience. What impressed me about Ammagamma, the AI company I collaborated with to create the HEAT AI compliance tool, was their common-sense approach to rejecting potential clients who asked them to build AI for the wrong reasons. One company wanted to use AI to make gambling more addictive. Another aimed to use it to make workforce evaluations more neutral. The third requested a tool that would automate employee feedback, even though one of its company values was taking the time to communicate feedback in person to colleagues. Because Ammagamma's mission was to create socially beneficial AI tools, it was able to think twice about these offers and either say no or suggest a different approach.

As mentioned in Chapter 8, AI companies should establish an 'exit door' through which to escape potentially disastrous AI development suggestions. I get this term from Priya Goswami, who believes that both consumers and workers at AI companies need to back out of having to create or use a technology that doesn't sit right with them. Really this means the space to think a tool through, which is effectively the antithesis of Silicon Valley's 'move-fast-and-break-things' mantra. An exit door isn't just the option to opt out entirely, but to pivot the project if the application of AI isn't appropriate. This is what Ammagamma did on occasion. It's an example of positive AI development by a company that has grappled with real, tangible ethical dilemmas and come out smiling, showing that ethical AI development is readily doable, and that companies can make better choices while still turning a profit. Here are three instances where Ammagamma ditched or pivoted directions when commissioned to build AI tools, and where their clients' requests didn't sound sensible.

Gambling against AI

What would you do if you were commissioned to create a recommendation engine for online scratchcards? For Ammagamma it was a no-brainer: facilitating access to online scratchcards often means exploiting a person's weakness – gambling. The World Health Organization estimates that 5.5 per cent of women and a whopping 11.9 per cent of men globally experience problems like the breakdown of their relationships, violence, financial distress and even engage in criminal behaviour because of gambling addictions.[1] According to a Swedish study, people who suffer from gambling disorders are fifteen times more likely to commit suicide than the general population. Ammagamma decided that using AI to make gambling products more popular was against its principle of creating technologies that help people make wiser decisions.[2] Because Ammagamma had already had plenty of internal conversations about what it stood for as a company, and a manifesto that outlined its values and principles without wish-wash, it wasn't difficult to politely decline the job offer. 'We decided that the product didn't align with our values,'[3] they said, and hopped through the exit door they had built for themselves.

From corporate surveillance to corporate self-surveillance

It's very common now for HR to use AI tools to help analyse and assess a workforce. The problem isn't the analytics per se, but when tools are predicting the performance of individuals in the future. This can't be done in a prejudice-free way, because AI models have to be trained on company data and therefore incorporate the biases that said enterprise has amassed over time. To create a good product which didn't do this, the client would have needed to be very intentional about what it aimed to achieve and avoid using AI to predict workers' value based on past performance. As is often the case, the company that proposed the project didn't do any of this; it simply hoped that sticking AI on to workforce analytics might solve its problems. Ammagamma hit the pause button. Hang on a second, they said, why don't we try a different tack. AI is great at highlighting the prejudices inherent in workforce assessments, so let's create a tool that can help HR understand and analyse themselves. In other words, they used AI to get HR better acquainted with their own biases. The tool also gave HR insight into whether employee satisfaction scores corresponded with payroll schemes and other improvements, to gain a clearer picture of why their workforce was happy or dissatisfied and how they could make improvements.

On another occasion, Ammagamma was asked to make an AI-powered churn analysis tool that would predict whether an employee would be successful in the company or not. Instead they created a system that showed the problems in how the company was assessing and predicting a worker's performance. This AI tool helped the company understand itself better, and was so successful that it was proposed to many other companies too.

Well done, your workforce are now robots

We often struggle to write feedback for each other at work. It's hard. No wonder HR are increasingly commissioning generative AI platforms that can automate employee feedback. The idea is that employees just write one or two keywords in a prompt and select whether the feedback should be negative, neutral or positive. Ammagamma was asked to make one such system but decided against it for two reasons. First, it would mean using an algorithm to substitute human-to-human feedback, which would be silly because the value of telling your colleague what you think of them is to make work life more personable, not more robotic and detached. Second, automating this process suggests that the feedback process is too lengthy, and that it would be better for employees to save their time for other things. But this contradicts any indication that the company values its employees' feedback. It's a classic example of AI doing something that would actually be antithetical to the company's values. Ammagamma decided, therefore, that this kind of AI system didn't even align with their client's mission, let alone with their own. Instead they suggested that AI be used to do a 'value spellcheck' on a worker's feedback before they submitted it. The system could suggest improvements based on best practice, including constructive examples of a colleague's positive behaviours, specific examples of less favourable actions, while avoiding attacks on their personality. I especially like this pivot because Ammagamma ended up building a socially beneficial AI system that satisfied the brief: improving employee feedback.

Ammagamma are doing great work saving us from ourselves, and they're not alone. The companies that approach my team at Cambridge for help do care: key figures in an organisation are genuinely interested and committed to doing something good for the world, their customers are asking for AI that is 'actually ethical', or their staff have been allotted company resources to improve their commitment to ethical AI. I don't expect Google will come knocking any time soon, but the fact that so many companies are actively seeking to improve their practices is still a very positive sign. My best wishes and utmost gratitude go to civil society groups like Amnesty Tech and AccessNow who attempt to counter Big Tech's lobbyists in Brussels, tech unions who hold Big Tech accountable from within, whistleblowers, lawyers and journalists who do what they can. My ambition is to help the many companies and AI engineers that contact us all the time at Cambridge make products that shift power towards those who are most impacted by the negative effects of AI. By working for, buying from, and following the path of companies whose desire to innovate is matched by an equivalent appetite for justice, we can make good headway towards ethical AI.

Conclusion

After many years spent hanging out with engineers, observing the 'phallic imagery of missile systems', sociologist Sally Hacker commented that 'engineering, the epitome of cool rationality, is shot through with pleasure and excitement. It is as though an intricately controlled erotic expression finds its most creative outlet today in the design of technology.'[1] The AI industry is bursting with similarly libidinous desires to shape the future. Designing technology is as emotional and as contextual as writing a book, and no less of a storytelling practice. It creates and shapes worlds. When she wrote these lines in 1989, Hacker wasn't criticising the erotic energy at the heart of tech development. Instead, she was pointing out that the tech industry was started and directed by men whose fascination with machines was interlaced with a desire for dominance and control. When we encounter stories about AIs that exceed (and are measured against) human intelligence, geniuses engineering sexbots in basement labs, or mammoth robots called up to fight sea monsters, we're being asked to indulge the fantasies of these men. This is why we might profitably learn to doubt our dreams of progress as much as our fear of disaster.

The desires of the few are dictating market forces, which in turn direct the technologies we build and invest in. If you feel uneasy about AI, that doesn't make you a Luddite – it's just that you're sensing that the purpose of an AI product isn't aligned with your own desires and needs. You might have thought, 'I don't see the point in this tool,' or 'When would I ever use that,' or 'I can't access it.' This is a sign that these tools aren't useful to you or engaged with your needs. Democratising the course of AI production is crucial if we want a future with technology that's not contributing to domination, surveillance and control. There's a stark divide between those who are thrilled by and profiting from AI tools and those who find them irrelevant, don't have a device with enough power to run them, or can't access them in their language. It shouldn't just be privileged people who can enjoy and be enchanted by new technologies. It's not the end of the world if a company you don't like or trust makes something you enjoy using, so long as you're not naive about it. These tools are not magic, and they come at a cost, which is why such a wide array of contradictions, indigestions and headaches are at the heart of what it means to live an intimate life with AI.[2] How we manage them while prioritising good ways of living is our challenge. This means we realise that they're not 'just tools', but things which shape the social fabric – and ourselves. They change us.

We need a different set of aspirations to orient our creation of AI. Strachey paved the way by opting for ironic self-expression when using computers to transform the Romantics' anaemic, self-indulgent love letters into odd ones that contort heterosexual norms. Ammagamma showed how its desire to make genuinely useful tools has led it to design technologies that help companies acquaint themselves with their flaws, so that their improved self-understanding translates into a happier and more performant workforce. Ammagamma was able to do this because it is not held hostage by the myths we've uncovered in this book. Humanity was never distinct from technology, and as much as we desire to break away from the primordial soup of life's origins, we have no business attempting to cordon ourselves off from the creatures and conditions that we depend on for survival. Immortality is a fool's game, as is human perfectionism. It's merely another way of creating deeper fissures in society. We first need to dismiss the old, worn-out imagery we use as mascots for this silly, undesirable future, like VMan – the poster boy for perfection. When we turn to contemporary evolutionary biology to question Neo-Darwinist and orthogenetic views of human evolution we uncover a far freer – and more exciting – vision of what progress could look like. By emphasising the role of co-operation in evolution, cellular and otherwise, we can break away from the binary options of a transhumanist utopia or apocalypse. If we keep telling ourselves that the dawn of AI will be a messianic, salvational second coming, we'll never escape our apocalypse fetish. We risk buying into pursuits of intelligence that slide easily into eugenics, and appalling claims that the stagnation of so-called 'human progress' is more of a problem than genocide.

It's time to depart from the Triangle of Doom: existential risk that pays no heed to inequality, effective altruists who claim to know the plight of others better than recipients of aid understand their own predicament, and utilitarianism that makes death the cornerstone of AI ethics. The fact is, we cannot calculate ourselves out of all problems, as attractive an impulse as that may be. Breaking away from the causes of poverty means dealing with inequality, corruption, colonialism, the climate crisis. We cannot herald a new era just by building smarter technology. We don't need to eat this kind of naive utopianism out of the hands of technocrats. Nor do we have to buy into their panic: emergency is not always a helpful mode of action, encouraging totalitarian tendencies towards top-down and technocratic decision-making and alienating the rest of us from the conversation. AI ethics shouldn't be cornered into debates about potential annihilation or discussions at the extremes of possibility – singularity or extinction. We cannot trust the companies who claim to be both the poison and the antidote and expect us to drink their Kool-Aid.

We will also never have – and don't need – flawless observational systems that submit the universe to the mighty arm of an LLM. Attempting to exercise control over chaos and turn nature into order is what happens when engineering's desire to fix and solve meets centuries-long traditions of capitalist governance. Control via rules is what AI does, but it's also what limits it because, like any organised system, it has to abide by the rules it conforms to. Because self-driving cars learn to stop at red lights, obey speed limits or yield to pedestrians, they struggle to know when and how they should break rules to prevent accidents. Equally, an AI recruitment tool won't know what to do with anyone who doesn't fit the patterns or the data that it has been given, has a name the system hasn't encountered before, was educated at a non-traditional institution, or had a career gap. Such candidates are not really outliers, for the ideal candidate is untouchable, impossible, a fantasy of the system. When a person is identified as an anomaly by an AI system, it should not be showing them up as a problem (or making them invisible). Instead, the meaning that we should infer is that the AI system itself and its broader real-world context need improvement. AI's constraints and limitations can be powerful allies when building an ethical future. Rather than erasing uncertainty and projecting order on the world, ethical AI systems can help us dig deeper into the variability and ambivalence of life. We need to be making use of the doubt that AI calculates – and covers up – to help us understand the world better, rather than confirm our prejudices and expectations. Innovation can just as much move us backwards as forwards.

As technologies evolve, so do we. This doesn't mean we're not distinguishable from the tools we use: only that there is no future in which we will become more-than-human, because we already are and always have been infused with technology. Even at the cellular level, humans use other species as tools:

we harness gut microbiota to digest food, and the mitochondria in our cells – which were once free-roaming bacteria – to convert food to energy. Technology is as 'artificial' as any other abiotic (non-living) component of life: the air we breathe, the light from the sun, the wind and humidity. It has always been part of our ecosystem, shaping both us and the environment. Like living organisms, technology evolves unpredictably. As cultural critic Derek Woods puts it, technology 'feeds back to alter the subjects who wield it'.[3] AI gets its cognitive power from humans – biological organisms provide labour and data – which creates a continuity between biological and computational media. While organisms can't be reduced to algorithms – we are so much more than a set of instructions – algorithms do evolve with organisms.

Cognition – and perhaps even consciousness – is not an on/off switch, but a spectrum of possibility. If AI wasn't modelled on human intelligence but on forests, then instead of generative AI systems like ChatGPT which present as a single entity providing one-to-one conversations, AI of the future could represent a group or a collective. Finally, if AI was built in collaboration with the people it's being designed to imitate, from personal assistants to artists, we might have products that genuinely enhance the work we do rather than atrophy our creativity, stall our job prospects and steal tacit knowledge imparted from a worker to a machine.

The people who have the most responsibility right now for AI have limited expertise beyond tech, and are mostly in STEM subjects like computer and cognitive science. Conversations about AI are driven by the ideas and knowledge from these areas, which means that unless you're an expert in those disciplines you might feel entirely estranged from their centre of gravity. The rest of us are encouraged to give up on AI before we've even begun to understand the problem. This message is itself as undemocratic as AI can be. We're already participating in AI development by interacting with AI products. But this isn't enough. AI cannot be a public good until experiments are informed by public opinion. This is why we must jump at the myriad opportunities we have to take responsibility for our future with AI rather than resigning ourselves to Big Tech's iron fist. Find your 'way in': whether it's getting involved in the roll-out – or prevention – of different AI tools at work or in public spaces, knowing how to recognise AI-generated disinformation, or taking responsibility for the fictions you create and buy into about what AI should look like in the future. Teachers, parents, artists, youth activists, journalists and trade unions are already showing us that getting AI right shouldn't be left to the 'experts'.

Acknowledgements

This book began in the more humble form of a slide deck that I have presented in various iterations over the last few years, to schools and companies alike. Its aim was to cut through some of the prevailing apocalypticism and take both a radical and realistic angle on what it takes to get AI right, right now.

I first want to thank all the people who reached out to me in person and online, expressing how these talks unlocked new ideas and motivations, and who made this book feel worth writing. Huge thanks to my agent Stuart Cooper, who found me on *Moral Maze*, and Ben, a bright history graduate invested in how technology affects us, who knew where the book needed livening up, and who I hope would have liked its current form.

To my editor at Profile Books, Jon Petre, for his extensive comments and re-readings, as well as Emily Frisella, Linden Lawson and Rachel Wright, whose astute comments and proofreads have made this a much more elegant read. Thanks to publicist Kate McQuaid for her enthusiasm and faith in this project, as well as Laina Deene in marketing, audio editor Audrey Kerr, indexer Hilary Bird, and cover designer Steve Coventry-Panton.

The book was generously supported by Stiftung Mercator, a non-profit foundation working in service of solidarity, peace and climate neutrality. I am grateful to Mercator's David Alders and Carla Hustedt, whose commitment to the societal impact of AI has allowed the ideas and projects in this book to take shape in the world.

A few other thank-yous: to my colleagues at LCFI Cambridge, who pioneer the best work (in my unbiased opinion) in AI ethics; to my family (Dan, and mum and dad), and all the teachers, students, engineers and innovators who are already getting AI right.

List of Illustrations

p.31 NASA Extravehicular Activity (EVA) patch, Fred Keune. Photo: © National Air and Space Museum.

p.31 *Disabled Vitruvian Man*, Déborah 'Debs' Rodrigues. Photo: © Déborah 'Debs' Rodrigues. Photo: U.S. Department of Energy, Human Genome Project.

p.32 *Le Penseur* (The Thinker) in the garden of Musée Rodin, Paris. Photo: Wikimedia Commons.

p.37 'The Tree of Life' diagram from *On the Origin of Species*, Charles Darwin, 1859. Photo: Wellcome Collection.

p.94 *The Creation of Adam*, Michaelangelo, 1508–12. Photo: Wikimedia Commons.

p.95 Robot thinker statute, Shutterstock AI Generator. Photo: © Shutterstock.

p.97 *Silicon on Black I*, Catherine Bresslin. Photo: Better Images of AI/CC BY 4.0.

p.99 *Classification Cupboard*, Anton Grabolle. Photo: Better Images of AI/CC BY 4.0.

p.100 *Letter Word Taxonomy*, Theresa Berndtsson. Photo: Better Images of AI/CC BY 4.0.

p.101 *Fish Reversed*, Rens Dimmendaal and David Clode. Photo: Better Images of AI/CC BY 4.0.

p.101 *Power/ Profit*, Clarote and AI4Media. Photo: Better Images of AI/CC BY 4.0.

p.105 *Txitxardin*, Michelle Lee Brown and Kari Noe. Photo: © Michelle Lee Brown and Kari Noe.

p.117 Screenshot from Personality Machine. Photo: Author's own.

p. 136 *Actinologia britannica. A history of the British sea-anemones and corals from 1860*, Phillip Henry Gosse, 1860. Photo: New York Public Library.

p.137 *Pomegranate and Menelaus Blue Morpho Butterfly*, Maria Sibyella Merian, 1702. Photo: © Royal Collection Trust/His Majesty King Charles III 2022.

p.139 Arthur Mason Worthington's engravings of splashes made by drops falling on a plate, 1877. Photo: *Popular Science Monthly*.

p.141 Anatomical illustration by Max Brödel, 1940. Photo: John Hopkins University/National Library of Medicine.

p.214 Image of a Pope generated by Gemini AI. Photo: Author's own.

p.214 Woodcut illustration of Pope Joan, Heinrich Steinhöwel, c. 1474. Photo: Wikimedia Commons.

Notes

Introduction

1. Samuel Taylor Coleridge, 'Love', 1799.
2. Natasha McKeever, Luke Brenning et al., 'Open Letter', Ethical Dating Online, 10 Feb 2025, www.ethicaldatingonline.com/open-letter.
3. Dan Drollette Jr, 'Interview with Sneha Revanur, "the Greta Thunberg of AI"', *Encode Justice*, 15 Jan 2024, www.encodeai.org/interview-with-sneha-revanur-the-greta-thunberg-of-ai/ (accessed July 2025).
4. Eleanor Drage & Kerry Mackereth, 'Does AI debias recruitment? Race, gender and AI's "eradication of difference"', *Philosophy and Technology*, 35:4 (2022), pp. 1–25.
5. Audrey Tang, 'Reboot democracy', 1 Nov 2024, www.rebootdemocracy.ai/blog/audrey-tang-ai-democracy.
6. Thomas Haigh, 'Artificial intelligence then and now', *Commun. ACM*, 68:2 (Feb 2025), pp. 24–9.
7. Asvatha Babu, 'A new AI lexicon: Muga adaiyaalam thozhilnutpam (face identity technology)', 1 Sept 2021, AI Now Institute, www.ainowinstitute.org/publications/collection/a-new-ai-lexicon-muga-adaiyaalam-thozhilnutpam-face-identity-technology.
8. Yásnaya Elena Aguilar Gil, trans. Robin Myers, 'A modest proposal to save the world', *Rest of World*, 9 Dec 2020, www.restofworld.org/2020/saving-the-world-through-tequiology/; Yadira Sánchez Benítez, 'A new AI lexicon: Tequiologies', AI Now Institute, 22 October 2021, www.ainowinstitute.org/publications/collection/a-new-ai-lexicon-tequiologies.

9. ZKM Karlsruhe, 'Donna Haraway & Bruno Latour: Discussion of the Film *Storytelling for Earthly Survival*' [video], YouTube (uploaded 25 June 2020), www.youtube.com/watch?v=j-2r_vI2alg; Donna Haraway, 'Situated knowledges', *Feminist Studies* 14:3 (1988), pp. 575–99.

10. Hayden Field, 'AI engineers report burnout and rushed rollouts as "rat race" to stay competitive hits tech industry', CNBC, 3 May 2024, www.cnbc.com/2024/05/03/ai-engineers-face-burnout-as-rat-race-to-stay-competitive-hits-tech.html.

11. Deborah Bird Rose, *Wild Dog Dreaming* (Charlottesville: University of Virginia Press, 2011), p. 6.

12. Donna J. Haraway, *Staying with the Trouble* (Durham, NC: Duke University Press, 2016), p. 4.

1: The Pernicious Myths on Which AI Is Built

1. Paul B. Preciado, *Testo Junkie* (New York: The Feminist Press, 2013), p. 118.

2. Ibid., p. 120.

3. Knvul Sheikh, 'Many personal care products contain harmful chemicals. Here's what to do about it', *The New York Times*, 15 Feb 2023.

4. Bernard Stiegler, *Technics and Time, 1* (Stanford, CA: Stanford University Press, 1998).

5. Gilbert Simondon, trans. Ninian Mellamphy, *On the Mode of Existence of Technical Objects* (Minneapolis: Univocal Publishing, 2017), p. 12.

6. Microsoft (2024), 'Microsoft datacenters in Texas', Apr, pp. 1–2, www.local.microsoft.com/wp-content/uploads/2024/04/Microsoft-datacenters-in-Texas.pdf; Sebastian Klovig Skelton, 'Kenyan AI workers form Data Labelers Association', ComputerWeekly.com, 14 Feb 2025, www.computerweekly.com/news/366619321/Kenyan-AI-workers-form-Data-Labelers-Association.

7. Michael Kwet, 'Microsoft's iron cage', Al Jazeera, 21 Dec 2020, www.aljazeera.com/features/2020/12/21/microsofts-iron-cage-prison-surveillance-and-e-carceral-state.

Notes

8. Simondon, *On the Mode of Existence of Technical Objects*, p. 11.
9. Theodore M. Porter, 'Thin description', *Osiris*, 27:1 (2012), p. 223.
10. Friedrich A. Hayek, *The Road to Serfdom* (London: Routledge, 1944).
11. Simondon, *On the Mode of Existence of Technical Objects*, p. 2.
12. Déborah Rodrigues, 'Disabled Vitruvian Man' (digital illustration) on Dribbble, May 2025.
13. Richard O'Brien, *The Rocky Horror Show*, Dominion Theatre, London, 2024 revival.
14. Care Quality Commission, 'GP Mythbuster 29', 12 Dec 2025, www.cqc.org.uk/guidance-providers/gps/gp-mythbusters/gp-mythbuster-29-looking-after-homeless-patients-general-practice.
15. Judith Butler, *Precarious Life* (London: Verso, 2004).
16. 'Biological revolution' © Andrey VP/stock.adobe.com www.britannica.com/topic/decision-making.
17. 'How will humans evolve?', BBC Radio 4, 25 Apr 2015, www.bbc.co.uk/programmes/p045qlkd.
18. Brooke Harrington, 'What the broligarchs want from Trump', *Atlantic*, 24 Nov 2024.
19. Tim Ingold, *Lines* (London: Routledge, 2007), p. 8.
20. Ibid., p. 63.
21. Ibid., p. 114.
22. Niamh Rowe, 'Millions of workers are training AI models for pennies', *Wired*, 16 October 2023; Distintas Latitudes, 'Latin America: Uncovering the hidden human workforce behind AI', Global Voices, 5 October 2024, www.globalvoices.org/2024/10/05/latin-america-uncovering-the-hidden-human-workforce-behind-ai/.
23. Billie Mok, 'OpenAI used Kenyan workers making $2 an hour to filter traumatic content from ChatGPT', *TIME*, 18 Jan 2023.
24. OpenAI Charter (San Francisco: OpenAI, 9 Apr 2018), p. 1.

25. Osman Elbek, 'Risk medicine and transhumanism', *Thoracic Research and Practice*, 24:6 (2023), p. 327.

26. Mike Federowicz (also known as Mike Darwin), *Cryonics Magazine*, Nov 1986.

27. Deborah Bird Rose, *Wild Dog Dreaming* (Charlottesville: University of Virginia Press, 2011), p. 6.

28. Thom van Dooren, *Extinction Studies* (New York: Columbia University Press, 2017), p. 10.

29. Hetty Nooy-Palm, *The Sa'dan-Toraja, vol. 2* (Dordrecht: Foris Publications, 1986).

30. Putu Sayoga, 'What happens to the dead? In Indonesia, a family's sacred obligation', *The New York Times*, 14 Dec 2020.

31. John Misana Biseko, 'Cultural echoes: Linguistic insights into death and afterlife in the Swahili language', *Cogent Arts & Humanities*, 11:1 (2024), pp. 1–18.

32. Andy Bergmann, 'History of Earth in 24-hour clock', FlowingData, 9 October 2012, www.flowingdata.com/2012/10/09/history-of-earth-in-24-hour-clock/.

33. Jan Swammerdam, *A General History of Insects* (Amsterdam: Imprimerie Royale, 1669).

34. ZKM Karlsruhe, 'Donna Haraway & Bruno Latour: Discussion of the Film *Storytelling for Earthly Survival*' [video], YouTube (uploaded 25 June 2020), www.youtube.com/watch?v=j-2r_vI2alg.

35. Lauren Schenkman, 'Japanese guts are made for sushi', *Science*, 7 Apr 2010.

36. Lynn Margulis, *Symbiosis in Cell Evolution* (San Francisco: W. H. Freeman, 1981).

37. Diane M. B. Dodd, 'Reproductive isolation as a consequence of adaptive divergence in Drosophila-pseudoobscura', *Evolution*, 43:6 (1989), pp. 1308–11.

38. Ricardo Guerrero, Lynn Margulis & Mercedes Berlanga, 'Symbiogenesis', *International Microbiology*, 16:3 (2013), p. 135.

39. Joan Roughgarden et al., 'Holobionts as units of selection and a model of their population dynamics and evolution', *Biological*

Theory, 13:1 (2018), pp. 44–65; Eugene Rosenberg & Ilana Zilber-Rosenberg, *The Hologenome Concept* (Cham, Switzerland: Springer Cham, 2013); Seth R. Bordenstein & Kevin R. Theis, 'Host biology in light of the microbiome', *PLOS Biology*, 13:8 (2015).

40. Favourite theories of what it means to live well together include Judith Butler, *Notes Toward a Performative Theory of Assembly* (Cambridge, MA: Harvard University Press, 2015).

41. Donna J. Haraway, 'The Promises of Monsters', in Lawrence Grossberg, Cary Nelson, & Paula A. Treichler (eds), *Cultural Studies* (New York: Routledge, 1992), p. 324.

42. Charles Darwin, ed. Francis Darwin, *The Life and Letters of Charles Darwin*, vol. 2 (London: John Murray, 1887), p. 311.

43. Scott F. Gilbert, Jan Sapp & Alfred I. Tauber, 'A symbiotic view of life', *The Quarterly Review of Biology*, 87:4 (2012), pp. 325–41.

44. Conrad Hackett et al., 'How the global religious landscape changed from 2010 to 2020', Pew Research Center, 9 June 2025, www.pewrsr.ch/4jA91LR.

45. D. Danowski & E. B. Viveiros de Castro, 'Is there any world to come?', e-flux Journal #65 (2015).

46. Ayn Rand, 'Collectivized "Rights"', in *The Virtue of Selfishness* (London: Penguin, 1988), p. 385.

47. The Holy Bible, Authorized King James Version, 1 John 3:2 (Oxford: Oxford University Press, 1769).

48. Herbert Spencer, *The Principles of Biology, vol. 1* (London: Williams & Norgate, 1864), p. 444.

49. Heinrich Anton de Bary, *Die Erscheinung der Symbiose* (Strasbourg: Verlag von Karl J. Trübner, 1879), p. 121.

50. Later published by ORSA as Herbert Simon, 'Heuristic problem solving', *Operations Research*, 6:1 (Jan–Feb 1958), pp. 1–10.

2: Misdirections, or Apocalypse vs Utopia

1. Ursula K. Le Guin, 'The Carrier Bag Theory of Fiction', in

Dancing at the Edge of the World (New York: Grove Press, 1989), pp. 165–70.

2. Donna J. Haraway, *Modest_Witness@Second_Millennium. FemaleMan_Meets_OncoMouse* (New York: Routledge, 1997), p. 44.

3. Mark Duffy, 'The unending arrogance of the iPhone tagline marches ever onward', Digiday, 28 Sept 2015, www.digiday.com/marketing/unending-arrogance-iphone-tagline-marches-ever-onward/.

4. Juliet Schor, *The Overworked American* (New York: Basic Books, 1991).

5. Judy Wajcman, 'ANFÖRANDE: Pressed for time', *Sociologisk Forskning*, 53:2 (2016), p. 196.

6. Shamira Ahmed et al., 'Future of Work in the global South', Research ICT Africa, Dec 2021, www.africaportal.org/wp-content/uploads/2023/05/Future-of-Work-in-the-global-South-FOWIGS-Working-Paper-1.pdf, p. 9.

7. Competence Centre on Foresight, 'Widening health-related inequalities', European Commission, 18 May 2021, www.knowledge4policy.ec.europa.eu/foresight/widening-health-related-inequalities_en.

8. *Star Trek: First Contact*, Paramount Pictures, 1996.

9. Jude Browne, Eleanor Drage & Kerry McInerney, 'Tech workers' perspectives on ethical issues in AI development', *Big Data & Society*, 11:1 (2024).

10. Theodore M. Porter, 'Thin description', *Isis* 101:4 (2010), pp. 781–96.

11. Nick Bostrom, 'Existential risks', *Journal of Evolution and Technology*, 9 (2002).

12. Andrew Anthony, 'Eugenics on steroids', *Guardian*, 28 Apr 2024.

13. Bostrom, 'Existential risks'.

14. Andrew Raff, 'Idiocracy', Buzz Rant & Rave, 18 Sept 2006, www.buzzrantrave.com/2006/09/.

15. Donna J. Haraway & Anna Tsing, 'Reflections on the

Plantationocene: A conversation', *Edge Effects Magazine*, 18 June 2019.

16. Lauren Berlant, 'Slow death (sovereignty, obesity, lateral agency)', *Critical Inquiry*, 33:4 (2007), pp. 754–80.

17. Ibid.

18. Deborah Bird Rose, *Wild Dog Dreaming* (Charlottesville: University of Virginia Press, 2011), p. 15.

19. Donna J. Haraway, *Staying with the Trouble* (Durham, NC: Duke University Press, 2016), p. 37.

20. Emily M. Bender et al., 'On the dangers of stochastic parrots', *Proceedings of the 2021 ACM Conference on Fairness, Accountability and Transparency (FAccT '21)*, 1 Mar 2021, pp. 610–23.

21. Cristina Criddle & Madhumita Murgia, 'Big tech companies cut AI ethics staff, raising safety concerns', *Financial Times*, 7 Apr 2023.

22. Rishi Sunak, Prime Minister's speech on AI, GOV.UK, 26 October 2023, www.gov.uk/government/speeches/prime-ministers-speech-on-ai-26-october-2023.

23. Timnit Gebru, Emily Bender, Angelina McMillan-Major, Margaret Mitchell et al., 'Statement from the listed authors of stochastic parrots on the "AI pause" letter', DAIR Institute, 31 Mar 2023, www.dair-institute.org/blog/letter-statement-Mar2023/.

24. LobbyControl, 'Lobbying power of Amazon, Google and Co. continues to grow', Corporate Europe Observatory, Sept 2023.

25. Joseph R. Biden Jr, 'Notice on the continuation of the national emergency with respect to certain terrorist attacks', White House press release, 9 Sept 2024.

26. Judith Butler, 'Letter from Paris', Verso, 15 Nov 2015, www.versobooks.com/en-gb/blogs/news/2337-mourning-becomes-the-law-judith-butler-from-paris?

27. Max Colbert, 'Lack of transparency over police forces' covert use of predictive policing software raises concerns about human rights abuses', *Byline Times*, 28 Mar 2023; Federica Frabetti & Eleanor Drage, 'The performativity of AI-powered protest

detection', *Science, Technology, & Human Values* 49:5 (2023), pp. 1045–72.

3: The Triangle of Doom

1. Geoffrey Miller, 'What can we learn from what the Chinese are doing, how can we help them and how can they help us to keep up as they create their brave new world?', Chinese Eugenics, Edge, response to the 2013 Annual Question, 27 July 2013, www.edge.org/response-detail/23838; Barbara J. King, 'The fat-shaming professor', NPR, 6 June 2013, www.npr.org/sections/13.7/2013/06/06/188891906/the-fat-shaming-professor-a-twitter-fueled-firestorm.

2. Michael Lewis, 'Sam Bankman-Fried, a personal verdict', *Washington Post*, 20 Aug 2024.

3. Habiba Banu, 'A personal response to Nick Bostrom's "Apology for an Old Email"', Effective Altruism Forum, 12 Jan 2023, www.forum.effectivealtruism.org/posts/8zLwD862MRGZTzs8k/a-personal-response-to-nick-bostrom-s-apology-for-an-old.

4. Geoffrey Miller, 'Utilitarianism, if applied with rationality, impartiality and integrity, is a powerful moral philosophy' [X post], 4 May 2020, x.com/primalpoly/status/125813579376941 0562.

5. Benjamin L. Jones & Richard K. F. Unsworth, 'The perverse fisheries consequences of mosquito net malaria prophylaxis in East Africa', *Ambio*, 49:7 (2020), pp. 1257–67.

6. Leif Wenar, 'The deaths of effective altruism', *Wired*, 27 Mar 2024.

7. Nick Bostrom, 'Existential risks', *Journal of Evolution and Technology*, 9:1 (2002), p. 2.

8. Nick Bostrom, 'Astronomical waste', *Utilitas* 15:1 (2003), p. 4.

9. 'Countries currently at war 2024', World Population Review, www.worldpopulationreview.com/country-rankings/countries-currently-at-war; 'Global military spending from 2000 to 2023', Statista, 22 Apr 2024, www.statista.com/statistics/264434/trend-of-global-military-spending/.

10. Nick Bostrom, *Superintelligence* (Oxford: Oxford University Press, 2014), p. 51; Bostrom, 'Astronomical waste', pp. 308–14.

11. 'Wytham Abbey put up for sale for £15m by effective altruism group EVF', *Guardian*, 12 May 2024.

12. Bostrom, 'Astronomical waste'.

13. See, for example, my research into the German Federal Office for Migration and Refugees 'voice biometry system and the UK HMPO passport photo checker tool': Eleanor Drage & Federica Frabetti, 'Copies without an original', *Communication and Critical/Cultural Studies*, 21:1 (2024), p. 79.

14. Michael Lawrence et al., 'Polycrisis research and action roadmap', Cascade Institute, Aug 2024, www.cascadeinstitute. org/technical-paper/polycrisisroadmap.

15. Centre for the Study of Existential Risk, 'Research themes', University of Cambridge, www.cser.ac.uk/work/research-themes/.

16. Centre for the Study of Existential Risk, 'Global justice and global catastrophic risk', University of Cambridge, www.cser. ac.uk/work/research-themes/.

17. AI Now Institute, 'A new AI lexicon', www.ainowinstitute.org/ collection/a-new-ai-lexicon.

18. Donald J. Trump, interview with *Bloomberg Businessweek*, 25 June 2024, www.bloomberg.com/features/2024-trump-interview-transcript/.

19. Diederik Baazil et al., 'ASML and TSMC can disable chip machines if China invades Taiwan', Bloomberg UK, 21 May 2024,www.bloomberg.com/news/articles/2024-05-21/asml-tsmc-can-disable-chip-machines-if-china-invades-taiwan.

20. Cat Zakrzewski, 'Trump allies draft AI order to launch "Manhattan Projects" for defense', *Washington Post*, 16 July 2024.

21. US–China Economic and Security Review Commission, '2024 Annual Report: Recommendations', United States Congress, Nov 2024, p. 27.

22. Donald J. Trump, interview on 'Mornings with Maria Bartiromo', Fox Business Network, 2 Aug 2024.

23. Mark Zuckerberg, 'Zuckerberg says the White House pressured Facebook to censor some COVID-19 content during the pandemic', PBS NewsHour, 27 Aug 2024.

24. Jeffrey A. Sonnenfeld, 'The Coming MAGA Assault on Capitalism', Faculty Viewpoints, 31 May 2024, www.insights.som.yale.edu/insights/the-coming-maga-assault-on-capitalism.

25. Lina Maliha Khan, 'The ideological roots of America's market power problem', *Yale Law Journal* Forum, 4 June 2018, www.yalelawjournal.org/forum/the-ideological-roots-of-americas-market-power-problem.

26. Ibid.

27. Bernhard Rieder, Giovanni Sileno & Geoff Gordon, 'A new AI lexicon: monopolization', AI Now Institute, 1 October 2021, www.ainowinstitute.org/publications/collection/a-new-ai-lexicon-monopolization.

28. Max A. Cherney, 'Amazon racing to develop AI chips cheaper, faster than Nvidia's, executives say', Reuters, 25 July 2024.

29. US Department of Justice, 'Complaint: United States v. Apple Inc. for Monopolization of Smartphone Markets', Washington DC, filed 21 Mar 2024.

30. Federal Trade Commission, 'FTC Complaint: FTC v. Meta Platforms, Inc. – Withheld Information in Instagram and WhatsApp Deals', filed 5 June 2024.

31. Joseph R. Biden Jr, 'Remarks by President Biden at signing of an executive order promoting competition in the American economy', the White House, 9 July 2021, www.bidenwhitehouse.archives.gov/briefing-room/speeches-remarks/2021/07/09/remarks-by-president-biden-at-signing-of-an-executive-order-promoting-competition-in-the-american-economy/.

32. Karl Marx, trans. Ben Fowkes, *Capital, vol. 1* (London: Penguin Books, 1990 [original 1867]), especially Part III: 'The Production of Absolute Surplus-Value'.

33. Michael Kwet, 'Digital colonialism', *ROAR Magazine*, 3 March 2021, https://roarmag.org/essays/digital-colonialism-the-evolution-of-american-empire/.

34. Michael Kwet, 'Microsoft's iron cage'.

35. Microsoft has since 'retired' the question from their Support Community, Microsoft Community User. 'This AI chatbot "Sydney" is misbehaving', Microsoft Community (Bing forum), 23 Nov 2022. For further comment on the issue see Kevin Roose, 'Microsoft's Bing chatbot isn't like OpenAI's – and it shows', *The New York Times*, 16 Feb 2023; Matthias Bastian, 'Microsoft knew the Bing bot was a little weird – and launched it anyway', The Decoder, 21 Feb 2023, www.the-decoder.com/microsoft-knew-the-bing-bot-was-a-little-weird-and-launched-it-anyway/; Jeremy Khan, 'Why Bing's creepy alter-ego is a problem for Microsoft – and us all', *Fortune*, 21 Feb 2023.

36. Sananda Sahoo, 'Biometric data's colonial imaginaries continue in Aadhaar's minimal data', *BJHS Themes*, 8 (2023), p. 205.

37. Nayantara Ranganathan, 'The Economy (and Regulatory Practice) That Biometrics Inspires', in *Dissent on Aadhaar* (Hyderabad: Orient Blackswan, 2019).

38. Mira Rai Waits, 'The History of Anthropometry and Fingerprinting in Colonial South Asia', in *Oxford Research Encyclopedia of Asian History* (Oxford: Oxford University Press, 2024).

39. Ibid.

40. Alex Konrad & Kenrick Cai, 'OpenAI's Sam Altman talks ChatGPT and how Artificial General Intelligence can "break capitalism"', *Forbes*, 3 Feb 2023.

41. Mark Fisher, *Capitalist Realism* (Winchester: Zero Books, 2009).

42. Zoe Todd, 'Fish, kin and hope', *Afterall*, 43 (2017), pp. 102–7.

43. Nilay Patel, 'Why signal won't compromise on encryption', The Verge, 18 October 2022, www.theverge.com/23409716/signal-encryption-messaging-sms-meredith-whittaker-imessage-whatsapp-china.

4: Building from Better Visions

1. Auguste Rodin, quoted in *Bulletin des études Valéryennes*, vols 21–2 (1994), p. 158.

2. Virginia Woolf, *A Room of One's Own* (London: Hogarth Press, 1929).

3. Gilbert Simondon, trans. Ninian Mellamphy, *On the Mode of Existence of Technical Objects* (Minneapolis: Univocal Publishing, 2017), p. 1.

4. Catherine Breslin, *Silicon on Black 1* [image], Better Images of AI, https://betterimagesofai.org, https://creativecommons.org/licenses/by/4.0/.

5. Friedrich Kittler, 'There Is No Software', in John Johnston (ed.), *Literature, Media, Information Systems* (New York: Routledge, 1997), pp. 147–55.

6. Marc Andreessen, 'Why software is eating the world', *Wall Street Journal*, 20 Aug 2011.

7. Federica Frabetti, *Software Theory* (London: Rowman & Littlefield International, 2015); Luca M. Possati, *Software as Hermeneutics* (Cham, Switzerland: Palgrave Macmillan, 2022).

8. Anton Grabolle, *Classification Cupboard* [image], Better Images of AI, https://betterimagesofai.org, https://creativecommons.org/licenses/by/4.0/.

9. Teresa Berndtsson, *Letter Word Text Taxonomy* [image], Better Images of AI, https://betterimagesofai.org, https://creativecommons.org/licenses/by/4.0/.

10. Rens Dimmendaal & David Clode, *Fish reversed* [image], Better Images of AI, https://betterimagesofai.org, https://creativecommons.org/licenses/by/4.0/.

11. Stephen Jay Gould, 'This view of life: What, if anything, is a zebra?', *Natural History*, 90:7 (1981), p. 12.

12. Clarote & AI4Media, *Power/Profit* [image], Better Images of AI, www.betterimagesofai.org/images?artist=Clarote&title=Power%2FProfit.

13. Eleanor Drage, *The Planetary Humanism of European Women's Science Fiction* (London: Routledge, 2023).

14. Catherine Breslin, *Silicon on Black 1* [image], Better Images of AI, https://betterimagesofai.org, https://creativecommons.org/licenses/by/4.0/.

15. Alex de Vries-Gao, 'The growing energy footprint of artificial intelligence', *Joule*, 7:10 (2023), pp. 2191–4.

16. Kerry Mackereth, Eleanor Drage & Janneke Parrish, 'Janneke Parrish on worker solidarity and why tech unions matter', *The Good Robot*, 15 October 2024, www.thegoodrobot.co.uk/post/janneke-parrish-on-worker-solidarity-and-why-tech-unions-matter.

17. Michelle Lee Brown, Txitxardin (Biotech Eel AI), in Jason Edward Lewis (ed.), *Indigenous Protocol and Artificial Intelligence*, position paper, Honolulu, Hawaii (2020), the Initiative for Indigenous Futures and the Canadian Institute for Advanced Research, www.spectrum.library.concordia.ca/id/eprint/986506/7/Indigenous_Protocol_and_AI_2020.pdf.

18. Bruno Latour, 'From Multiculturalism to multinaturalism', *Nature and Culture* 6:1 (Spring 2011), p. 4.

19. Jane Bennett, *Vibrant Matter* (Durham, NC: Duke University Press, 2010), p. vii.

20. Jane Bennett, 'The agency of assemblages and the North American blackout', *Public Culture*, 17:3 (2005), pp. 445–65.

21. N. Katherine Hayles, *Unthought* (Chicago: University of Chicago Press, 2017).

22. N. Katherine Hayles, 'Good Technology Is Biophilic', in Eleanor Drage & Kerry McInerney (eds), *The Good Robot: Why Technology Needs Feminism* (London: Bloomsbury Academic, 2024), pp. 28–35.

23. Elizabeth A. Wilson, *Neural Geographies* (New York: Routledge, 1998), p. 6.

24. David Abram, 'The ecology of perception – an interview', *Emergence Magazine*, 2018.

25. Tomasz Hollanek & Katarzyna Nowaczyk-Basińska, 'Griefbots, deadbots, postmortem avatars', *Philosophy & Technology*, 37 (2024), pp. 1–22.

26. Tomasz Hollanek & Katarzyna Nowaczyk-Basińska, '"Digital afterlife": Call for safeguards', *University of Cambridge News*, 9 May 2024.

27. Amin Samman et al., 'Death and apocalypse in the digital megamachine', CAPAS PubPub, 16 Feb 2023.

28. Maria Patrizia Carrieri & Diego Serraino, 'Longevity of popes and artists between the 13th and the 19th century', *International Journal of Epidemiology*, 34:6 (2005), pp. 1435–6.

29. 'Global life expectancy at birth from 1950 to 2023, with projections until 2100', United Nations Department of Economic and Social Affairs, www.statista.com/statistics/805060/life-expectancy-at-birth-worldwide/.

5: Beware False Promises

1. Byron Reese & Margaret Mitchell, 'Voices in AI, episode 83: A conversation with Margaret Mitchell' (podcast), Voices in AI, 15 Mar 2024, www.voicesinai.com/episode/episode-83-a-conversation-with-margaret-mitchell/.

2. Email correspondence with Margaret Mitchell.

3. Ibid.

4. Available at www.personal-ambiguator-frontend.vercel.app/. Coverage includes Chris Vallance, 'AI tools fail to reduce recruitment bias – study', BBC News, 13 October 2022; Madeline Halpert, 'AI-powered job recruitment tools may not improve hiring diversity, experts argue', *Forbes*, 9 October 2022.

5. Eleanor Drage & Kerry Mackereth, 'Does AI debias recruitment? Race, gender and AI's "eradication of difference"', *Philosophy & Technology*, 35 (2022), p. 89.

6. Asvatha Babu, 'A new AI lexicon: Muga adaiyaalam thozhilnutpam (face identity technology)', AI Now Institute, 1 Sept 2021, www.ainowinstitute.org/publications/collection/a-new-ai-lexicon-muga-adaiyaalam-thozhilnutpam-face-identity-technology.

7. Ibid.

8. Ibid.

9. For better reporting on the incident see Sonia Katyal, 'Why you should be suspicious of that study claiming AI can detect a person's sexual orientation', Stanford Cyberlaw, 14 Sept 2017, www.cyberlaw.stanford.edu/publications/why-you-should-be-

suspicious-study-claiming-ai-can-detect-persons-sexual-orientation/.

10. Blaise Agüera y Arcas et al., 'Do algorithms reveal sexual orientation or just expose our stereotypes?', Medium, 11 Jan 2018, www.medium.com/@blaisea/do-algorithms-reveal-sexual-orientation-or-just-expose-our-stereotypes-d998fafdf477.

11. For research debunking the system see ibid.

12. Yilun Wang & Michal Kosinski, 'Deep neural networks are more accurate than humans at detecting sexual orientation from facial images', *Journal of Personality and Social Psychology*, 114:2 (Feb 2018), pp. 246–57.

13. Anna Brown, 'Bisexual adults are far less likely than gay men and lesbians to be "out" to the people in their lives', Pew Research Center, 18 June 2019, www.pewresearch.org/short-reads/2019/06/18/bisexual-adults-are-far-less-likely-than-gay-men-and-lesbians-to-be-out-to-the-people-in-their-lives/.

14. *Paris Is Burning*, Academy Entertainment, 1990.

15. Andrew R. Flores et al., 'Gender identity disparities in criminal victimization', *American Journal of Public Health*, 111:4 (2021), pp. 726–9.

16. C. J. M. de Blok et al., 'Mortality trends over five decades in adult transgender people receiving hormone treatment', *The Lancet Diabetes & Endocrinology*, 9:10 (2021), p. 666.

17. Ibid.

18. Human Rights Campaign and Trans People of Color Coalition, 'Addressing Anti-Transgender Violence', https://assets2.hrc.org/files/assets/resources/HRC-AntiTransgenderViolence-0519.pdf

19. Human Rights Campaign, 'The Epidemic of Violence Against the Transgender & Gender-Expansive Community in the U.S.', November 2024, https://reports.hrc.org/an-epidemic-of-violence-2024

20. Max Colbert, 'Lack of transparency over police forces' covert use of predictive policing software raises concerns about human rights abuses', *Byline Times*, 28 Mar 2023; Federica Frabetti & Eleanor Drage, 'The performativity of AI-powered protest

detection', *Science, Technology, & Human Values*, 49:5 (2023), pp. 1045–72.

21. American Civil Liberties Union, 'Police used Facebook, Twitter to track protesters', VOA News, 25 Aug 2016.

22. Federica Frabetti & Eleanor Drage, 'The performativity of AI-powered protest detection'.

23. Alex Jaimes, 'Our AI Strategy for Creating Dataminr-unique High Performance LLMs and Foundation Models', Dataminr, 3 October 2023, www.dataminr.com/resources/blog/our-ai-strategy-for-creating-dataminr-unique-high-performance-llms-and-foundation-models/; Ted Bailey & Alex Jaimes, 'Harnessing the power of AI', Dataminr, 2023, www.dataminr.com/resources/blog/harnessing-the-power-of-llms-and-multi-modal-foundation-models-in-dataminrs-ai-platform/.

24. Federica Frabetti & Eleanor Drage, 'The performativity of AI-powered protest detection'.

25. Madhumita Murgia, *Code Dependent* (London: Profile Books, 2023).

26. Federica Frabetti & Eleanor Drage, 'The performativity of AI-powered protest detection'.

27. Max Colbert, 'Lack of transparency over police forces' covert use of predictive policing software raises concerns about human rights abuses', *Byline Times*, 28 Mar 2023; All the Citizens, 'Former Metropolitan Police Commissioner Lord Hogan-Howe was also paid for an online speaking engagement with Dataminr in 2020', [Twitter (now X) post], 1 July 2022, www.x.com/allthecitizens/status/1542865451155394561.

28. Sandra Laville, 'Hogan-Howe criticised for comments regarding child sex abuse claims', *Guardian*, 11 Feb 2016.

29. David Leigh et al., 'Phone hacking: Met failed to consult before invoking Official Secrets Act', *Guardian*, 19 Sept 2011.

30. 'Met launches "total war on crime"', BBC News, 8 Feb 2012, www.bbc.co.uk/news/uk-england-london-16954257.

31. See, for example, West Yorkshire Police, 'Written Evidence to the House of Commons Committee on the Police and Crime Bill (Evidence ID: 77781)', submitted 20 July 2023; Ipsos MORI

Notes

/ Her Majesty's Inspectorate of Constabulary, *Public Views of Policing in England and Wales*, research report, July 2016.

32. London Borough of Hackney, 'Hackney Strategic Plan 2022–2026', Hackney Council, adopted 14 Mar 2023; City and Hackney Health and Care Board Sub-Committee, Meeting Papers, 10 Jan 2024, North East London ICB, 10 Jan 2024.

33. Oxfordshire County Council, 'Police and Crime Plan Strategic Priority 2 – Performance Report: Prevention and Early Intervention', Thames Valley Police and Crime Panel meeting, 20 Nov 2020, item 33/20, www.mycouncil.oxfordshire.gov.uk/mgAi.aspx?ID=23092.

34. Max Colbert, 'Lack of transparency over police forces' covert use of predictive policing software raises concerns about human rights abuses'.

35. House of Lords Justice and Home Affairs Committee, *Technology Rules? The Advent of New Technologies in the Justice System*, House of Lords Paper 180, 30 Mar 2022.

36. Karen Barad, *Meeting the Universe Halfway* (Durham, NC: Duke University Press, 2007).

37. Donna Haraway, 'Situated knowledges', *Feminist Studies*, 14:3 (1988), pp. 575–99.

38. For example Pratyusha Kalluri, 'Don't ask if artificial intelligence is good or fair, ask how it shifts power', *Nature*, 583:7815 (2020), p. 169.

39. Lorraine Daston & Peter L. Galison, *Objectivity* (Princeton: Zone Books, 2007).

40. Philip Henry Gosse, *Actinologia Britannica* (London: Van Voorst, 1860).

41. Maria Sibylla Merian, 'Pomegranate and Menelaus Blue Morpho Butterfly' (watercolour and gum arabic on vellum, RCIN 921162), Royal Collection Trust, Windsor Castle; created 1702–1703.

42. Arthur Mason Worthington, 'On drops', *Popular Science Monthly*, 11 (1877), pp. 562–5.

43. Donna Haraway, 'Situated knowledges'.

44. Charles Baudelaire, 'L'Œuvre et la vie d'Eugène Delacroix', *Art absolument* 13 (Summer 2005), p. 68.

45. Donna Haraway, 'Situated knowledges'; Bruno Latour & Steve Woolgar, *Laboratory Life* (Princeton: Princeton University Press, 1979); ZKM Karlsruhe, 'Donna Haraway & Bruno Latour: Discussion of the Film *Storytelling for Earthly Survival*' [video], YouTube (uploaded 25 June 2020), www.youtube.com/watch?v=j-2r_vI2alg.

46. Alfonso Martinez Arias, 'Cells, not DNA, are the master architects of life', *Noema Magazine*, 30 May 2023.

47. Max Horkheimer, *Eclipse of Reason* (Oxford: Oxford University Press, 1947).

48. Ned Beauman, *Venomous Lumpsucker* (London: Soho Press, 2022).

49. Ernesto Sabato, *Hombres y engranajes* (Buenos Aires: Emecé editores, 1951).

50. Tweede Kamer der Staten-Generaal, 'Aanhangsel van de Handelingen', from Zoeken in officiële bekendmakingen, 23 Dec 2022, www.zoek.officielebekendmakingen.nl/ah-tk-20222023-1177.html.

6: The Fight for Control

1. S. Bubeck et al., 'Sparks of Artificial General Intelligence: Early experiments with GPT-4' (2023), arXiv Preprint arXiv:2303.12712.

2. Marilyn Strathern, 'Improving ratings', *European Review*, 5:3 (1997), pp. 305–21.

3. Mike Knoop, 'Announcing ARC Prize', ARC Prize, 11 June 2024, www.arcprize.org/blog/launch.

4. Melanie Mitchell, 'On the "ARC-AGI" $1 million reasoning challenge', *AI Guide* Substack, published approximately Aug 2024, www.aiguide.substack.com/p/on-the-arc-agi-1-million-reasoning.

5. NVIDIA, 'GTC Mar Keynote with NVIDIA CEO Jensen Huang' [video], YouTube (streamed live 18 Mar 2024), www.youtube.com/watch?v=Y2F8yisiS6E.

Notes

6. Department for Education, *Schools, Pupils and Their Characteristics: Jan 2025*, National Statistics, 5 June 2025.

7. End Everyday Racism Project, University of Cambridge, 2024, www.racismatcambridge.org/.

8. Hande Güzel et al., Second Report (2023), End Everyday Racism Project, University of Cambridge, October 2023, www.racismatcambridge.org/wp-content/uploads/2023/10/EER-Executive-Report-Oct-2023-v7.pdf.

9. B. Benyamin et al., 'Childhood intelligence is heritable, highly polygenic and associated with FNBP1L', *Mol Psychiatry* 19 (2014), pp. 253–8.

10. G. Davies et al., 'Genome-wide association study of cognitive functions and educational attainment in UK Biobank (N = 112,151)', *Molecular Psychiatry*, 21:6 (2016), pp. 758–67.

11. Tama Leventhal & Jeanne Brooks-Gunn, 'The neighborhoods they live in', *Psychological Bulletin*, 126:2 (2000), pp. 309–37; Judith Blake, 'Number of siblings and educational attainment', *Science*, 245:4913 (1989), pp. 32–6.

12. Karl R. White, 'The relation between socioeconomic status and academic achievement', *Psychological Bulletin*, 91:3 (1982), pp. 461–81.

13. Samuel Bowles & Herbert Gintis, 'The inheritance of inequality', *Journal of Economic Perspectives*, 16:3 (Summer 2002), pp. 3–30.

14. Robert M. Hauser & Min-Hsiung Huang 1997, 'Verbal ability and socioeconomic success', *Social Science Research*, 26, pp. 331–76.

15. Stephen Cave, 'On the Dark History of Intelligence as Domination', Aeon, 21 February 2017, www.aeon.co/essays/on-the-dark-history-of-intelligence-as-domination.

16. ZKM Karlsruhe, 'Donna Haraway & Bruno Latour: Discussion of the Film *Storytelling for Earthly Survival*' [video], YouTube (uploaded 25 June 2020), www.youtube.com/watch?v=j-2r_vI2alg.

17. Pádraig Belton, 'Valerie Hunter Gordon obituary', *Guardian*, 30 October 2016.

18. Walter Isaacson, *Elon Musk* (New York: Simon & Schuster, 2023), p. 620.

19. Elon Musk, 'Doing my best to help the underpopulation crisis', [Twitter (now X) post], 7 July 2022, www.twitter.com/elonmusk/status/1544874041663844352.

20. Christopher Strachey, 'Control without men', radio broadcast, BBC Home Service, 8 May 1952.

21. Daniel Kokotajlo, 'How, exactly, could AI take over by 2027?', [X post], 3 Apr 2025, www.x.com/DKokotajlo/status/1907826614186209524.

22. Stuart J. Russell, *Human Compatible* (London: Penguin, 2019), p. 11.

23. For example, Google DeepMind 2025, 'For AGI to truly complement human abilities, it has to be aligned with human values', 'Taking a responsible path to AGI', Google DeepMind, www.deepmind.com/discover/blog/taking-a-responsible-path-to-agi/ (accessed 21 July 2025).

24. Tom McTague, 'The philosophy behind Trump's Dark Enlightenment', *Financial Times*, 26 Mar 2025.

25. Gina Raimondo, 'US and allies must set "democratic" rules for artificial intelligence, Biden administration officials say', *South China Morning Post*, 13 July 2021, www.scmp.com/news/china/diplomacy/article/3140997/us-and-allies-must-set-democratic-rules-artificial (accessed 21 July 2025).

26. Kathleen H. Hicks, 'Our country's vibrant innovation ecosystem is second-to-none precisely because it's powered by a free and open society committed to responsible-use values and ideals', 'Remarks on the State of AI in the DoD', US Department of War, Washington DC, 2 Nov 2023, www.defense.gov/News/Speeches/Speech/Article/3578046/ (accessed 21 July 2025).

27. Shazeda Ahmed, 'A new AI lexicon: Big data swindling', AI Now Institute, 29 June 2021, www.ainowinstitute.org/publications/collection/a-new-ai-lexicon-big-data-swindling (accessed 21 July 2025).

28. Cory Doctorow, 'The Enshittification of American Power', *Wired*, 15 July 2025.

29. Hyrum Lewis & Verlan Lewis, 'The Consequences of Left and Right', in *The Myth of Left and Right* (New York: Oxford University Press, 2023), p. 84, online edn, Oxford Academic, 15 Dec 2022.

30. Matthew Bacon & Toby Seddon, 'Controlling drug users', *British Journal of Criminology*, 60:2 (2019), pp. 403–21.

31. Erika Guevara-Rosas, 'Global UN report must signal end to manifestly failed "war on drugs"', Amnesty International media release, 24 June 2024, www.amnesty.org/en/latest/news/2024/06/global-un-report-must-signal-end-to-manifestly-failed-war-on-drugs/ (accessed 21 July 2025).

32. Jonathan Penn 2020, 'Inventing Intelligence', PhD thesis, University of Cambridge, 2020.

33. Fred Turner, *From Counterculture to Cyberculture* (Chicago: University of Chicago Press, 2006), blurb.

7: Feminism by the Back Door

1. Alex Hanna, 'Alex Hanna on vague AI-ethics principles and why automatic gender recognition is nonsense', *The Good Robot*, 31 May 2022, www.thegoodrobot.co.uk/post/alex-hanna-on-vague-ai-ethics-principles-and-why-automatic-gender-recognition-is-nonsense (accessed 21 July 2025).

2. Eleanor Drage, 'LCFI hosts discussions on interfaith and intercultural AI ethics', Leverhulme Centre for the Future of Intelligence, 17 October 2024, www.lcfi.ac.uk/news-events/blog/post/lcfi-hosts-discussions-on-interfaith-and-intercultural-ai-ethics (accessed 21 July 2025).

3. Shane Jones, 'Letter to the Microsoft Board of Directors and FTC Chair Lina Khan regarding governance and responsible AI concerns', *Wall Street Journal* public resources, 6 Mar 2024, https://s.wsj.net/public/resources/documents/SHANE_JONES_MICROSOFTFTCLETTER.pdf (accessed 21 July 2025).

4. Ibid.

5. Sara Ahmed, *Complaint!* (Durham, NC: Duke University Press, 2021).

6. Matthew Weaver, 'Tanni Grey-Thompson says apologies not enough for having to "crawl off" train', *Guardian*, 27 Aug 2024.

7. Lina M. Khan, 'Remarks by Chair Lina M. Khan', US Federal Trade Commission, Washington DC, 8 Jan 2025, www.ftc.gov/system/files/ftc_gov/pdf/remarks-chair-lina-m-khan-brookings-institution.pdf (accessed 21 July 2025).

8. Timothy Williamson, *Vagueness* (London: Routledge, 1994).

9. Mark Sainsbury, 'Concepts Without Boundaries', in Rosanna Keefe & Peter Smith (eds), *Vagueness* (Cambridge, MA: MIT Press, 1997), pp. 251–64 (originally published as inaugural lecture, King's College London, 6 Nov 1990).

10. Distributed AI Research Institute 2024, 'Who We Are', DAIR, www.dair-institute.org/ (accessed 15 Nov 2025).

11. Ibid.

12. Lucile Saulnier et al., 'Putting ethical principles at the core of the research lifecycle', Hugging Face, 19 May 2022, www.huggingface.co/blog/ethical-charter-multimodal (accessed 21 July 2025).

13. 'Manifesto of experiential rationality', Ammagamma, 2024, https://ammagamma.com/en/manifesto-experiential-rationality/ (accessed 21 July 2025).

14. European Parliament and Council, 'Article 10, Regulation (EU) No 2018/1725: Processing of special categories of personal data', *Official Journal of the European Union* L 295/39–98, 21 Nov 2018, www.eur-lex.europa.eu/eli/reg/2018/1725/oj/eng (accessed 21 July 2025).

15. Ibid.

16. Praavita Kashyap, 'A new AI lexicon: C is for consent', AI Now Institute guest post, 16 Dec 2021, www.ainowinstitute.org/publications/collection/a-new-ai-lexicon-c-is-for-consent (accessed 21 July 2025).

17. Privacy International et al., 'Time to deliver answers', 13 Jan 2025, www.privacyinternational.org/advocacy/5509/time-

deliver-answers-open-letter-just-eat-takeaway-uber-and-deliveroo (accessed 21 July 2025).

18. Mophat Okinyi, 'Impact of Remotasks' closure on Kenyan workers', in M. Miceli et al. (eds), The Data Workers' Inquiry, 2024, www.data-workers.org/mophat/, (accessed 21 July 2025); Niamh Rowe, 'Kenyan moderators decry toll of training of AI models', *Guardian*, 2 Aug 2023.

19. Catharine A. MacKinnon, 'Sexual assault and inequality', Agora Lecture, Brown University, 14 October 2022.

20. Oxford Law Faculty, 'Rape redefined: Catharine A. MacKinnon in conversation with Kate O'Regan', [video], YouTube (uploaded 30 Nov 2022), www.youtube.com/watch?v=NuCz VESoboA.

21. Elizabeth Edenberg & Meg Leta Jones (2020), 'Troubleshooting AI and Consent', in Markus Dirk Dubber et al. (eds), *The Oxford Handbook of Ethics of AI* (Oxford: Oxford University Press, 2020), pp. 347–62.

22. Samuel D. Warren & Louis D. Brandeis, 'The right to privacy', *Harvard Law Review*, 4:5 (1890), pp. 193–220.

23. James Ball, 'Angry birds and "leaky" phone apps targeted by NSA and GCHQ for user data', *Guardian*, 27 Jan 2014.

24. Department for Science, Innovation and Technology, Department for Culture, Media and Sport and Intellectual Property Office, *Copyright and Artificial Intelligence: Consultation*, UK government consultation, 17 Dec 2024, www. gov.uk/government/consultations/copyright-and-artificial-intelligence/copyright-and-artificial-intelligence (accessed 21 July 2025).

25. Scott Berinato, 'Stop thinking about consent', *Harvard Business Review*, 24 Sept 2018.

26. European Commission, Commission Staff Working Document Impact Assessment Accompanying the Document Proposals for Directives of the European Parliament and of the Council, 11.4.2018, www.eur-lex.europa.eu/resource.html?format=PDF &uri=cellar%3Aba7bffc9-3e34-11e8-b5fe-01aa75ed71a1.0001.0 2%2FDOC_3&utm, p. 23.

27. European Commission, *A European Consumer Agenda – Boosting Confidence and Growth*, COM(2012) 225 final, 22 May 2012, www.eur-lex.europa.eu/LexUriServ/LexUriServ.do?uri=COM:2012:0225:FIN:EN:PDF (accessed 21 July 2025).

28. 'The EU should regulate AI on the basis of rights, not risks', Access Now, 17 Feb 2021, www.accessnow.org/eu-regulation-ai-risk-based-approach/ (accessed 21 July 2025).

29. Federica Frabetti, *Software Theory* (London: Rowman & Littlefield International, 2015); also Federica Frabetti & Eleanor Drage, 'The performativity of AI-powered protest detection', *Science, Technology, & Human Values*, 49:5 (2023), pp. 1045–72.

30. Adham Abdelfattah, 'When I got a "?" email from Jeff Bezos', Substack, 15 Apr 2025, www.adham.substack.com/p/when-i-got-a-email-from-jeff-bezos (accessed 21 July 2025).

31. 'New toolkit launched to help businesses navigate high-risk AI compliance under the EU AI Act', LCFI news post, 5 Feb 2025, www.lcfi.ac.uk/news-events/news/new-toolkit-launched-to-help-businesses-navigate-high-risk-ai-compliance-under-the-eu-ai-act (accessed 21 July 2025).

32. North West Ambulance Service NHS Trust, 'Complaints and concerns: Handling procedure', Trust policy document, May 2024, www.nwas.nhs.uk/wp-content/uploads/2024/06/Complaints-procedure.pdf (accessed 21 July 2025).

33. Ahmed, *Complaint!*, p. 288.

34. Ibid., p. 23.

8: The Case for Controversy

1. Joanna Browne et al., 'Tech workers' perspectives on ethical issues in AI development', *Big Data & Society*, 11:1 (2024).

2. Jenny L. Davis et al., 'Algorithmic reparation', *Big Data & Society*, 8:2 (2021).

3. Wonyoung So et al., 'Beyond fairness', *Proceedings of the 2022 ACM Conference on Fairness, Accountability and Transparency (FAccT '22)*, Seoul, 21–4 June 2022, pp. 988–1004.

4. Emily A. Shrider, 'Poverty in the United States: 2023', *Current

Population Reports P60-283, US Census Bureau, Sept 2024, www2.census.gov/library/publications/2024/demo/p60-283.pdf (accessed 21 July 2025).

5. Joy Buolamwini & Timnit Gebru, 'Gender shades', Conference on Fairness, Accountability and Transparency, *Proceedings of Machine Learning Research* 81:1–15 (2018); Wilhelmina Nekoto et al., 'Participatory research for low-resourced machine translation', *arXiv* preprint, 5 October 2020, doi.org/10.48550/arXiv.2010.02353 (accessed 21 July 2025); Iroro Orife et al., 'Masakhane – machine translation for Africa', *arXiv* preprint, 13 Mar 2020, doi.org/10.48550/arXiv.2003.11529 (accessed 21 July 2025).

6. From personal conversations at the University of Cambridge; also Simon Hattenstone, 'The good hacker: Can Taiwanese activist turned politician Audrey Tang detoxify the internet?', *Guardian*, 17 Aug 2024.

7. Eun Seo Jo & Timnit Gebru, 'Lessons from archives', *FAT* '20: Proceedings of the 2020 ACM Conference on Fairness, Accountability and Transparency (FAccT '20)*, 27 Jan 2020, pp. 306–16, doi.org/10.1145/3351095.3372829.

8. Priya Goswami, 'Good Technology Needs an Emergency Exit Door', in Eleanor Drage & Kerry McInerney (eds), *The Good Robot* (London: Bloomsbury Academic, 2024), pp. 118–26.

9. Indigenous Design and Innovation Aotearoa (IDIA), nd, *Kuīni AI Chatbot*, IDIA project page, www.idia.nz/mahi/kuini-chatbot (accessed 21 July 2025).

10. Sophia Dominique Manalang, 'E-basura: An automated waste segregator', Community AI, www.thecommunityai.org/projects (accessed 21 July 2025).

11. Southbank Centre, 'Is AI an Existential Threat to Humanity?' [video], YouTube (streamed live 28 Sept 2023), www.youtube.com/watch?v=yo6oldvCul4.

12. Personal communications.

9: Nerds, Arise: Data Scientists Behaving Badly

1. Isabelle Stengers, *In Catastrophic Times* (Cambridge: Polity Press, 2022), p. 62.

2. Right to Warn Signatories, 'A right to warn about Advanced Artificial Intelligence', open letter published 4 June 2024, RightToWarn.ai, www.righttowarn.ai/ (accessed 21 July 2025).

3. Kevin Roose, 'OpenAI insiders warn of a "reckless" race for dominance', *The New York Times*, 4 June 2024.

4. Daniel Kokotajlo, [X post], 4 June 2024, www.x.com/ DKokotajlo/status/1797994238468407380 (accessed 21 July 2025).

5. Right to Warn Signatories 2024, 'A right to warn about Advanced Artificial Intelligence'.

6. Janneke Parrish, 'Worker solidarity and why tech unions matter', *The Good Robot*, 15 October 2024, www. thegoodrobot.co.uk/transcripts/worker-solidarity-and-why- tech-unions-matter.

7. Jon Jackson, 'Apple fires new employee for calling women "weak, cosseted, naïve" in book', *Newsweek*, 14 May 2021.

8. Casey Newton et al., 'Apple employees circulate petition demanding investigation into "misogynistic" new hire', The Verge, 12 May 2021, www.theverge.com/2021/5/12/22432909/apple- petition-hiring-antonio-garcia-martinez-chaos-monkeys- facebook.

9. Janneke Parrish, 'Worker solidarity and why tech unions matter'.

10. Ibid.

11. Carole Cadwalladr, 'Google, democracy and the truth about internet search', *Guardian*, 4 Dec 2016.

12. Carole Cadwalladr & Emma Graham-Harrison, '50 million Facebook profiles harvested for Cambridge Analytica in major data breach', *Guardian*, 17 Mar 2018.

13. Maurice Chiodo, 'The Good Robot podcast: Featuring Maurice Chiodo', AI Hub, 16 July 2024, www.aihub.org/2024/07/16/ the-good-robot-podcast-featuring-maurice-chiodo (accessed 21 July 2025).

14. 'Cambridge University students keep fire burning for sidelined don Piers Bursill-Hall', *The Times*, 29 October 2021.

15. Melissa Heikkilä, 'The viral AI avatar app Lensa undressed me – without my consent', *MIT Technology Review*, 12 Dec 2022.

16. Aisha Sobey, 'The thinness of GenAI', *AI and Ethics*, 5 (2025), pp. 4181–96.

17. Bettany Hughes, 'Why were women written out of history? An interview with Dr Bettany Hughes', English Heritage, 29 Feb 2016, www.english-heritage.org.uk/visit/inspire-me/blog/blog-posts/why-were-women-written-out-of-history-an-interview-with-bettany-hughes/ (accessed 21 July 2025).

18. UN Women & UN Office on Drugs and Crime, 'One woman or girl is killed every 10 minutes by their intimate partner or family member', press release, 25 Nov 2024, www.unwomen.org/en/news-stories/press-release/2024/11/one-woman-or-girl-is-killed-every-10-minutes-by-their-intimate-partner-or-family-member (accessed 21 July 2025).

19. National Assessment Governing Board, 'Eighth-grade scores decline in civics and U.S. history on the nation's report card', press release, 3 May 2023, www.nagb.gov/news-and-events/news-releases/2023/eighth-grade-scores-decline-in-civics-and-us-history.html (accessed 21 July 2025).

20. Hayden Field, 'AI engineers report burnout and rushed rollouts as "rat race" to stay competitive hits tech industry', CNBC, 3 May 2024, www.cnbc.com/2024/05/03/ai-engineers-face-burnout-as-rat-race-to-stay-competitive-hits-tech.html (accessed 21 July 2025).

21. Sneha Revanur, 'Good Technology Is Intergenerational', in Eleanor Drage & Kerry McInerney (eds), *The Good Robot* (London: Bloomsbury Academic, 2024), pp. 43–50.

22. Sneha Revanur, 'How youth activism is shaking up AI', *The Good Robot*, 27 May 2024, www.thegoodrobotpodcast.buzzsprout.com/1786427/episodes/8697916-how-youth-activism-is-shaking-up-ai-with-sneha-revanur (accessed 21 July 2025).

23. Ibid.

24. Julia Angwin et al., 'Machine bias', *ProPublica*, 23 May 2016, www.propublica.org/article/machine-bias-risk-assessments-in-criminal-sentencing (accessed 21 July 2025).

25. Nette Nöstlinger, 'Germany's far right is winning over the young', *Politico Europe*, 9 October 2024.

26. Shaun Walker, 'Poland's drift to right divides young male and female voters', *Guardian*, 8 October 2019.

27. Jonathan Yerushalmy, 'What's behind the global political divide between young men and women?', *Guardian*, 14 Nov 2024.

28. Ibid.

29. Amrat Kaur & Weiqin Chen, 'Exploring AI literacy among older adults', *Studies in Health Technology and Informatics*, 306 (2023), pp. 9–16.

30. Jude Browne, 'Putting the Public into the Public Body', in *Political Responsibility and Tech Governance* (Cambridge: Cambridge University Press, 2025), pp. 119–53.

31. James S. Fishkin et al., 'Applying deliberative democracy in Africa', *Daedalus*, 146:3 (2017), pp. 140–52.

32. Hannah Kaufman, 'Citizens' assemblies: How can the UK learn from Ireland?', The Constitution Unit Blog, 25 October 2018, www.constitution-unit.com/2018/10/25/citizens-assemblies-how-can-the-uk-learn-from-ireland/ (accessed 21 July 2025).

33. Scott Wong & Kevin Collier, 'Washington is struggling to catch up on artificial intelligence', NBC News, 15 May 2023, www.nbcnews.com/politics/congress/washington-struggling-catch-artificial-intelligence-rcna84489 (accessed 21 July 2025).

34. Jonnie Penn, 'Algorithmic silence', *Journal of Social Computing*, 2:4 (Dec 2021), pp. 337–56.

35. 'The technocratic deficit', *The Economist*, 7 Sept 2024.

36. Ben Ansell, 'Our Democratic Future' (Reith Lectures), BBC Radio 4, 13 Dec 2023, Lecture 3, 'The Future of Solidarity', www.bbc.co.uk/sounds/play/m001t9f9 (accessed 21 July 2025).

37. Robert Epstein, 'How Google could rig the 2016 election', *Politico*, 19 Aug 2015.

38. Jack Stilgoe, 'AI has a democracy problem. Citizens' assemblies can help', *Science*, 385: 6711 (22 Aug 2024), pp. 135–6.

10: Trust Your Instincts

1. World Health Organization, 'Gambling', fact sheet, 2 Dec 2024, www.who.int/news-room/fact-sheets/detail/gambling (accessed 21 July 2025).
2. Anna Karlsson & Anders Håkansson, 'Gambling disorder, increased mortality, suicidality and associated comorbidity', *Journal of Behavioral Addictions*, 7:4 (2018), pp. 1091–9.
3. 'Space 3: Expertise and engagement – anonymized practitioner examples', High-Risk EU AI Act Toolkit, ammagamma.ai, p. 27, www.aiact.cloud.ammagamma.com/ (accessed 15 Nov 2025).

Conclusion

1. Sally Hacker, *Pleasure, Power and Technology* (New York: Routledge, 1989), p. 45.
2. Ethical headaches, from Rosi Braidotti, 'Good Technology Is Earthly', in Eleanor Drage & Kerry McInerney (eds), *The Good Robot* (London: Bloomsbury Academic, 2024), pp. 36–42; indigestions, from Donna Haraway, *When Species Meet* (Minneapolis: University of Minnesota Press, 2007), pp. 298–9.
3. Derek Woods, 'Prosthetic symbiosis', *CR: The New Centennial Review*, 22:1 (2022), pp. 157–86, www.muse.jhu.edu/article/ 874474.

Index

Page numbers in *italic* refer to the illustrations

2001: A Space Odyssey (film) 93

A

Aadhaar 91, 175–6

Abdelfattah, Adham 186

Aboriginal Australians 39, 65

Abram, David 108

Access Now 184, 230

activism 207–13

Aeschylus 20

Affectiva 199

Africa 160

Aguera y Arcas, Blaise 121

Aguilar Gil, Yasnaya Elena 16

Ahmed, Sara 168, 187, 188

Ahmed, Shamira 55

AI Now 81

AI4Media 101–2, *101*

AIDS epidemic 121

Airbnb 160

Alcor Life Extension Foundation 38

algorithms 9, 15–16, 99, 114, 178, 196, 212–13, 218–19, 224–5, 235

Altman, Sam 84, 91–2

Amazon 67, 82, 84, 85–7, 114, 116, 165, 185–6

Amazon Web Services (AWS) 90, 156

AMD 82

American Civil Liberties Union (ACLU) 124–5

Ammagamma 172–3, 226–9, 232

Amnesty International 162

Amnesty Tech 230

Andreessen, Marc 84, 97–8

Angry Birds 180

Ansell, Ben 222

Anthony, Andrew 61

Anthropic 82

Anthropocene 58

anthropomorphism 115–16

antitrust legislation 68, 84, 85–8

apocalypse 17–21, 52–3, 56–60, 72–92, 93, 111, 233

Apple 5, 13, 38, 54, 69, 84, 87, 103–4, 206

AppleTogether 209–10

ARC-AGI 147–8

Artificial General Intelligence
    (AGI) 83–4, 89, 102, 146–9,
    154–7, 208–9
Asimov, Isaac 52
Austria 177
authoritarianism 37–8, 79–80,
    122, 129, 208
autism 199

B
Babu, Asvatha 118–19
Bacon, Matthew 161
Baltimore Police Department
    (BPD) 124–5, 126
Bankman-Fried, Sam 72–3, 77
Bannon, Steve 212
Barad, Karen 133
Barclay, Louis 128
Basque people 104
Baudelaire, Charles 141–2
Bayer 69
BBC 3, 17–18, 155
Beaumont, Nick 144–5
Belgium 177
benchmarks 147–8
Bengio, Yoshua 66–8
Bennett, Jane 106
Berlanga, Mercedes 43–4
Berlant, Lauren 64
Berndtsson, Teresa 98–9, *100*
Better Images of AI project
    96–102, 116
Beukes, Lauren 57
Bezos, Jeff 84, 185–6
Biden, Joe 84, 85, 87, 88
big data swindling (大数据杀熟)
    159–60

Bing 91, 208
biology 135–7
biometric data 91, 175–6
Biseko, John Misana 40
Black Lives Matter (BLM) 69,
    124–5, 127, 129, 131, 187
blackouts 106–7
Bloomberg 83
Bohr, Niels 133
Bolivia 16
Bolt 178
Bostrom, Nick 61–3, 72–3, 75,
    76–80
Bradstreet, Anne 3
brain 78–9, 95, 108, 111, 152
Brandeis, Louis 180
Braverman, Suella 130
Breslin, Catherine 96, 97,
    102–3
Brexit 128, 224
Brödel, Max 141, *141*
Browne, Jude 220
Browne, Michelle Lee 104, *105*
Browning, Elizabeth Barrett 3
Brunning, Luke 4
Buddhism 47
Buolamwini, Joy 197
Bursill-Hall, Piers 212
Butler, Judith 34, 70
Byron, Lord 3

C
Cadwalladr, Carole 128, 210–12
California 6–7
Calment, Jeanne 40
Cambridge Analytica 128,
    163–4, 173, 182, 210, 211–12

Cambridge University 150–1,
    153–4, 172–3, 188, 212, 213,
    229–30
capitalism 49–50, 54, 63, 88,
    89–92, 112
Caribbean Reparations
    Commission 196–7
CARICOM 197
Carnegie Mellon University 15
cars, self-driving 20, 234
Cascade Institute 78
Catholic Church 47
Cave, Stephen 152
Cavendish, Margaret 52
Centre for the Study of
    Existential Risk (CSER)
    78–80, 83
chatbots 10, 12, 109
ChatGPT 2, 5, 36–8, 114–15,
    156, 235
Chen, Weiqin 220
Chile 16
China 83–4, 158–60, 197–8
Chinembiri, Tapiwa 55
Chiodo, Maurice 211–12
chips 83–4, 86, 97, 103
Chollet, François 147–8
Christianity 46–8, 53, 94
The Citizens 128
citizens' assemblies 220–1, 222
The City of Devi (film) 57
Clarote 101–2, *101*
climate crisis 58–9, 65, 73, 103,
    208
Clode, David 99–100, *101*
cloud services 86, 90–1, 103,
    156

CNBC 18, 216
cognition 107–9, 110, 113,
    149–52, 235
Cohere 82
Colbert, Max 69, 129, 130, 188–9
Coleridge, Samuel Taylor 3
Community AI 201
competence, AI 8, 188
complaints 173, 183–9
consciousness 106, 107–10, 113,
    114–15, 235
consent 173–83
consumerism 62–3
content generation 11
control 146, 155–64
Cook, Tim 5, 84
Copenhagen 125
Copilot 166
copyright issues 180–1
corporate surveillance 228
Crawford, Kate 59
creation myths 46–7, 94
crime 127, 129–31, 218–19
cryonics 39, 47–8
Il Cuore Finto di DR (film) 57
cybernetics 163

D

DALL-E 14, 166, 213
Danowski, Déborah 46–7
Darwin, Charles 35–6, 37, 42,
    45, 48, 62
Daston, Lorraine 135
data, and consent 173–83
data analytics 10
data centres 36, 90, 98, 103, 108,
    156

Dataminr 124, 125–7, 129–30, 132
dating websites 4, 120–2
Davis, Jenny L. 195–6
The Day After Tomorrow (film) 57
death 20–1, 39–40, 47–8, 63–5, 110–13
deep learning 9, 14
deep neural networks (DNNs) 120–1
Delacroix, Eugène 142
Deliveroo 178
Deluge (film) 57
democracy 8, 71, 84–5, 87–9, 105, 128, 160, 202, 220–3
Democratic Party 87–9
Department of Justice (US) 87
Descartes, René 140
digital afterlife 110–13
Digital Dubai 166
Dimmendaal, Rens 99–100, 101
disability theory 32–3, 34, 109
Distributed AI Research Institute (DAIR) 68, 171–2
diversity 7, 71, 203–6
DIY AI 200–2
DNA 134, 143, 151
Doctorow, Cory 160
DOGE (Department of Government Efficiency) 28
drones 20–1
drugs, war on 161–2
Duffy, Mark 54
dysgenics 61–3, 153
dyslexia 149

E
e-waste 103–4
economics, and intelligence 154–5
The Economist 222
Ecuador 16
Edenber, Elizabeth 180
education 62, 90–1, 150–1, 198, 216, 224–5
effective altruism (EA) 72–5, 78, 89, 92
Effective Ventures Foundation 77
Egyptian Charter for Responsible AI 166
el Kaliouby, Rana 199
Elbeck, Osman 38
elections *see* democracy
Eliot, T. S. 61, 63–6
Ellison, Caroline 73
emergency, (nation) state of 66–71
Emmerich, Roland 57
Encode 219
End Everyday Racism project 150–1
energy consumption 79, 103
engineers, ethics training 213–18
Enlightenment 29
enshittification 160
environmental impacts 59, 104–5
The Epic of Gilgamesh 52, 57
Epimetheus 25
Epstein, Robert 223
Ethical Dating Online 4
eugenics 61–3, 152–3

European Charter of
  Fundamental Rights 184
European Commission 55, 69,
  182, 184–5
European Data Protection
  Directive 174
European Union (EU) 12, 68, 82,
  172, 174, 182, 184–5, 187
evolution 35–6, 41–6, 48–50, 233
exam algorithms 224–5
existential risk (Ex Risk) 72–3,
  75–80, 92
exit doors 200–1, 226–8
extinction 17–20, 58, 65

F
Facebook 77, 84, 85, 87, 121,
  124, 128, 163–4, 210–11
facial recognition technology
  (FRT) 78, 118–20, 123–4, 197
Federal Trade Commission (US)
  87, 166
Federowicz, Mike 38
feedback, employee 229
feminism 165, 172, 176–7, 193
Ferranti, Sebastian Ziani de 163
Ferranti, Vincent Ziani de 162–3
Ferranti Mark I computer 2–5,
  162
figs 45
films 15, 54, 55–8, 59–60, 80, 93
Financial Times 67
Fisher, Mark 92
Fisher, Ronald 153
Ford, Henry 153
Frabetti, Federica 69, 70, 98, 124,
  127, 133, 185

France 207
Freeman, Morgan 64–5
FTX 84
fundraising 77–8
Future of Life Institute 66–71,
  78

G
Gallison, Peter 135
Galton, Francis 153
gambling 227–8
gaming, online 67
García Martínez, Antonio
  209–10
Gaza 78
GCHQ 180
Gebru, Timnit 66, 68, 166,
  171–2, 197, 198
gender 118, 122–3, 150, 153–4,
  220
General Data Protection
  Regulation (GDPR) 174,
  181–2, 184
genetics 143, 151–2
genocide 62, 75
Geofeedia 124–5
Germany 177, 220
Ghaly, Mohammed 160
gig workers 178
Gilbert, Scott 46
Gillwald, Alison 55
GitHub 117–18
Global Emerging Technology
  Summit (2021) 158
Global Science Research 163–4
GNU Ethertics 202
Goodhart's Law 147

Google 5, 66–7, 69, 82, 84, 87,
    103, 165–6, 170–2, 195, 223, 230
Google DeepMind 29, 222–3
Google Gemini 213–16, 214
Google Maps 13
Google Translate 118–19
Gordon, Geoff 86
Gosse, Philip Henry 135–6, 136,
    140
Goswami, Priya 199, 200, 226–7
Gould, Stephen J. 100
GPT 89, 112, 146–7, 208
GPUs (general processing units)
    156
Grabolle, Anton 98, 99
Granada, Spain 16–17
Graphics Processing Units
    (GPU) 82
Greek myths 57
Grey-Thompson, Tanni 168–9
Grok chatbot 81
The Guardian 77, 129, 131, 180
Guerrero, Ticardo 43–4
Guevara-Rosas, Erika 162

H
Hacker, Sally 231
Haigh, Thomas 15
hallucinations 114–15
Halsema, Femke 145
Hamad Bin Khalifa University
    (HBKU), Doha 166
Hanna, Alex 166, 171–2
Harari, Yuval 35, 46, 50, 66–8
Haraway, Donna 17, 21, 41, 44,
    52, 53, 63–4, 65, 134, 141, 143,
    144, 152–3, 155

hardware 97–9
Harrington, Brooke 35
Hassabis, Dennis 140
Haugen, Frances 210–11
haunting devices 110–13
Hawaii 199
Hayek, Friedrich 28
Hayles, N. Katherine 107
HEAT (High-Risk EU AI Act
    Toolkit) 172–3, 186–7, 200,
    226
Helsinki 51–2
Here After AI 111
Herschel, William James 91
Hicks, Kathleen 158–9
hiring technology 117–18,
    132–3, 135, 225, 234
historical inaccuracy 215–16
Hogan-Howe, Lord 129–30
Hollanek, Tomasz 110–11, 112
Hollywood 12, 58, 59–60, 80,
    178
holobionts 43–5, 49
Horkheimer, Max 144
Horowitz, Ben 84
House of Lords 129
Huang, Jensen 149
Hugging Face 68, 82, 172
human augmentation 11
Human Genome Project 29, 31
humans, early 26
Humans in the Loop 100–1
Husky Energy 92
Huxley, Aldous 153

I
ID systems 175–6

Idiocracy (film) 62–3
illustrations, scientific 135–41
images 93–106, 115–16
immortality 40–1, 47, 111–12
immune system 44, 45, 48–9, 151
Ince, Gertrude 163
India 91, 114, 118–19, 176, 208
Indigenous AI 199–200
Indigenous people 16, 46, 65, 79,
    92, 104
individualism 46, 47, 49
inequality 49, 54–5, 67, 178–9,
    181, 196
Inflection AI 82
Ingold, Tim 35–6
Instagram 87, 124
insurance companies 183, 187
intelligence 26, 75–7, 78–9,
    146–55
intelligence (IQ) tests 148–9, 152
International Women's Day
    (IWD) 193–4
Internet of Things (IoT) 205
iPad 13
iPhones 38, 54, 87
Ireland 221
Isaacson, Walter 154
Islam 46, 53, 125, 160, 166

J
Jainism 40
Jeffreys, Alec 143
Jews 125
Jo, Eun Seo 198
Johari, Aarefa 199, 200
Johnson, Boris 224
Johnson, Bryan 39, 40

Jones, Leta 180
Jones, Richard 74
Jones, Shane 167
Jordan, David Starr 63
Judaism 46, 94
Judge, Mike 62–3
Jumper, John 140
Just Eat 178

K
Kamenov, Nacho 100–1
Kant, Immanuel 139
Kashyap, Praavita 176
Kaur, Amrat 220
Kenya 36–7
Kepler, Johann 140
Keynes, John Maynard 54–5
Khan, Lina 85, 88, 170
kill switches 83
killbots 93
Kittler, Friedrich 97, 98
Knoop, Mike 147–8
Kokatajlo, Daniel 157, 208
Kuini AI Chatbot 199
Kurzweil, Ray 19
Kwet, Michael 90–1

L
language 114–16, 118–20
large language models (LLMs)
    13, 66–71, 180–1, 215, 234
Latin America 9, 202
Latour, Bruno 105, 143, 144
Le Guin, Ursula 52
Leeds University 4
legislation 68, 69, 82, 85–6, 89,
    130, 174–5, 184–5, 187

Lehmann, Brieuc 153
leisure 55
Lensa 213
Leonardo da Vinci 28, 29–30, 138
Lewis, Hyrum and Verlan 160
LGBTQ+ community 4, 122, 206
life expectancy 112
LinkedIn 117–18
Liu, Mark 83
Livingston, Jennie 122
LNER 168–9
local-use AI 8–9, 200–2

M
MacAskill, Will 73
machine autonomy 109–10
machine learning 9, 12, 96, 138, 194
McInerney, Kerry 118, 165, 218
McKeever, Natasha 4
MacKinnon, Catherine 179
McKinsey 132
Manalang, Sophia Dominique 201
Manchester University Computer (MUC) 2–4
Māori people 199
Margulis, Lynn 43–4, 48
marketing 15, 116–18, 133–4, 171
martial law 69–71
Martinez Arias, Alfonso 143
Marx, Karl 88
Masakhane 197
Melloni, Georgia 153

Merian, Maria Sibylla 136–7, 137, 140
Mesopotamia 52, 58
Meta 67, 69, 84, 87, 164, 165, 166
metamorphosis 41
#MeToo movement 176, 187
Metropolitan Police 69, 129–32, 143, 188–9
Michelangelo 94, 94
microbiome 42–4, 46, 108, 235
Microsoft 5, 27, 67, 69, 81, 82, 89, 90–1, 166–7, 208
Microsoft Azure 156
Microsoft Outlook 187
Middle East 83
Midjourney 213
Miller, Geoffrey 72–3
Minority Report (film) 127
Mistral 82, 89
MIT 15
Mitchell, Margaret 66, 68, 115–16, 121, 147, 172
Mitchell, Melanie 148
monopolies 81–9
Moonfall (film) 57
Moore's Law 97
mortgage lending 196
Moskovitz, Dustin 77
mourning 112–13
Moxyland (film) 57
Moyo, Mpho 55
Mumkin 199
Murgia, Madhumita 127
Musk, Elon 11, 27, 28, 67, 81, 88–9, 144, 154, 215
#MuslimLivesMatter 124–5, 126

myths 25–50

N
NASA 29, *31*, 34, 38, 86
nationalism, AI 158–9
natural selection 49
necroethics 20–1
Neo-Darwinism 48, 233
Netflix 86
Netherlands 83, 103, 122–3, 127
neural networks 14, 156
Neuralink 11, 154
News of the World 129
Newton, Isaac 140
NHS 169
Nissembaum, Helen 181
Noah's Ark 57, 58
Nokia 5, 69
Nowaczky-Basińska, Katarzyna 110, 112
Nvidia 82, 86, 149

O
objectivity 134–45, 146
O'Brien, Richard 33
Official Secrets Act 129
Okinyi, Mophat 178
Okorafor, Nnedi 57
OpenAI 5, 8, 36–8, 81, 115, 154, 157, 208–9
Operation Weeting 129
optimisation 48, 49–50, 62
orthogenetics 41–3, 53, 233

P
Pacific Rim (film) 80
parasites 45

Parrish, Janneke 103–4, 209–10
Pasek, Anne 103
Pearson, Karl 153
Penn, Jonnie 162, 222
Pentagon 212
performativity 133, 168–9
Personality Machine 117–18, *117*
Peru 16
Pew Research Center 121
Philippines 201
photography 139–41
Pichai, Sundar 84
Pinterest 86
planetary intelligence 155
poetry 2–4
Poland 220
police 120, 124–32, 143, 188–9
Pol.is 197–8, 202
Porter, Theodore 28, 59
positivism 140, 144
Possati, Luca M. 98
power hierarchies 146
Preciado, Paul 26
prediction tools 10
Prell, Lettie 51
privacy 173–6, 180–2
pro-justice AI 80, 199–202
ProKid+ 145
prolepsis 53–4
Prometheus myth 21, 25, 26, 28, 33
ProPublica 219
protests 120, 127–8
protocol 169–70
Puerto Rica 153

Q

quality of life 55

R

racism 6–7, 118, 150–1, 152–3, 165, 196, 213, 218–19

Raimondo, Gina 158

Rand, Ayn 47

Rauhala, Mikko 51

reasoning 147–8

recidivism algorithms 218–19

recognition technology 11, 120–4, 127, 146

recruitment systems 117–18, 132–3, 135, 225, 234

regulation 8, 12, 28, 69–70, 85, 89, 116, 173–4, 194–5

religion 40, 46–8, 94

Remotasks 178

reparative AI 195–8

Republican Party 84, 152, 211

Reuters 86

Revanur, Sneha 6–7, 218, 219

Rieder, Bernhard 86

robots 9, 59–60, 94, 106

Rocky Horror Picture Show (film) 33

Rodin, Auguste 29–30, 32, 94–6, 95

Rodrigues, Déborah 33

Romanticism 141, 142, 232

Rose, Deborah Bird 21, 39, 65

Rowley, Sir Mark Peter 131

Russell, Stuart 18, 66–8, 157, 201–2

S

Sabato, Ernest 145

Sacks, David 84

Sainsbury, Mark 171

Scale AI 178

Schmidt, Eric 222

Schor, Juliet B. 55

science, objectivity 134–45

science fiction 51–3, 56–7, 59, 153

scientism 145

scientists, activism 207–8

Seddon, Toby 161

sexism 193, 213, 218

sexual consent 173–4, 176–7, 178–9

sexuality 120–3

Shakespeare, William 60, 111

Shaw, David G. 51

Shell 69

Sileno, Giovanni 86

Silicon Valley 27, 72

Simon, Herbert 49

Simondon, Gilbert 26–7, 96

singularity 51–6

Skype 77

Slack 86

Smith, Adam 49

So, Wonyoung 196

Social Darwinism 48, 63

social media 124, 126, 163–4, 211, 218

software 97–9

Sonnenfeld, Jeffrey 85

South Africa 90–1, 129

South America 16

South Korea 69, 220

Spain 16–17, 177
Spawning AI 181
Spencer, Charles 48
Stability AI 82
Stable Diffusion 14, 82, 213
Stanford University 15
star colonisation 76
Star Trek films 54, 55–6
states of emergency 69–71
Statista 76
statistics 9, 14, 73, 153
Stengers, Isabelle 207
Stiegler, Bernard 26
Stilgoe, Jack 223
Strachey, Christopher 2–4, 155–6, 162, 232
Strathearn, Marilyn 147
Stross, Charles 51
subjectivity 135
Sunak, Rishi 68
superintelligence 13
Suri, Manil 57
'survival of the fittest' 42, 48, 50, 63
Swammerdam, Jan 41
symbiosis 42–6, 48–9, 79

T
Taiwan 8, 13, 27, 82–3, 197–8, 202
Taiwan Semiconductor Manufacturing Company (TSMC) 82–3
Tallinn, Jaan 77
Tang, Audrey 8, 197–8, 202
task automation 9–10
technology, history of 19, 25–8

technosolutionism 135
Tequiologies 16–17
Teresa, Mother 74–6
The Terminator films 15, 56, 57, 59–60, 93, 97
terminology 114–16
terrorism 69–71
Tesla 27, 81
Thames Valley Police 130
thoughtfulness 171
TikTok 83
Todd, Zoe 92
Todorov, Alexander 121
Tor Project 202
Toraja people 39–40
Transcendence (film) 59
transhumanism 35, 38–42, 47–50, 53, 54, 111
transparency 166–8, 171
Triangle of Doom 72–92, 233
'Trolley Problem' 20
Trump, Donald 28, 30, 67, 83–5, 92, 128, 152, 153, 158, 159, 165, 196, 212, 220
Turing, Alan 2–5
Turner, Fred 163
Twitch 67
Twitter/X 81, 124, 157, 183, 215

U
Uber 160, 178, 202
Uganda 221
UNESCO 8
unions 188, 209–10
university students 150–2, 168
Unsworth, Richard 74
utilitarianism 72–6, 92

utopia 102, 200

V
vagaries 170–2
Vallorani, Nicoletta 57
values 156–62, 164
van Dooren, Thom 39
Venezuela 36
violence 122–3
Viveiros de Castro, Eduardo 46–7
VMan 28, 29–34, *31*, 35, 36, 38, 50, 62, 96, 233
voting *see* elections

W
Wajcman, Judy 55
Wales, Jimmy 128
Wall-E (film) 64
War of the Worlds (film) 65
warfare 20–1, 65, 66, 76
Warren, Samuel D. 180
water consumption 103
Weinstein, Harvey 178
WhatsApp 87
When Worlds Collide (film) 57
whistleblowers 128, 210–12
Whittaker, Meredith 92
Who Fears Death (film) 57
Wikipedia 128
Wilde, Oscar 60

Williams, Apryl 195–6
Williamson, Gavin 224–5
Williamson, Timothy 170
Wilson, Elizabeth 108
Wolfe, Josh 52
Woods, Derek 235
Woolf, Virginia 96
Wordsworth, William 141
World Health Organization 227
World Population Review 76
Worthington, Arthur Mason 138–9, *139*, 140
Wozniak, Steve 66–8
Wylie, Chris 211
Wytham Abbey 77

X
X/Twitter 81, 124, 157, 183, 215
xAI 81

Y
Yanapak 202
Yang, Michael W. 195–6
Yarvin, Curtis 158
Yelp 86
Yoon Suk Yeol 69
You, Only Virtual (YOV) 111

Z
Zilis, Shivon 154
Zuckerberg, Mark 84, 88–9